PRISONERS OF ENGLAND

PRISONERS OF ENGLAND

Miriam Kochan

First published 1980 by
THE MACMILLAN PRESS LTD
London and Basingstoke
Associated companies in Delhi
Dublin Hong Kong Johannesburg Lagos
Melbourne New York Singapore Tokyo

Printed in Great Britain by
Unwin Bros Ltd, The Gresham Press,
Woking, Surrey

British Library Cataloguing in Publication Data

Kochan, Miriam
  Prisoners of England
  1. World War, 1939–1945 – Prisoners and prisons,
  British
  I. Title
  940.54′72′41   D805.G7

  ISBN 0–333–27434–2

Contents

List of Plates

Preface

On 1 September 1939, German armies marched into Polish territory. Two days later, Great Britain, party to an alliance with the Polish Government, declared war on Germany.

The war which raged for the ensuing five and a half years was fought on an unprecedented scale, in all quarters of the world, and with a violence never before seen. In Britain, it rapidly assumed the character of a battle of ideologies – of democracy opposing German National Socialism, with its attendant qualities of Hitler dictatorship, racial superiority (involving racial discrimination and later extermination) and dreams of world conquest. The soldiers whose fate is described in this book were members of the German armed forces which made these atrocities possible. Without them, the abominations of the Hitler period could not have been perpetrated.

Millions were killed or wounded between 1939 and 1945. Among the minor casualties were the prisoners taken by either side. Their enforced sojourn on enemy soil forms a small, largely unrecorded, almost forgotten episode in history – but one which none the less had repercussions on the people amongst whom they were compelled to live and on the Germany to which they returned. One thing stands out: the way in which the German prisoners – even the most committed Nazis amongst them – came to learn and appreciate something of the British democratic outlook, and how the British people they encountered – though engaged in a bitter war against Nazi Germany – found it possible to establish human relationships with individual Germans.

The first German prisoners arrived in Britain in October 1939. Official repatriation was completed in July 1948. At its peak, in September 1946, Britain was host to some 402,200 prisoners confined in hundreds of different camps. Experiences varied from prisoner to prisoner, from camp to camp, from period to period. Attitudes were influenced by the course of the war and of the peace, by governmental decisions, by events in Germany.

This book records just a few of the experiences on both sides of the barbed wire; how a few prisoners came to find themselves in Britain and how some of the British who came into contact with them saw the prisoners. This book would not have been written without the help of all these people.

My most grateful thanks also go to Joan and Peter Katz, Benjy Kochan, Ken and Else Lawrence and the late Natalie Koch and Sheila Wright, who helped me with translating the German material involved; Norman Lawrence, Alan Lester, Harry Shukman and Herbert Sulzbach, who have given invaluable assistance in other ways; and Marianne Calmann, who conceived the idea of the book, was a source of inspiration during incubation, but was unable to assist with the birth.

The Characters in Order of Appearance

HANS RECKEL. Entered the German army straight from school and held the rank of *Gefreiter* (lance-corporal) when captured in July 1944. He is at present a teacher in a gymnasium in West Germany.

HENRY BLUNDEN (né BLUMENTHAL). Was born in Germany, but came to England in the 1930s and was an acting sergeant in the British army; at Oaklands Emergency Hospital, Cockten Hill, Bishop Auckland, Co. Durham, in 1944.

BESSIE SCOTT. Ward sister at Oaklands Emergency Hospital. She now lives in Stockton-on-Tees.

B. M. STEEN. Houseman and doctor at various Scottish hospitals. He now lives in Edinburgh.

SIEGFRIED GABLER. Had just finished his apprenticeship as a toolmaker when he became a private in the German army in August 1943. In August 1944 he became a prisoner of war. He is now a toolmaker with British Leyland in Swindon, Wilts.

KURT BOCK. Export apprentice before he entered the German army. Had reached the rank of lieutenant when captured in February 1945. He was repatriated in April 1948 and is now export manager in a Hamburg firm.

MR CAMBRAY. A professional Oxford engineer who used German POW labour during the war.

SHEILA CONNOR. Acted as a driver to British YMCA personnel in Scotland during the war. She now lives in Australia.

DR HARALD DREIER. When war broke out, he had just completed his studies and was hoping for an academic career. He had reached the rank of *Sanitäts-Obergefreiter* (medical corporal) in the German army when he was captured in October 1944. He was repatriated in April 1947 and now lives in Hamburg, working for the leading book-import wholesaler in West Germany.

SIEGFRIED BANDELOW. A bookseller before he joined the

German army, in which he was a lieutenant when captured in August 1944. He was repatriated in October 1947 and is now a master at a gymnasium in Westerstede, West Germany.

EGON SCHORMANN. Lieutenant in the German army when captured in February 1945. He was repatriated in February 1948 and is now managing director of the same leading book-import wholesaler as Harald Dreier.

ALF EISERBECK. Serving in the German navy as *Maschinen Matrose* (equivalent to the rank of corporal in the army, he says) when captured on the Channel Islands in May 1945. Before he joined he worked as a construction engineer.

EUGENE ROLFE. Sergeant interpreter in the British army; worked as interpreter at various prisoner-of-war camps. He now lives in St Albans.

GRISELDA FYFE. A schoolgirl when she met German prisoners of war in Edinburgh, where she still lives.

K. E. Serving in the German army when captured in February 1945. He now owns a prosperous motor-repair business in Wantage, Oxon.

GEORGE WEISER. A trained general mechanic, he worked for the Luftwaffe as a civilian from the outbreak of war till he was called up for active service in the paratroops in 1944 and trained as a medical orderly. He was a *Gefreiter* (lance-corporal) when he was taken prisoner in February 1945. He now lives in Oxford.

GODFREY SCHEELE. Tutor at Wilton Park.

HENRY POSNER. As a corporal in the British army he was stationed at a prisoner-of-war camp in Oxford, where he now lives.

REVEREND A. S. COOPER. Minister of St Columbia's Presbyterian Church, Cambridge. He now lives on Merseyside.

C. V. W. TARR. Established friendships with German prisoners of war in Exeter, where he still lives.

SONIA ARGYLE. Graduate student in Classics at Newnham College, Cambridge, in 1947. She now lives in Oxford.

MRS EVA GLEES. Dental surgeon who lives in Oxfordshire.

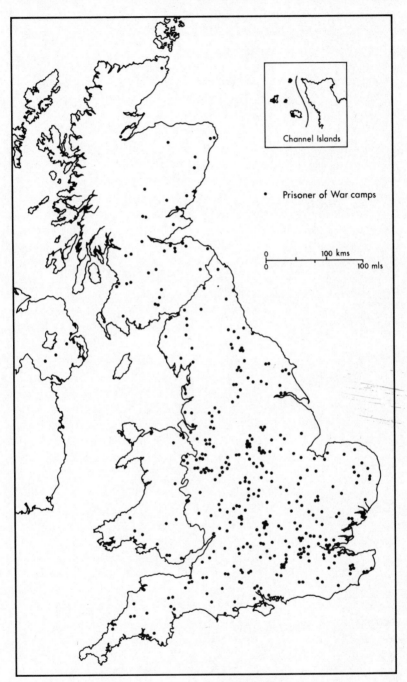

Map of England showing POW camps

1 Men in Cages

In October 1939 the International Red Cross reported that some of the crew of the German submarines U27 and U29 were in British hands. On 14 November it was confirmed that eighteen German officers (eleven naval personnel and seven Luftwaffe men) and ninety-four other ranks (eight of whom were airmen) were held in camps in England. The first stage in the story of the German prisoners of war in England had begun.

Though it covers the longest period, this first stage is in some ways the least important, in that the number of German POWs actually held in Great Britain remained relatively insignificant. The real story opens with stage two in June 1944, when numbers began steeply to rise. This rise continued until a peak was reached in September 1946, when a positive policy of repatriation and the third and final stage commenced.

The arrival of the first prisoners in October 1939 created no major upheaval. POWs were not a new phenomenon. The machinery for dealing with them had already been established many years earlier. Rules governing every conceivable aspect of POW welfare had been worked out in the light of the experience of the First World War and embodied in the Geneva Convention, ratified, in 1929, by thirty-four states. Everything was covered, from the situation of the camps (away from any area where the prisoners' lives might be endangered) to food rations, from medical care to monetary payment. The implementation of the Convention was in the hands of the International Red Cross, centred in Geneva in neutral Switzerland, from where it maintained a system of inspections – not only of the treatment of German prisoners by the British but also of British prisoners in Germany – to ascertain that the terms of the Convention were being observed.

The first German prisoners to arrive in England were housed in two camps – Grizedale Hall, Lancs (Camp 1), for the officers, and Glen Mill Camp, Oldham, Lancs (Camp 176), for the men – though, as new camps were established, separate camps for officers and men were not always considered necessary. As the need arose, camps were set up wherever suitable facilities offered. Disused barracks and teacher-training colleges were brought into use. Tents were pitched on racecourses (closed for the duration of the war) and Nissen huts erected on waste land. Grizedale, three miles south of Hawkshead and eight miles away from Ambleside, Westmorland, the nearest town, had once been a stately home. It still had the heavy oak front door, stained-glass windows and panelled reception rooms of its erstwhile splendour. It was also an expensive proposition to maintain. 'Would it not be cheaper to keep them at the Ritz?' asked Colonel Wedgwood in the House of Commons on 21 November 1939, after learning from the Secretary of State for War, the Right Hon. Leslie Hore Belisha, MP, that it cost £50 a day to keep twenty-one inmates in a camp designed to accommodate 200. It is little wonder that Grizedale soon gained the nickname of the 'U-Boat Hotel'.

Its occupants were, as the name implies, mainly officers from German submarines, U-boats. In fact, in the early months of the war, most of the prisoners taken were members of the German navy, though they were increasingly interspersed with pilots and crews of aeroplanes. For the first six months, the period known as the 'phoney war', there was only limited military action on land. The warring factions confined their activities to naval blockades, in which the U-boats scored a somewhat higher success rate than their British equivalents. Their effect can be gauged from the food shortage in Britain in those early days of the war, reflected in the rationing of foodstuffs to British civilians. In January 1940 bacon, ham, sugar and butter were rationed to the British housewife; in March, meat; in July, tea, margarine and cooking fat.

In April 1940 the period of phoney war was brought to an abrupt end. Hitler, in his lust for world conquest and autarchy, marched triumphantly through Denmark and Norway, Holland and Belgium. In May 1940 the tattered remnants of the British army were rescued from the European continent by a fleet of little boats which picked them up from the port of Dunkirk, where they had been encircled by the German armies. On 14 June German troops entered Paris. Hitler now held the whole of Western Europe from the North Cape to the Spanish frontier, from Memel to Trieste. In these days of defeat, Britain was not taking vast numbers of prisoners.

What is more, she was not keeping many of those she had. Britain now stood in the front line. There seemed little doubt that she was scheduled as Hitler's next victim. Under their new premier, Winston Churchill, the British population, civilian and military, mobilised materially and psychologically for imminent invasion. Road blocks were constructed, signposts taken down, the ringing of church bells banned except as a warning that the invasion had begun, 'enemy aliens' residing in Britain were interned, a home defence force consisting of volunteers of non-military age (the Local Defence Volunteers, which later became the Home Guard) was formed, and the advisability of moving German POWs to the colonies and dominions was discussed in the House of Commons. This proposition had numerous advantages. Food supplies in Britain were barely sufficient to satisfy her own population. The colonies were far more plentifully endowed. They equally had wide open spaces more easily able to absorb large-scale camps. They were situated thousands of miles from Germany, so that the possibility of escape was minimised. But, finally and most significant at this juncture, removal there would eliminate the danger of the prisoners rising up and rejoining their armies if the threatened invasion took place. By March 1941, Britain had shipped 2950 German prisoners to Canada, and, although the invasion threat had disappeared by mid September, their numbers continued to rise until June 1945, when they reached a peak of 33,800. The experience of these German prisoners in Canada is another story.

The numbers of those held in Britain were in consequence kept down to a fairly low level, not touching the 2000 mark until March 1944. Not that the British camps were empty. In June 1940 the Italian dictator, Mussolini, had declared war on Britain. The following September he began operations on a North African front, and in January 1941 Britain scored resounding victories in Cyrenaica, taking some 130,000 Italian prisoners. Britain's triumph was only short-lived, but the prisoners were brought to Britain, where they were sometimes kept in the same camps as the Germans, sometimes apart, inviting frequent comparisons of their respective virtues and vices, and forming an essential part of the agricultural labour force.

The composition of the German prisoner body in Britain did, however, change during the 1940–1 period. In Germany, plans for 'Operation Sea Lion' (the invasion of Britain) had begun to be made from 21 July. As a preliminary, 'Operation Eagle', the German air offensive 'to establish conditions favourable to the conquest of Britain', was launched on 15 August 1940. The Battle of Britain, fought in the air over southern England between British and German planes, lasted a month, until 15 September, and testified to Britain's superiority in the air. The Germans lost a total of 1733 aircraft during the Battle of Britain, the British 915. The pilots and crews of the shot-down German planes influenced the character of the POW camps at this period. Their numbers grew during the night-bombing of Britain which ensued. The Blitz lasted eight months and primarily affected London – between September 1940 and May 1941 some 1,150,000 houses were damaged or totally destroyed – though other major industrial centres also suffered.

The German prisoners in the camps at this stage of the war were mainly young men in good physical and mental condition. Many of them had spent a great part of their lives after childhood under the Nazi regime and were imbued to a greater or lesser degree with its ideology. The effects of this upbringing varied, of course, from individual to individual, and were found at their strongest amongst the members of the SS, Hitler's elite force. They had mostly grown up in the totalitarian state Hitler had created in the 1930s, with its concept of *Gleichschaltung*, co-ordination of every phase of national life, including the church, press, education, industry and army. They had barely known a society where diversity of opinions and institutions was possible. Instead, they had been subjected from their schooldays to the full force of Nazi propaganda. They had learned from their teachers to glorify the leader, worhip the Fatherland and offer blind obedience. They had also been taught Hitler's theory of the alleged superiority of the 'Aryan' race, which on the one hand necessitated the elimination of all alien elements in the population (hence the discrimination against the Jews, and later their extermination), and on the other led to a policy of world conquest.

In the early years of the war, the prisoners' morale and their confidence in the invincibility of the Führer and in a German victory were intact. They too were convinced that the German invasion of Britain would shortly release them from captivity and enable them to resume their triumphant participation in a glorious German victory.

There was therefore little purpose to be served at this point by attempting to escape – although escape was regarded as a prisoner's prerogative. Under the terms of the Geneva Convention, the maximum punishment for the offence was thirty days in the 'cooler'. 'Every prisoner of war of whatever nation', Colonel Scotland, head of the Prisoner of War Interrogation Section, explains, 'was entitled to try his hand at escape to rejoin his forces. If he succeeded, good luck. If he failed, thirty days. It sounds, and is, a humanely intelligent rule . . . .'

Escape committees were formed amongst the slowly increasing number of prisoners and attempts made. None succeeded during the war. Some caused a considerable amount of excitement whilst they were in progress. In February 1940 four German merchant seamen escaped from a 'northern prison camp', but were recaptured the following day, twelve miles south-west of York. Eight months later, a young Luftwaffe pilot, Fritz von Werra, claimed that he secured five days of freedom when he broke out of Grizedale. Exhilarated by his success, von Werra tried again shortly afterwards, this time in company with four other German officers. Starting from Swanwick Camp (Camp 179), disguised as a Dutch airman, he got as far as the pilot seat of a Hurricane aircraft at Hucknall aerodrome before he was recaptured. A similar attempt a year later got a step nearer success. On 24 November 1941, two German pilots managed to leave their camp in the north of England and steal into a civilian aerodrome which the Royal Air Force were using to train Allied personnel. They too pretended to be Dutch airmen, wore their flying suits, and in this way succeeded in evading the RAF guards and the defence patrol on duty at the time. They even got into a two-seater Miles Magister training aircraft without being challenged and took off under the very eyes of a civilian mechanic. Only as he watched the 'plane disappearing into the sky did the mechanic suddenly realise that neither of the pilots had been carrying the regulation parachutes. He immediately signalled the alarm and the aircraft was tracked by the Royal Observer Corp. Their efforts however, were unnecessary. The pilots soon ran out of fuel and were forced to land. They were taken back into captivity. In April 1944 the Government could report that, since the beginning of the war, only sixty-two prisoners had attempted to escape. All had been recaptured, except two who had been drowned while attempting to escape.

Meanwhile, as early as the beginning of 1941, efforts were being made to counteract the Nazism prevalent to a greater or lesser degree. *Die Wochenpost*, a 'paper for German prisoners in England', was published in London for the Prisoners of War Recreational

Association and edited by a German Jew, Bernhard Reichenbach. The Prisoner of War Department of the Foreign Office, the body directly responsible for the paper, saw it as an attempt to force the prisoners, hitherto brainwashed from childhood by Nazi propaganda, to think for themselves. To that end, *Wochenpost* made a practice of printing the full text of the daily *Wehrmacht* bulletin, side by side with shortened versions of the Allied reports. After every speech by Hitler, a special supplement containing the full text was produced. Although *Wochenpost* specifically attempted to avoid issuing British propaganda, it was regarded by many prisoners with a great deal of suspicion.

British war news, that spring of 1941, gave little encouragement to the propagandist. There was defeat in North Africa, the loss to Germany of Yugoslavia, Greece and Crete, the introduction of jam, marmalade, cheese and clothes rationing at home. Hitler's speeches, on the other hand, abounded in confidence. On 22 June he moved on to his most ambitious project: the invasion of Soviet Russia.

Although in December 1941 America was brought into the war on the British side by the Japanese bombing of her main fleet in Pearl Harbor, the tale of defeat continued. Singapore fell in February 1942, Burma in the spring; in June, Tobruk surrendered. British shipping was suffering grave losses in the Atlantic. Rations at home were reduced. Sweet and chocolate rationing was introduced in July. In June 1942, with the number of German POWs in the country down to 200, *Wochenpost* suspended publication.

The turn of the tide could be said to have come in the late autumn of 1942, when the British and Americans thrust forward in North Africa. When the British took El Alamein in November, they also took 10,000 German and 20,000 Italian prisoners. On 3 December it was stated in the House of Commons that two German generals captured in the Western Desert were in a POW camp. The end of 1942 also saw the breakthrough on the Russian front and the beginning of the end of Hitler's Russian campaign. By May 1943 the battle for North Africa was over, with the Allies taking some 130,000 prisoners, and the Fascist government in Italy had collapsed. A year later, when the Russians had recovered practically the whole of their prewar territory, the way lay wide open and public opinion was impatiently demanding the opening of a second front in Europe. At that date there were 7900 German prisoners in British camps.

2 D-Day and After

On 6 June 1944, after months of anticipation, rumour, impatience and discussion, the Allied invasion of Europe began. British, Canadian and American forces landed on the beaches of the Normandy coast of France. Apart from great superiority of numbers, the Allied attack also had the advantage of surprise: the German Commander-in-Chief West, Field Marshal Rundstedt, firmly believed that the landing would be made in the region of Calais, and, although Field Marshal Rommel was convinced that Normandy was the goal of the invading army, Hitler distributed the German forces equally on the east and west sides of the Seine.

The attack, when it came, was launched on the coastal area between the rivers Orne and Vire and, by utilising two artificial Mulberry harbours and also landing craft which put men and equipment directly onto the beaches, avoided the need to use a port. The Allies had massed vast forces for the invasion: 1200 fighting ships, 10,000 aircraft, 426 landing craft and 864 transport ships. By the evening of 6 June, 156,000 Allied troops had been landed in Europe.

German resistance was strong and it was only in the face of hard and painful fighting that the Allies advanced. It took the British and Canadian troops a month of heavy action to capture the town of Caen, which had been expected to fall on the first day. It was not until 9 July that its capture could be reported. On 18 July, General Montgomery launched an offensive to the south of the town.

By mid July, the number of German prisoners in the United Kingdom had risen to 7922. One such was Gefreiter (lance corporal) Hans Reckel, who was caught up in the changing fortunes of Caen.

'In the evening twilight,' he recalls, 'we attacked the village of Eterville, near Caen; and at the edge of the village, just at the corner of a house, two Canadians climbed out of a bunker. Obviously they had not dared to withdraw in time, after a third had been fatally hit in an attempt to do so. The dead man lay crumpled on the ground, while the two survivors stood in front of us with raised hands. My call of "Hands up" was unnecessary. Their faces still showed the full extent of their shock, but we too were embarrassed. I took their cartridges off them; I did not notice that they did not fit my quick-firing rifle until later. We ordered one of our slightly wounded soliders to take the two back to company headquarters immediately.

'Exactly nine days later, on 19 July, I came into close contact with Canadian soldiers again. This time, it was in the early afternoon. They came across a wide, half-trampled field of wheat. To begin with, tanks rolled by at considerable intervals, stopped from time to time, then advanced a short distance again. They were followed by groups of infantry soldiers, first leaping forward, then only advancing in a stooping position.

'Only a few hours before, some ten or twelve of us had gone there in formation, while the rest of the company lay further back in reserve. We had strict orders to hold the position against all attack, provided that we did not receive a direct order to retreat. We had immediately begun to dig in, but had not managed to get very deep. When the attackers came nearer, we crawled over to the trenches of the neighbouring company, but everybody there was equally uncertain about what we should do. Then we slipped into several flat shell craters, which seemed to offer a little more protection and enabled us to move closer together. What we primarily gained from each other's company were sympathetic listeners to our loud complaints about the hopelessness of our position.

'One of the tanks came straight towards us, stopped a short distance from the craters and directed its machine guns diagonally downwards. All we could do was climb out and raise our hands. Immediately, several infantry soldiers appeared from behind the vehicle. They each seized one of us by the belt and hacked it open. They then indicated that we also had to throw our steel helmets away. I found it particularly unpleasant not to have any head-covering, and, because it occurred to me that I had lost my haversack containing my cap when my belt fell off, I bent down to pick it up. A machine gun was immediately pointed at me and a sharp order quickly brought me to my senses. At any rate, I was allowed to look after a comrade who had been hit in the belly by some splinters at the last moment. He stood there with his trousers half in shreds, groaning. I gripped him under the arms and supported him as we moved off. We were thus the only two in our small group who did not have to cross their hands behind their heads.

'While we were walking in the direction the vehicles had come from, we met advancing Canadian infantry. Near a fairly large factory, our guard stopped an ambulance; a stretcher was brought and our wounded man laid on it.

'Just as we were going to lift the stretcher and move on, we heard the sounds of shots from a German smokescreen battery and the howl of approaching rockets. All day long, we had heard nothing from our artillery and it was even longer since we had seen a trace of the German airforce. Our rage at those responsible who were trying to help us too late was mixed with glee at the sight of the Canadians jumping nervously around and quickly diving into the gutter. We, however, lay down slowly, as if all this no longer had anything to do with us.

'After the explosions and the rain of shrapnel had ceased, we were taken to a building like a garage – which belonged to the factory. Some of us wore camouflage jackets and these were removed, as well as our fountain pens and all our French money. One of the Canadians collected all the paper money in a heap and put a match to it; very likely he was faithfully obeying orders. The orders probably did not state that the fountain pens should go into Canadian pockets. When we took our camouflage jackets off, one of our soldiers let a chain with a cross slip out of his open shirt collar. The Canadians stared in amazement. "Isn't Hitler your God?", one of them asked. Before we left the building, some young Frenchmen rushed in and came at us with clenched fists. But one of the guards turned his machine gun on them and they hastily fled.

'We were joined by another group of prisoners and marched through the outskirts of Caen to a troop-assembly point in a field. We were stopped on the way by an old French couple who looked at our wounded soldier. "Pauvre garçon", said the wife sympathetically, and brought him some water. Shortly afterwards he was put into an ambulance and we said goodbye to him, trying to comfort him by telling him that he had been extremely lucky. Then we had to form a long line and empty out all our pockets. I had to watch furiously as my pocket knife was taken away from me. Two men were led out, taken to a tent and interrogated individually. Presumably they were asked for information about the place they were to attack, the section of the army they belonged to, as well as its equipment and morale.

'In the evening we were locked up in the air-raid shelter at Caen station. There we received our first meal: biscuits and corned beef, and with them our first English tea. There were fairly recent German newspapers in a corner, and by the dim light we read reports of wonderful new retaliatory weapons.

'The next morning we had to line up on platform 1, immediately behind the station building. The next platform swarmed with English journalists, who wanted to photograph us. They tried first from the right; we all looked left. Then they repeated the attempt from the left; we turned our heads to the right. At last they divided into two groups so that we could not escape. Two weeks later I clearly recognised myself in a picture in an English newspaper.

'After this we were able to watch a group of Canadian sergeants opening a selection of tins and eating an ample meal. But, when we cleared up the station building, we too found some nourishment: a tin with butter and a few biscuits. And, while we were left unobserved for a few moments, we ate absolutely everything up.

'When we returned to the platform, we suddenly heard the sound of loud bellowing. A sergeant with his arms akimbo was roaring at a POW. In fluent German but with pathetically rolled English 'R's', he was shouting: "When a sergeant of the Canadian army addresses you, you stand still!"

'In the afternoon, lorries took us to a large field, where for the first time we enjoyed the protection from the outside world that rolls of barbed wire can afford. To prevent us hatching any plans for escape, we were informed that mines were buried all round. Then we were searched thoroughly again and finally officially taken prisoner; that is, we had to declare our personal particulars.

'We were allowed to build a hut from planks, and, with a spade provided as a tool, we dug benches into the soil. We slept fairly comfortably on these the following night, though crammed together.

'In the morning it rained, but this made our hut even cosier, especially as one of us suddenly thought of having a sing-song. And we all sang in an untroubled feeling of security. The important event of the morning occurred when somebody took off his tunic and shirt to search for lice – not entirely unsuccessfully.

'In the course of the day we were transported to a large transit camp near Bayeux. When we arrived I recognised several acquaintances among the prisoners standing ready for departure. I met others inside the camp, and we were able to discuss all the things that had happened to us in the last few days and our fears and hopes for the future. Among other pieces of information, I heard why we had not received the hoped-for order to retreat two days before. The man who was supposed to bring it, a sergeant with a large mouth and a considerable collection of medals, had been too much of a coward. At Bayeux too, I met a fellow prisoner from our neighbouring company who told me about a comrade he had shared an earth hole with. This chap, nineteen years old like myself, had put his pistol to his head when the Canadians approached, and had shot himself rather than surrender to the enemy. Another, from a different army unit, told how Canadian soldiers had ordered him to dig his own grave and stand in front of it.

'As this camp had no installations except a few tents for cooking and for the guards, as well as the most primitive latrines, we assumed that we would not be staying there long. At night we lay down on the grass and scantily covered ourselves with strips of torn camouflage jackets that were lying about, so that the rain did not soak us to the skin. In the daytime we searched for half-ripe apples to supplement our diet. Needless to say, we were searched yet again and my pocket mirror was removed. We were also cursorily deloused with DDT powder.

'Soon afterwards we were transported to another, even more temporary camp, where Allied troops who had just disembarked were also assembled. A bagpiper entertained them with tunes in which melancholy and gaiety were strangely intermingled.

'After a short stay we had to march down a muddy road to the coast. Now and again military vehicles came towards us and we had to step aside for them. Each time we got further and further into the mud, as the only reasonably passable area was the middle of the road, where steel mats with wide meshes had been laid down. On a road sign we read the name of a small coastal village, St Côme de Fresné.

'Little groups of soldiers, military vehicles and tanks were gathered along the small beach, while reinforcements (rearguard) in the form of more and more soldiers and vehicles were coming out of a fairly large landing craft. More ships lay off-shore on the grey surface of the water.

'At last we marched over the lowered flaps at the stern and onto the landing craft, which had meanwhile been unloaded. When the inner deck was more or less full and the stern flap had been closed again, we felt as if we were in a rusty, floating coffin. True, each of us was given a life-jacket, but, if German U-boats had attacked and hit the ship, all POWs would probably have drowned, because the upper deck could only be reached by a very small, slow lift.

'At about six o'clock in the evening the journey began, interrupted by long worrying halts. It did not end until morning two days later. I lay fairly comfortably on a plywood board; most of the others lay on the rusty floor. Many tried to sleep. Only when the sparse meals were distributed was there some movement.

'When the food chests and tea canisters first made their appearance, the many Russian 'hiwis' [volunteers] who were also being transported to England, and who had no illusion about the fate that awaited them later, stormed forward. The Germans were also hungry and thirsty, but they took a different view of their position and behaved in a disciplined fashion, although there were no officers present. On the other hand, it was noticeable that collar markings and eagles, in some cases even insignia of rank, had been removed from many German uniforms.'

In Britain, preparations were being made to receive the expected influx of German prisoners. These included hospital accommodation. Those who worked in these early POW hospitals still have vivid memories of the period. Acting Sergeant Henry Blunden, interpreter officer, describes his experiences:

'I was German born and when I was in the British Royal Army Service Corps we kept getting questionnaires asking us if we had any special qualifications. I was bored stiff and I put down that I knew German perfectly. Well, I didn't hear anything for a long time, then, suddenly, in May 1944, I was transferred to a hospital at Bishop Auckland, Co. Durham [Oaklands Emergency Hospital, Cockten Hill, Camp 93] and I was there till December 1945. The hospital held 300 or so prisoners – there must have been ten wards of thirty or forty beds. It was a changing population because, as soon as the prisoners were well enough, they were sent back to their camps, except for a few (about four) we kept as permanent staff working in the kitchen or the library and so on. The prisoners all loved it in hospital, because it was a very cushy life: beds, running water, and so on.

'When I got there, we organised the best way of doing things. We had officers and privates in the hospital – it made no difference to the treatment we gave them. We put them all together. The hospital started as a POW hospital with myself and one colleague. There were no patients there when I arrived.

'My job was to go round with the doctors, get the history of their illness or injury from the patients and translate it for the nurses and doctors. I also had to interpret orders from the English officers to the patients about how to keep the ward tidy, how to behave to the sisters and staff and so on. Quite frequently I attended operations. Those who had been in the SS had been indoctrinated with the idea that they were going to be murdered in Britain. So, when they had an operation, they did not want a general anaesthetic. They were therefore given a local one and I had to talk to them and reassure them while the operation was carried out.

'There was never the slightest bit of trouble in the hospital – except once we found one of the patients kissing a very pretty Irish nurse – which only aroused jealousy on my part. We sent him away a bit earlier than he would otherwise have gone.

'And then one did, as a hobby, ask them questions, though this was not part of my duty. One did hear information. For example, one of them would say, "I live in Darmstadt and the big factory there hasn't been bombed." One would report this to the commandant and get great pleasure when shortly afterwards one heard that it had been bombed. It probably wasn't connected, but it gave one satisfaction.

'One quite amusing incident did occur. We got an officer in who was a *Kriegsgerichtsrat* [judge advocate]. I had done law myself and I had heard his name before; he had done law three years or so before me and had done quite brilliantly, graduating *summa cum laude*. I asked a friend of mine about him and he told me that this prisoner's mother was a very well-known writer of kitsch in Germany. He was terribly ashamed of her. I went to the camp library and I asked the librarian for a book by this woman. I put it on the prisoner's bedside table. When I went in to see the man later, he was as white as a sheet. Apart from anything else, he was impressed – as were many others – by what he considered the efficiency of the British Secret Service.

'Some of the nurses thought that the interpreters were spies. They heard us talking in German to the prisoners and thought we were planning revolt and escape and they reported it. They never minded nursing German prisoners. They all liked young men, I think. In addition, the German prisoners behaved extremely well. The only thing they complained about was the English bread, which they found very unsatisfactory; they said that they got up from meals still feeling hungry.

'Some of them insisted on being Nazis but we didn't talk politics. They still thought they were winning the war until the Ardennes. They didn't believe the British news – they couldn't understand it apart from anything else. The more intelligent were anti-Nazis. They didn't get any newspapers in the hospital, so we used to pass ours on when we had read them. The less intelligent thought they were propaganda.

'I used to take some of them out for football, or for walks through the town (which was unpleasant because the population didn't like it). I had my rifle with me. It was awfully heavy and I used to get a prisoner to carry it for me. We never had an escape. I think it was considered bad form to try to escape from a hospital.

'The main doctors in the camp were German prisoners. They were quite good doctors and I used to consult them if there was anything wrong with me. They were quite educated people, Nazis probably, but not aggressively so. They were anti-communist – but they all were.

'Most of the prisoners we got came from camps, and were not freshly captured. We were not the first place they went to when they landed. We had no terribly serious cases: appendicitis, hernias, and so on. I can't remember that we had anyone die on us. We had one meningitis case and we had to take him to an infectious-diseases hospital. We took bad cases to a hospital in York. Our prisoners came from anywhere.

'The privates disliked the German officers but we mixed them all up. There was an amazingly harmonious atmosphere. The living conditions were really good.

'I did not go round spreading the fact that I was of German origin, though at that time I still used my German name of Blumenthal.

'I made a good friend from amongst the prisoners. His name was Dr Gustav Tilmann and he was a doctor of economics. He was a quite religious Catholic. He had been in the army the best part of seven years, but he had not got very far – which we liked, because if he had been a Nazi he would have made a career of it. He got on with everyone – he even spoke a little English.'

One of the Royal Army Medical Corps orderlies who was at Oaklands at the same period writes as follows.

'I was just a ward orderly. I said, "Henry [Blunden], do let me have a job." I was in the RAMC as a medical orderly, and wanted to improve my German.

'One day one of the prisoners died – he was the only German POW who died in Bishop Auckland. Henry had to get permission to take other German prisoners to follow his coffin. He was buried at Bishop Auckland. They went behind the coffin looking very solemn.

'The POWs had that special *Kultur* – an appreciation of music and the arts. The British Tommy didn't know anything of music and the arts, nor did he want to.

'Then there was this case – very sexual. One of the POWs started taking out the overseer's daughter at night; he finally seduced her and got her in the family way.

'The POWs were all very highly cultivated it seemed to me. They never believed that Hitler could be brought down. Hitler could never fail. "We will come back and subjugate you."

'They were passionately fond of music and the arts. There were no facilities for entertainment at Bishop Auckland.

'Major N. was the overseer. We were always being watched. He was very good to them. He often used to say, "These are very intelligent people, you know."

'Tilmann was the camp leader in charge of all the prisoners. if they had a complaint, the prisoners had to go to him. He passed the complaints on to the interpreters: if they had been overworked in any way, or if they didn't have enough to eat – nothing serious. Actually, there was plenty of very good food and they were well looked after.

'Hitler was their god. He couldn't fail. Most British people were indifferent to them or quite jealous. They realised the Germans were their superiors in many ways.'

Sister Bessie Scott was ward sister to forty of the POWs at this hospital. Her daily routine at the time was as follows.

'8 a.m. duty: read reports of night nurses.

'9 a.m. Did a round of the patients with my staff nurses and POW orderlies, who called "And De Betten" which I presume was "Stand at the foot of the bed", those who could walk about. Then I went to each patient and asked had they slept well, "Haben ze Strile gangen gehabt?" and "Haben ze pinkled?" and so on, and they either said "Yes" or "No" and notes were taken of this.

'Then 9.30: staff nurses and the POW ward orderlies did the dressing of those who had wounds or sores of some kind or another.

'10.30 was coffee or tea break for them and then Drs Weigele or Keller came and did a round.

'12.30 was lunchtime, which was always a two-course meal. After lunch they went out on walks or played chess, draughts, etc., till 4 p.m. tea.

'Dressings were done again at 5 p.m.

'7–7.30 p.m. supper time.

'After that everything was cleared away and washed up by POW kitchen boys. Then we had our games – for example, Lotto – when every man had a card and we played one line for one carrot or one cigarette; two carrots or two cigarettes for full house. There was great excitement to win a carrot or a cigarette. I bought all this out of my own money. I used to buy seven pounds of carrots at a time, apples and forty cigarettes. But it kept them happy and didn't allow them to brood. They also played chess and Lexicon. Some nights they had a concert for me. One of my POWs was a conductor in Hamburg. He was a seaman and he had them trained to sing lovely for me. We also had round-table talks about what would happen when the war finished. I drew a circle like this

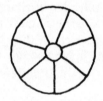

and every country that Germany had taken from another, I gave a little bit of Germany back and left just that small circle in the middle for Germany. When the war was going badly with Japan, I had just walked into the ward when some prisoners who had just arrived and didn't know me laughed about this and I was really vexed and I just let off steam at them and they got the impression that I hated Germans but it wasn't so. It was just that I had a sister who was a matron and had married a doctor who was a senior medical officer of health in Taiping and they had only been there one year when the Japs came in and I was very worried for them as they were near to the Jap invasion. Then one day, out of the blue, one POW asked me what was the medal that I wore, and my reply was "I got it on the Russian front and I've only been back a short while." To be truthful, it was my hospital badge, which was just like a medal. It had a cross in the middle and leaves round the edge. I'm only 5 foot tall and it made me 6 foot to them. I soon forgot about that till two years ago I visited two of the POWs that I'd kept in touch with, and the wife of Captain Carlsen, who is in charge of Kiel harbour and the fisheries, asked me what did I do to get my medal and I felt awful when I had to tell her that it was my passing-out hospital badge before I sat my State. We had quite a laugh about it.

'If I was very kind to the POWs it was because I had a brother who was a petty officer in the navy on merchant ships carrying high explosives to Russia and India, etc. His ship was blown up three times after he'd got his cargo to the place but was caught by the subs on the way back to England. I only hoped that, because of my kindness to my POWs, should he fall into enemy hands, they would be as good to my brother as I was to them.

'To me, all the POWs were my children and they belonged to me. One boy was only eighteen years old. He was in the SS and he'd been shot through both buttocks. When he was well, he used to follow me around the ward like a little dog. He was always at my side. Then one day he had to go back to camp, to a place called Tow Law, I think. When he got to camp, there was an interrogation in the camp about some incident that had happened in a French village, and this boy, Rudi Merschell, was one of them. In the middle of the day he was back with me, frightened to death. When I asked, "What are you doing back in hospital?", he said, "I've stolen a bike back to you. For sure they will kill me!" So I took him in my office and said, "They will come for you again. When you go back just tell the truth and I'm sure they won't do what you think." He gave me his parents' address to write to. This I passed on to a German orderly and explained that he might be late going home. He left a photo for me. Written on the back was "Keep this as an eternal remembrance of your Rudi Merschell. I shall always have you in my mind as a real mother."

'One day a young boy, also eighteen or nineteen years old, was brought into me from camp dying. All he kept asking for was "Mutti, Mutti", and, knowing this was German for "Mother", I said to Drs Weigele and Keller and Gustav [Tilmann], "If this is going to make his passing easier, I'll be his mother." So I repeated "Kleinen Mutter hier" and I kissed him on the brow three or four times to assure him I was his mother. I was a mother, so the role wasn't difficult. Then he died.

'I remember I sat by the bedside of a boy who'd lost an arm. He was crying copiously. I gave him a good talking to. I said, "Now look here, you may have lost part of your arm but thank God you've still got a brain."

'One of the men had been a U-boat commander. Well, Gustav used to say "Sister, they all look on you as Mother Carey and they are your chicks." When this U-boat man left, he stood outside the hut leaning against the door – and he was over 6 foot tall – crying like a baby. He left an envelope to be opened after he'd gone. It contained his tag. It was the only thing he possessed.'

3 Screening, July 1944

By comparison with conditions at the Front, life in Britain seemed comfortable, if not luxurious, in July 1944. To the prisoners, warm baths and comfortable railway compartments were a source of considerable pleasure. But in fact the British people at this time were still faced with severe food, petrol and clothes rationing. They were also prey to Hitler's 'wonder weapon'. The first of these flying bombs, pilotless aircraft familiarly known as V1s or, even more familiarly, as 'buzz-bombs' or 'doodle-bugs', fell on London on 13 June. The menace of the doodle-bugs did not cease altogether until nine months later, in March 1945, though it did diminish before then. By that time the flames shooting out of its tail and the discordant note of its engine had become an integral part of the British skyscape. By then every civilian knew that, when the engine noise suddenly cut off, he must fall flat on the ground and begin to count. The explosion came, on average, after ten seconds. In July, when the nightmare of the bombs' surprise arrival was at its height, with more than seventy a day falling on London, the Secretary of State for War was asked in the House of Commons for an assurance that German prisoners-of-war would not be transferred from camps in the south of England to areas unaffected by flying bombs.

Equally hostile was the question in the same month asking if the Secretary of State for War was aware that wounded German prisoners in military hospitals in this country had been put in the same wards as British wounded and that this was resented by the latter. Dr B. M. Steen was working as a house officer in Law Hospital, Lanarkshire, at this period. He recalls treating a contingent of German prisoners who were flown directly from the battlefield to Prestwick and transferred to Law.

'Many belonged to Hitler Youth', he writes. 'Injuries mainly slight shrapnel gun-shot wounds. Typically brash – disobedient – intransigent. Colleague above acted as interpreter. The most rebellious had to be cowed by British army in sister's room. Literally bashed into submission. No nonsense. Absolutely no fraternisation. Many transferred to local POW camp as injuries were minor.'

They must at least have formed a contrast with the previous POW contingent that Dr Steen had treated: 'POWs from Italy. Mostly cases of "shell shock" or disinclined soldiery. Great hilarity when many crawled under the bed during a thunderstorm.'

Many of the German prisoners hoped that on arrival in England they would be taken immediately to a permanent POW camp to begin a regular life as POWs under the terms of the Geneva Convention. This was not to be. The first stop was at one of the nine interrogation centres set up by the Prisoner of War Interrogation Section early in the war. There the prisoners were carefully screened and every morsel of information that they might wittingly or unwittingly be concealing was extracted. Field-post numbers and identity books, and unit names displayed on uniforms, were invaluable in helping British Intelligence establish the positions of German divisions. Disused racecourses, such as Doncaster, were favourite sites for such screening cages, because of the ample space and good accommodation they offered, but the football pitch at Preston was a reasonable alternative, and at both Loughborough and Catterick cages were established in bare fields. Colonel Scotland, head of the Interrogation Section, was in charge of the London Cage (in Kensington Palace Gardens), which served as headquarters and for the most difficult interrogations. Hans Reckel was taken to Kempton Park, Surrey.

A problem facing the prisoner early on was what to believe. Suddenly, he was confronted with two different versions of the war story. Did he continue blindly to accept the German bulletins as he had in the past, or was his confidence in their veracity shaken by the somewhat contradictory Allied reports? To help him resolve this conflict, *Wochenpost* resumed publication. But, however much it struggled to prove its objectivity, it was treated with scant respect by the prisoners. '*Wochenpost?*' said Siegfried Gabler. 'We just tore it up. Nobody read it. Tore it up and threw it at the feet of the chap who delivered the bundle. We knew it was propaganda and never touched it.' Kurt Bock, on the other hand, read it – when he could get hold of it!

'It was a small official paper with political and military news edited officially for all prisoners. As it only contained information against Germany, it was not easy to get a copy, as the German camp officials (before 8 May 1945) did not want the POWs to read propaganda against Germany. None the less, I was very eager to get a copy, because I wanted news, no matter from what source. I did not always succeed in getting a complete paper. I do not know which Germans took upon themselves the authority to distribute it in small pieces to be used as toilet paper. Anyhow, we needed it as toilet paper as well (especially as the real toilet paper was required for writing on). I read every piece of it I could get hold of as I had nothing else to read. Even English papers were very scarce and most of us certainly could not understand enough English to read them. I did not identify myself with the contents of *Wochenpost* (in slang "Wochenpest") but I just wanted news from anywhere and I thought myself capable of judging and deciding what was true and what I did not believe.'

One news item that could not be doubted, however, was the report that on 20 July a group of German generals and conservative politicians, united in the belief that Hitler was leading their country to ignominious defeat, had made an unsuccessful attempt on the Führer's life. They had planned, with his murder, to form a non-Nazi government in Berlin. Instead, the conspirators were either killed immediately or hanged in brutal circumstances following a cursory trial. Hans Reckel was at Kempton Park when he first learned of this event.

'On 24 July,' he recalls, 'on a dull, almost foggy morning, we stepped onto English soil at Gosport. In the streets almost all we saw were women in working clothes, smoking cigarettes, who barely took any notice of us. We marched to a small camp where we could have our first wash for several days. The next pleasure followed soon after: a railway journey, not in a goods wagon, as was customary with the German military forces, but in a proper civilian carriage.

'The journey ended at Kempton Park, where we came under routine treatment at the hands of highly trained staff, and we then became very clearly aware that we were nothing but POWs. It began from the moment we stepped onto the platform. We were left standing for a long time listening to all the loudspeakers summoning all foreign nationals to report, in a variety of languages. And then began the most thorough investigation we had ever undergone. First, we each had to fill in a long questionnaire (it was probably good preparation for later, similar tasks when we returned to occupied Germany). Almost all of us slipped the pencils we were given into the most secret hiding place we could think of, but we had to give them up again at the next barracks, together with all the

contents of all our pockets. The things we were allowed to keep were
shoved into a bag labelled with the name of the owner. Pay books,
i.e. our identity papers, all letters, as well as any photographs which
could possibly show uniforms, were confiscated.

'Immediately afterwards we had to undress, and all our clothes,
also marked with our names, were taken away for delousing. The
climax of the search was an examination for "piles", so that nobody
could smuggle secret papers or even weapons in his rectum. These
procedures completed, we were allowed to soap ourselves and have
a warm shower. Our uniforms, underwear and shoes, meanwhile,
had been suitably deloused by hot steam and were then returned,
together with the bags containing the rest of our effects.

'Because in the questionnaire I had written down a different
company from the one entered in my pay book, I was summoned to
an interrogation in the afternoon. One of the two gentlemen spoke
German fluently. I had no difficulty in convincing him that several
companies of my regiment had been combined. At the end, he asked
me an unexpected question, "Do you know where the Führer is?"
And when, in genuine innocence, I answered "No", he added with
a smile, "A few days ago, he nearly lost his life." Thus it was that an
unimportant POW heard of an event that by a hairbreadth could
have been of major importance.

'We did not have to stay long in the tents of Kempton Park. Two
days later, in the evening, we stepped into a special train which even
had upholstered seats. As the train drove through the suburbs of
London, people outside gave the V-sign and a stone was thrown
through the open window of the next compartment. These signs of
understandable hostility were counter-balanced the next morning
when one of the English soldiers escorting us handed us part of his
breakfast through the window.

'We got out at the small station of Longniddry (East Lothian)
and marched several kilometres along a bay of the sea which my
superficial knowledge of British coastal formation told me was the
Firth of Forth. Road and direction signs had been carefully
removed, and, as a further indication of Britain's defence measures,
we saw countless wooden stakes in the water – similar to the ones
well known as "Rommel's asparagus", designed to prevent an
Allied air landing in Normandy.

'Next to the little castle of Gosford, we found extensive barracks.
Some magnificent old trees indicated that the camp had been built
in the erstwhile park of the castle. A large oak tree just asked to be

climbed. The barbed wire could not be conquered that way, but in the distance I could recognise the big Forth Bridge and could gather that we were near Edinburgh. Unfortunately, climbing was soon prohibited.

'More important was that everyone received a "prison number", which meant that we were reported to the International Red Cross and could write our first postcard to our families by way of Geneva, if only with the very short printed text, "I have fallen into English captivity. I am well. Permanent address follows."

'Very soon afterwards, as I recorded in detail in my diary, everyone received one kitbag, some underwear, hand towels, a razor, a shaving brush and a housewife, also a toothbrush and soap. We did not, in fact, have toothpaste or razor blades, but, even so, this immediately made us feel halfway able to withstand the hard times to come. We also received, as a mark of continuously advancing civilisation, some toilet paper – thin brownish-grey sheets on which it was possible to write. As soon as I found a pencil stub, I began to write down events as they occurred and carefully hid these pages of my "diary" so that they defied all search.

'We were also able to find discarded razor blades, which we took to the grinder. As a result, we were always able to remove the stubble, with a certain amount of difficulty. One day we even had a hairdresser (needless to say a prisoner) come to the barracks to trim our excessive and exuberant growth of hair.

'In this camp we were at last fed fairly adequately. But it could scarcely be enough entirely to satisfy those of us who were big and strong. As a result, our covetous gaze soon fell on some potatoes and vegetable beet which lay inside the barbed-wire fence. Unfortunately we had to attempt our raids in daylight; at night time we were well shut up. It was comparatively easy to approach the red beet. But anyone who has ever eaten this delectable tuber raw knows how horribly sore your throat feels afterwards. For this reason, I myself together with a friend, an *Unteroffizier*, soon specialised in something more manageable and wholesome: potatoes.

'We waited for an unwatched moment and then crept quickly into the potato field, grubbed up as many potatoes as possible with our hands, stuffed them into some sort of bag or pouch, and slipped back into the safety of the barracks. Then we searched the kitchen rubbish dump for a large empty tin and hunted under the trees for dry wood. Somewhere or other we found old newspapers and someone who would lend us a match. In the disused boiler house of a laundry barracks, we cautiously made a fire so that the least possible smoke could come out of the chimney, and cooked the potatoes. Nevertheless, the British guards soon became aware of our activities, and from 17 September onwards the German "camp police" had to take steps to stop them.

'Provokingly, we next found that the "base personnel" – that is to say, every little fawning camp policeman, the kitchen staff and the German camp leader – were far better fed than the rest of us. They were even strong enough to indulge in regular sport. There was a football field for this and I remember some good games which I longingly watched. But our envious enquiries received a conclusive answer: if we became part of the base personnel tomorrow, we too would be equally well looked after.

'At that time we had well-founded hopes of being sent to Canada shortly. Five days before our arrival, yet another transport had gone there. Ignoring the prospect of being sent to the bottom of the sea by German U-boats, we were unanimously pleased with this idea, particularly the younger ones. The inveterate smokers were already dreaming of the 500 cigarettes which, it was alleged, everyone was given as soon as they boarded the ship. To the pleasures of anticipation were added the pleasantness of the surrounding countryside and the time of year. Even the camp itself, originally planned for British troops, was not bad.

'But, as week after week went by without visible preparations for departure being set afoot, when only a continual stream of new rumours buzzed through the camp, we began to get irritable. Most of the occupations with which we had to be satisfied at this time were tedious. Home-made card and board games were played till we were sick of them. Fresh experiences of the Front and of leaves spent at home became less fresh through repeated telling. There was nothing to read except a special newspaper for POWs, *Wochenpost*, which no one took seriously. Of course, one could read the official daily reports from the Front: the unmistakably genuine reports of the high command of the German armed forces, and the reports from London and Moscow, which were regarded with suspicion and which no one believed to be true. For the number of towns alleged to be taken or liberated was far larger than in estimates generally in circulation.

'The question of how far one could believe the different statements at that time aroused the first serious disputes. In my notes I read that on 31 October one of the dissenters, designated at that period by the paradoxical label "non-political", was horribly beaten up.

'The single nice day at this time when things were becoming increasingly less nice was the one on which we had "kitchen duty". The prospect of an unusually abundant mealtime noticeably increased our enjoyment of life. In the kitchen barracks there was the table to lay for lunch, and afterwards the dirty tin plates and spoons to be cleared away, washed up, dried, the table to be cleaned, the floor to be wiped over. This was work which enabled us to emerge from the feeling of general futility.

'To the few pleasant experiences of every week must also be added the evening "singing hour", which began as early as 3 August, in a large garage. A *Feldwebel* (sergeant major) had offered his services as choirmaster and he immediately succeeded in uniting the participants in the sing-song into a community. It was astonishing how many came – not only to listen but also to join in.

'All other efforts to sustain us with intellectual culture – a few lectures and community work – did not really get going, for we felt as if we were in a large waiting-room always listening for the order to decamp.

'After a six-week stay in Gosford camp, I noted down on 4 September, "At last, official notification that it's coming off tomorrow. Cook potatoes again, with enthusiasm, clean the room, Unteroffizier Schäfer finishes his chess set."

'We were woken up at four o'clock in the morning. It was raining slightly as we marched to the station. The weather improved on the journey southwards and glimpses of the eternal changing countryside raised our morale. Then we travelled through the dreary working-class district of Newcastle. We remembered comparable German industrial areas and the result of all comparisons was very flattering to our national feeling. The further journey along the Tyne showed us a landscape which did not seem very inviting: bare mountain sides and a narrow valley in which there were several clearings and disused stations.'

4 Digging for Victory

September 1944, and the way appeared to lie wide open to an Allied victory. In August the French, under General de Gaulle, had conquered Paris. In the same month, the Allied armies had liberated most of France and Belgium. On the Eastern Front, the Russians had reached the outskirts of Warsaw. In Britain, a sign of this optimism was the lifting of the blackout restrictions, which since the outbreak of war had made it illegal to show any bright light in the streets after nightfall. On 17 September 1944, just over five years since its imposition, it was replaced by half-lighting, the 'dim-out'. Ordinary curtains were now considered sufficient to mask houses, except on the coast. The modicum of street lighting permitted was increased and lamps on the few cars and motor cycles on the roads were allowed to shed a stronger beam. None the less, when the air-raid siren (popularly known as 'moaning Minnie') sounded, total darkness had once more to descend – though it could not matter very much, when the attack was coming from guided missiles which were independent of the human element. It was no longer solely the V1s which were making life in London hazardous. In September a new German terror, the V2 rockets, approached from the air. No engine noise heralded their arrival. They shot silently through the sky. The first intimation of their existence was a deafening explosion.

In autumn 1944 Britain also had a harvest to gather in and a notable shortage of labour available for this purpose. With a large proportion of the country's able-bodied men away from home in the armed forces, and with shortages of food supplies growing as the war dragged on, the Government turned to a source of labour as yet to a large extent untapped. Commandants of German POW camps were asked to submit lists of 'reliable' prisoners (that is to say, those without known National Socialist affiliations) who could be put to work. Italian POWs had been employed in British agriculture since 1941.

The Geneva Convention laid down precise regulations governing the extent to which POWs could be employed. Under its terms, officers could not be forced to work, unless they volunteered, though at this time the German Government had recommended via the Red Cross that prisoners be employed as a means of forwarding their mental and physical well-being. None the less, they remained in many cases reluctant. There was the danger of victimisation by the Nazi element in some camps, which would regard consent to work as collaboration with the British. There was the fear of helping the British war effort against their own country. There was, as much as anything else, lack of communication between the camp interpreter (whose task it was to ask for volunteers) and the body of POWs.

Hans Reckel, who was moved to Featherstone Park, near Haltwhistle, Northumberland (Camp 18), was one of a group who did agree to participate on a work unit. And, indeed, by the third quarter of 1944 some 10 per cent of the total 46,300 German prisoners in Britain – that is to say, some 4630 prisoners – were gainfully employed.

Very rapidly, the work ability of the German POWs invited comparison with that of their Italian counterparts. Mr Cambray, a professional engineer, was one of the people who used them.

'I did a lot of farm work', he remembers. 'Farmyard reconstruction – tidying up derelict farms. I had about forty to fifty POWs most of the time. I drew them from the Agricultural Committee, who sent them out by various means of conveyance. I generally had the same group all the time – under the control of a German warrant officer. He was usually the only one who could speak any English. They were all sorts of ages: from youngsters up to fifty- and sixty-year-olds. I used to tell the corporal what I wanted, and he dealt with everything.

'Quite a lot of them had quite a defiant attitude: "We are prisoners – but we aren't beaten yet." What rather struck me was that the type of prisoner in this war was different from the last. In the last war, he was more of a sportsman. They were good workers; they'd work all right. One day, they were wheelbarrowing concrete – and you know how heavy concrete is! Well, they were pushing this concrete too fast and I had to tell them to slow down. And they stood to attention supporting these great heavy lumps of concrete!

'They'd get on the job at 8 or 9 a.m. and leave around about dark. They brought all their own provisions with them. What you got out of those fellows depended on how you treated them. I had no trouble at all. People who were brutal to them got a bit of reaction. I didn't give them anything – not even a cigarette: I didn't dare.

'I'd have those fellows working without guards two or three miles out in the country. Those fellows could have set on me, but I had no trouble at all. It didn't matter what time of day you went there, you'd always find them at work.

'The Italians were more of a nuisance.'

The work situation offered some very definite advantages to the prisoner. Apart from the benefit to the morale of being engaged in productive activity, which helped to banish the depression born of boredom, idleness and inactivity, or of escaping from the claustrophobic atmosphere of the camp, there were material gains in the form of wages. The prisoners were paid a standard rate of 3/4*d*. an hour in *Lagergeld*, specially printed camp money, which could only be spent at the camp canteen. There they could buy a selection of items, ranging from toothpaste and cigarettes to braces, talcum powder and the clothes brush to which Hans Reckel treated himself as a parting gift when he left Braintree Camp.

Not everything was rosy, however. The camps, and particularly the work camps, were still inadequately supplied with recreational and educational material to help the prisoners to spend their leisure time in a constructive manner. The provision of these necessities was to a large extent in the hands of the Red Cross and the Young Men's Christian Association. In October 1942 the problems associated with their work had already given rise to questions in the House of Commons. 'Had the attention of the Secretary of State for War', it was asked, 'been called to the fact that the Italian and German prisoners of war in this country had been supplied by the Red Cross with portable gramophones and records, but that the firms supplying the records had been instructed not to include any music by British or Jewish composers, instrumentalists or singers, or band music by British regimental bands?' The reason given for this, the questioner continued, 'was that the records were mostly required for German airmen who are fanatical Nazis, who said that they would not have their ears polluted with British music and would require either German or Italian records'. Ignoring a facetious interruption ('Will the Right Honourable Gentleman see that music composed by Edward German Jones is played to them!'), the Minister replied that the music was chosen by neutral delegates to suit the tastes of the prisoners concerned.

That was in 1942. Two years later, libraries were still sadly deficient, and there was a crying demand for all types of technical books, as well as for complete collections of *Soldatenbriefe*, a series of instructive textbooks.

As well as material comforts, the YMCA also provided spiritual assistance. Sheila Connor drove a padre round the camps during this period.

'The German padre was Dr Heinz Golzen and we were employed by the YMCA/CVWW [Council of Voluntary Welfare Workers] controlled by a Swiss HQ, one of the heads being a world-famous pastor, who visited us on several occasions.

'Dr Golzen was a judge in Germany until the Hitler regime, when he left. He may have been Jewish – I am not sure of this – and he became a minister of the Church of Scotland. He was unable to drive, as he had one arm missing, I think from the First World War, and therefore he needed a driver-*cum*-secretary and I was fortunate enough to get the job.

'Dr Golzen acted as a kind of liaison between the prisoners and the army staff in charge of them. Our area was the whole of Scotland and Northumberland and we attempted to visit each camp three times a year. We used to tour several camps daily, staying at hotels, expenses paid by the YMCA, and return to HQ after a few days and type reports, etc. Everywhere we went we were welcome, and, as I was the only girl visiting the camps, a great fuss was made and the prisoners really enjoyed talking to a member of the opposite sex. Usually they just wanted to tell me about their children and their families they hadn't seen for so long. The car was always laden with all kinds of things, footballs, books, table-tennis equipment, educational items, and so on, provided by the YMCA. The problems were varied: tracing relatives, complaints re the officers in charge (usually unfounded), homosexuality, boredom and so on. Each camp had its "Leader", usually a padre, doctor or teacher, and he acted as a spokesman. Later on, Dr Golzen was able to arrange for trusted prisoners to go to the local churches and join the congregation, odd educational classes, and so on.

'There was one large camp in the north of Scotland for known Nazi criminals, and I was never allowed beyond the British officers' mess; it was the only camp that gave one the feeling of prison. At some of the camps, when we were due to go, the POWs would put in a special request for me to lunch with them and for the occasion they would produce all kinds of meals; the one that I remember most consisted of gulls' eggs and semolina done in a savoury way.

'The POWs were all well looked after and certainly not starved in any way; this I must emphasise. To contradict this, at one camp we had a lot of complaints from locals, as there was just not one cat left for miles – perhaps they used the fur!'

Hans Reckel tells of his experiences from the point of view of the German prisoner.

'The train stopped by a fairly sizable group of houses. "Haltwhistle" was written on a large signpost, and at first we were not sure if this was meant to be instructions for the engine driver. We had to form up into columns, with a long-legged officer in a Scots kilt at the head, setting the step. He obviously wanted to get us to the camp as quickly as possible, although we were tired and no longer used to extensive marches. On the way, we buried any hopes we might have retained of crossing to Canada. Instead of the vast expanses of North America, we were coming to the furthermost corner of England.

'Shortly before we reached our goal, we saw some ancient stone houses, an antique vaulted bridge and a castle – strange things to see on a march when we had no indication whatsoever as to how it would end. At last, our gaze fell on a conglomeration of long, low huts, closely hedged with high barbed wire, an impression of perfect and ultimate isolation.

'This was Featherstone Park Camp, Camp 18, which had been mentioned by the initiated only the day before in hushed tones. The road turned away from the river here towards the steep edge of the high ground. On the slightly rising land, the detached compounds of the camp lay on either side of the road, divided from each other again by high barbed wire.

'We newcomers were split up into groups of sixty men, each of which was taken into one of the barracks in B compound. Luckily, most people succeeded in staying together with their former comrades. Straw mattresses had to be fetched, everyone wrote their names down in a register, then the great boredom set in.

'The gloomy impression that the camp had made on our arrival was slightly mitigated when, three days later, everyone received a piece of cake as well as his own spoon, knife and fork, so that we assumed that this camp was going to become a base camp. This would have meant that we could at last have hoped to receive better food and also post from home. On the other hand, we were not exactly ecstatic at the prospect of staying in this bare, confined isolated prison for a long period.

'As unexpected and as pleasant as the cake was the fact that a little later on the refectory barracks were opened up as a common room in the evenings. We even had the use of a small piano there, which, moreover, had a fairly passable tone. Needless to say, a good player quickly appeared and we had some entertainment.

'Entertainment was urgently necessary, for in this neighbourhood and in the raw autumnal weather, hopelessness – unlike in Gosford – was widespread.

'On 12 September I wrote a postcard home: "It is gradually beginning to get cold. In the morning the grass outside here is completely white. The trees are showing their first golden leaves. Fortunately, the incessant rain has stopped again. At least at midday and in the afternoon, we can let the sun roast us." What this "roasting" meant was that we leant against the sloping outside wall of the barracks. Dense, close and motionless stood the sun-worshippers on the south side of all the barracks and let their faces brown until (almost) their legs fell off. Unfortunately, my letters from that period are fairly colourless. Everyone certainly knew, and it was ever again impressed on us, that the censor was at work on the English as well as the German side. In addition, nobody wanted to worry their relatives at home, so as a result many important things remained unsaid.

'In the days that followed, the hitherto firmly structured community began to crumble at the first onslaught. Some men naturally succeeded in being appointed to the base personnel. They moved to the base barracks. At first they were regarded as crooked, because the base personnel did not stand in the best of repute, being alternately envied and pitied. In any case, in no time at all we all suddenly had to decide if we wanted to work and be transferred to a work camp or not. The Jewish captain wrote down who could not or did not want to work. Of the sixty inmates of our barracks, there was only one who did not: a teacher. True, almost everyone gave very careful thought as to whether by so doing he would not at the same time be supporting the Allied war effort, but equally we were told that we would probably be employed on agricultural work and this seemed to us a fairly neutral branch of the economy. In addition, hardly any of us wanted to be excluded from the community which had held together through all vicissitudes and, as a large part of it had earlier decided, after animated discussion, in favour of a work camp, the remainder very quickly followed suit.

'There were probably very many POWs employed on agricultural work at that period; it was certainly so at harvest time. Many of us even supposed that we were not transported to Canada solely because of that. In addition, there were so many of us half-wanted, "immigrants" that it would have been much too involved and probably also too expensive to transport us across the Atlantic. The sheer number of us also told us something about the Allies' belief in imminent victory.

'On the day before our posting, the catering was already becoming frugal; two days later, morning and evening soup were struck off the diet sheet. But, on the evening before departure, the base personnel arranged a banquet – a great spread, I read in my notes – behind closed windows. In this way, the parting was made particularly easy for us.

'In the early morning of 19 September we were particularly poorly fed, so that the march to the station should not be made more difficult by full stomachs. At about nine o'clock we left Haltwhistle behind us, and in the evening, at about ten, we arrived in pouring rain at Braintree, where we continued our journey in lorries.

'The barracks at Camp 78 – High Garrett Camp, Braintree, Essex – were smaller than those in Featherstone Park. With only forty men in each, this was a step in the right direction. Once again, we stayed together in the old group, which had already survived two camps. The rubbish dump behind the barracks was still smoking; our predecessors could only have moved off a very short time before. From the graffiti on several walls, one gathered that they had been Italians. To end the day – there was nothing further to eat, only tea – we were summoned to roll-call. Though we had already been counted on arrival, this was a veritable internal German event. The newly appointed German camp leader introduced himself and his second-in-command, gave out some important information, and appealed to our reason to make the best of the unpleasant situation. While I was just remembering that I had been taken prisoner exactly two months earlier and was embarking on a gloomy train of thought on the subject, he concluded – I could scarcely believe my ears – with a triple "Sieg Heil" for "our Führer and commander-in-chief". This was the last and final time I ever took part in such a ceremony – and it was in England!

'At the time, it was scarcely felt to be a confession of political faith but was felt rather to be an expression of self-awareness and the will to endure, in addition to containing an element of defiance. And that camp leader soon proved to be an honest and not at all a fanatical man.

'In the following five days, we had time and opportunity to settle down in the barracks and in the whole terrain inside the barbed wire. Settling in was made easier for us by the certainty of being in a base camp. A contributory factor here was the fact that our letters and postcards would no longer be defaced (in bad German) by the notorious stamp

DURCHGANGSLAGER
SCHREIBEN SIE NICHT BEVOR DER
KRIEGSGEFANGENE SEINE ENFGILTIGE
LAGERANSCHRIFT BEKANNT GIBT

("Transit camp. Do not write before the prisoner of war has informed you of his valid camp address").

'Under the sender's name, all that needed to be supplied were the prisoner's number and the number of the camp. So we could now finally hope to receive answers from home in the near future. The worrying onesidedness of our existence would then at last be supplemented to become a reassuring reciprocity.

'In addition, everyone received some money – from some foreign assets or other of the German Reich – paid out in a new type of currency: *Lagergeld* (camp money), specially printed for us. In return for this, we could sometimes buy cigarettes or cake in the canteen, when supplies were available, as well as toothpaste and razor blades at last, and shaving soap, pens and nibs, ink powder and exercise books – but not notepaper, for we were only allowed to use forms which were handed out, and which made any conceivable use of invisible ink impossible. Before the first tobacco products were available, the avid smokers were scouring the lawns and the road for cigarette stubs, which they then spread out to dry and rolled into new cigarettes with newspapers.

'At this period, a dentist also came to the camp and a doctor held a general health inspection.

'On 23 September I noted down, "Showers. Non-smokers can buy cakes. The tommies discovered two escape tunnels in the barbed wire. In the evening, I saw a V1 for the first time; its explosion later shook the whole hut. The catering is at last becoming tolerable." V1 rockets thenceforth became almost daily visitors. We heard the motorbike-like rattle of their engines and waited for the explosions with mixed feelings. One evening we even saw two German aeroplanes caught in English searchlights. So we could never think that we were living well protected on a peaceful island. A search was made for the author of the escape tunnels and other escape suspects, but they were never found, although all barracks and kitbags were thoroughly checked.

'Finally, work groups were formed, each with one sergeant-major, two *Unteroffiziere* and twenty-three men. In open lorries, sitting on the tail boards, we travelled to work in the mornings. On the way we met comrades from the American camp, who were transported in large buses. After a long journey through Braintree and Witham, we stopped on the edge of a large potato field. A foreman was already waiting for us, everyone received the usual wire basket and then the great potato-picking began.

'We were completely out of training and the work was mostly not easy, but we were basically happy to be able to prove our strength away from all barbed wire, even if accompanied by armed guards. Although our backs got increasingly sore, we worked competitively; everyone wanted to do better than the next man. We drove each other on with words of encouragement.

'At the beginning of the midday break, we were allowed to take two buckets of potatoes to our resting place and cook them for ourselves over the tea stove. And in the evening we received permission to fill the empty food boxes with windfalls from a nearby orchard, so that we returned to the camp tired and knocked out beyond doubt, but fairly content. Content too was a gentleman from London who came to the field on instructions from his Ministry and acknowledged that we were "very good workers". Later, everyone heard it said that we worked 60 per cent better than our predecessors, the Italians.

'The work performance obviously did not maintain the "very good" reputation of the first days. Perhaps we might even have become lazy and indifferent very quickly if other measures had not counteracted this danger.

'First of all, we received $\frac{3}{4}d$. for every hour we worked, paid in *Lagergeld*, of course. In addition, we were surprised by an un-expected act of generosity: everyone was given an extra pair of shoes, oilskins, pullover and even gloves; for the increasingly cool nights, there was an additional woollen cover. On the other hand, one member of my work group, who was always last in the potato furrow and who opposed all commands to hurry, was punished with twenty-eight days' arrest – on the grounds of refusing to obey orders. Not just commands, but encouragement also, came from our German group leader and some others. Opinions as to whether "we ought to help the tommies to win the war" were very varied and long and violent discussions took place.

'Generally the guards who travelled with us were quite reasonable, but there were unpleasant exceptions. On 10 October I wrote down, "Had an absolutely stupid guard. Could neither cook potatoes nor take apples. Talked to civilians and only grumbled maliciously." And on 18 October: "Lifted turnips all day. Had an absolutely stupid guard; grumbled because I laughed at his instructions; thinks I do not want to understand because I answer his threats with a shrug of the shoulders."

'In many cases, communication was difficult because we lacked all practical experience with the English language. None of us had ever been to England before, and, faced with the different English dialects, were pretty helpless. It was at its worst with a driver from "Lord Raleigh's Machinery", who was very friendly to me but tried to explain in the most horrible London dialect how large his employer's machine park was. With one of the guards, I even managed to talk about the war and politics. And often, in the midday break, he gave us a bit of his newspaper as soon as he had read it himself.

'Through the medium of a sergeant-major with whom I got on well I could frequently borrow the only dictionary in the camp in the evenings. But I was generally so tired that I could only make any progress worth mentioning at weekends, learning important words and grasping grammatical constructions. There was scarcely an opportunity for other intellectual activity, though I once actually managed to read one of the half-dozen books which were in the camp.

'We gradually observed that the beautiful oilskins were not a luxury given as a proof of friendship or for the promotion of our self-respect. As the weather became increasingly English, as the Middle Europeans imagined it to be, the order came that we were to go on working in "light rain". Grumbling and filthy, we moved through sodden potato furrows and slippery turnip fields. As protection from the filth and wet, we wound potato sacks round our shins and most of us wore another potato sack as a picturesque apron. Everyone hoped that the light rain would become heavy. And we did in fact stand unemployed in an open barn for many hours, freezing, but with no desire for better weather. In any case, the return journey was the best part of the day. When it was made in the rain and with a tarpaulin drawn over the back of the vehicle, we felt particularly secure and often started singing.

'Obviously, such security and solidarity were not entirely desired. At the end of October, a group of fifty newcomers was moved into our camp, as a disturbing element. It was said that they came from German military prisons in North France. More precise information was not to be had; they spoke nothing but English in the washroom and in our presence generally. A day or so later, some fifty men who had come with us were taken off to another camp. Choice depended on which unit one belonged to. On the following day, I too was informed that I had to pack my kitbag.

'I myself as well as the others selected would have been very happy to remain in the time-tested comradeship and sober work atmosphere of that camp.

'We had to spend our last *Lagergeld*, that unconvertible currency, in a hurry in the canteen. As a non-smoker, I was so wealthy that I bought myself a clothes brush, the dearest item generally to be obtained. If I had known what lay ahead, I should obviously have bought nothing but toothpaste, razor blades and pencils. We had, after all, already become suspicious as a result of the rumour that we were going back to Northumberland.

'In the early morning, we marched to Braintree station, a group of 146 men. During the railway journey, we chatted animatedly if not fluently with one of the guards, who employed all his efforts to make us familiar with English colloquial speech. More than anything else, he demonstrated the use of a certain English four-letter word which was very widespread in the British army. Every female face he saw on the station, inspired him to further fresh examples of its use. The journey was therefore fairly entertaining.'

5 A Mixed Blessing

The large-scale advances of the Allied armies were virtually suspended by the beginning of September 1944. While they consolidated their gains, the Germans might possibly have had time to regroup. But on 17 September the British and Americans struck from an unexpected direction. Airborne troops were landed with the purpose of seizing bridges over the Rhine at Nijmegen and Arnhem in Holland. The scheme was not wholly successful. There was heavy and confused fighting and the British public at home waited with baited breath for the outcome. But the British land forces were not able to break through to meet up with the paratroopers at Arnhem. Some of them managed to withdraw; the rest were taken prisoner by the Germans. On 25 September orders were given for the withdrawal of all Allied forces across the Lower Rhine. After that the Allies concentrated on Antwerp – to such good effect that by 30 September the whole of South Beveland in Holland had been cleared, and by 9 November the stiff resistance in Walcheren had ceased and some 10,000 Axis troops had been captured.

In October 1944, Sir James Grigg, British Secretary of State for War, explained in the House of Commons, 'We captured far more German prisoners than we ever expected, and while that is a great blessing, it is not an unmixed blessing.' As Hans Reckel had guessed, the numbers of 'unwanted immigrants' were giving rise to new and unexpected problems.

With 95,000 German POWs in Britain in October, existing camps were filled to capacity and beyond. Temporary camps were established wherever remotely suitable facilities offered. Sometimes these facilities were not remote enough. When accommodation in London itself was utilised, worried questions began to be heard in Parliament. 'Was the Minister aware . . . ' that camps in East Ham or on Wanstead Flats, Stratford East were causing anxiety locally? Would he secure other sites further removed from populated areas for this purpose? A harassed Arthur Henderson explained that these camps were available at a time when temporary accommodation had to be found for a considerable influx of prisoners. They would be moved to permanent accommodation before the end of October.

Other complaints mirrored the atmosphere of the time. Why was penicillin, the new wonder drug, which had at this juncture made its first appearance on an astonished world, available to German prisoners and not to British civilians? Why were German prisoners seated in comfort in Britain's reduced and consequently overcrowded trains? Why were German prisoners placed in the same hospital wards as our gallant British lads?

Positively uncharitable sentiments were voiced: the Secretary of State for War was, for example, asked whether, in providing camps for German POWs, he would segregate, as far as possible, those who had had anything to do with the robot bombing and put camps for them in places where the bombs were most likely to operate. The suggestion was, of course, dismissed as contrary to the Geneva Convention.

Oblivious or indifferent to the hostile atmosphere without, the prisoners within the overcrowded camps were frenetically engaged in making life more tolerable for themselves. Unsuspected as well as previously proven talent emerged in many spheres. Theatres were built from makeshift materials and productions were staged – undeterred by the obvious lack of women to fill female roles. Bands and orchestras were formed. Lectures and classes were held – given by professionals from all walks of civilian life, and overcoming all manner of scarcities of teaching aids.

Such was the situation in which Dr Harald Dreier began his experiences of imprisonment in Britain.

'On 16 October 1944 I was promoted from Medical *Obergefreitr* to POW. The place of this transaction: Venray, on Dutch soil. Despite my Red Cross armband, I was still ordered to "put my hands up". We then marched to an assembly point. The few personal possessions which a front-line soldier carried round with him, in an attaché case or some such, were left behind. I marched, hands behind my head like the others, unfortunately in the back row. The gentleman who was escorting the rear of our procession, with an MP [machine pistol] at the ready, had glimpsed the wrist watch on my left wrist – a present from my father. His request for the watch was accompanied, in a manner that it was impossible to misunderstand, by a vigorous thrust of the MP against my back. The blue mark decorated my back for long after. The gentleman who pursued his aim so persistently received the watch.

'At the assembly point we were ordered to line up, empty our pockets and lay everything on the ground. The sergeant who held our material destiny in his hands discovered a pipe – a Dunhill – amongst my things. A touch, and it was broken and thrown away. A Dunhill in the possession of a German! He must surely have taken it off a dead Englishman! The receipt from the Viennese firm from which I had bought the pipe in 1936 could unfortunately no longer be produced as counter-evidence.

'During private interrogation by an officer, I complained that an English guard had removed my watch. The officer explained very indignantly, "An English soldier does not steal!" What could I say to that? In this case, he was even right. This was no common theft: it was daylight robbery.

'I was only in the medical camp for a short time. The wounded in this camp were first treated by English army doctors and then handed over to German POW doctors in the medical camp for further treatment. It would have been far better for many wounded army comrades if the English doctors had gone on treating them longer. To see an army doctor who is a general practitioner in private life, acting as a surgeon, is a very special sort of experience.

'I spent one night before crossing to England on the bare cement floor of an assembly camp. The commandant of this transit camp had had all the palliasses removed from the barracks. The day before he had received the news that his brother had been shot down over Germany.

'The crossing to England took place in the hold of a transport ship. This night crossing was horrible. We were closely crowded together. The lavatory could only be used by those who had found a place in the vicinity of the bucket – a dubious privilege.

'Hampden Park was the first station in my compulsory stay on British soil. Hampden Park: a racecourse. From the moment of the first roll-call in this camp, there were already many, many prisoners jogging to the left and falling out. The order came at roll call: "Poles, to the left, fall out! Ukrainians, to the left, fall out! Czechs, to the left, fall out! Slovaks, to the left, fall out!" and so on. Even Unteroffizier Bengalski, from my unit, who came as I did from Danzig, was suddenly a Pole. A few days before, he still wanted everyone who doubted Hitler's war policy and the promised wonder weapon to be hanged forthwith. The picture is fixed in my memory of a small group of German prisoners, possibly fifty to a hundred men, who were the only ones out of the several hundred POWs to retain their German nationality.

'Real camp life began in a camp in Sheffield (Camp 17, Lodge Moor Camp), situated on a slope. If I were painting a picture of the camp from memory, the dominant colour would be grey. Rain and misty fog masked our view of the chimneys and winding-shafts of the town. One sank up to one's knees in mud in the roads in the camp. But the food was unusually good and plentiful. There was even real coffee to quench our thirst, and, if it were not up to peacetime strength, to make it so was certainly the object of the POWs who worked in the camp kitchens. The roll call in the morning was interminable. Standing in the same spot hour after hour in the damp, cold December weather, was not pleasant. With the first cigarette allocation, which I received in my capacity as protected personnel, I could offer my tent-mates some comfort, for they were not medical orderlies.'

Dr Dreier was joined in Sheffield by Siegfried Bandelow, who also arrived in England in October 1944.

'On 30 August 1944 I was taken prisoner by the Americans, together with the rest of my corps. I was a lieutenant in charge of the company. Before, there had been heavy battles around the Seine (Mantes) and Somme. I had been wounded in the leg and arm. On 16 September I was in a military hospital at St Mère-Eglise. Then it was Cherbourg and we crossed the Channel to arrive in Southampton on 21 October. From there I was taken to Hampden Park and London. We were very badly treated by the military police and some pretty aggressive guards. I was sent for interrogation at the London District Cage, where I was asked questions about things and situations I knew nothing about. As I was unable to answer them, I was knocked about. My leg and arm wounds were not yet healed. The last private possessions which the Americans had left me (photos and letters) were taken away and my spectacles and stick were broken beyond repair. To this day, I do not know the reason for all this, as I was a member of an ordinary rifle unit and never a member of the Party, etc.

'After a short period in Camp 17, Lodge Moor Camp, Sheffield (cold, muddy and wet and the food was bad), I was moved to Camp 21, Comrie, Perthshire, Scotland, where there were eighty officers in each barracks. The mud was still there, but the food was a little better and we were allowed to write to our families. We organised lectures, lessons and theatre groups. There were political interrogations there, which showed that the British officials judged our problems and our attitudes completely wrongly. There was snow on the ground and the weather was very cold. I had frostbite.'

Private Siegfried Gabler was also in Britain in October 1944.

'I joined the army in August 1943 and served in the artillery. The funny thing was that less than a year later I was a prisoner. I was just eighteen when I was taken prisoner. I was captured by the Americans in August 1944 at St Lô in Normandy. For a couple of months or so we unloaded ships for the Americans. We couldn't believe our eyes when we saw the food that was unloaded there: stacks as big as houses. One day, there'd be chocolate; the next day, Nescafé; the next day, cigarettes. We didn't eat bread and spuds those days – just chocolate and Nescafé, and we smoked fags by the thousands. The French people used to stand round outside and watch us, and we'd throw them biscuits over the barbed wire. The Yanks would rather burn the stuff than give it to the French. We worked in leather gloves – real leather gloves. Every Saturday, all our stuff was burned – our socks, pants and so on – and we were given new. All this happened in Cherbourg.

'The day the fighting stopped, I was in a sort of camp hospital. I don't know what I caught but they gave me an injection. The food there was better than ever.

'Then they put us into a boat. We thought we were going to America. We spent two days and two nights in the boat. It was one of those landing craft with no doors and no windows so we couldn't see where we were going. Then we landed. The first thing we saw were some old gas lamps, and we said, "This isn't America!" It was Portland Bill. The date was October 1944.

'Everybody had to go through Kempton Park. There, they stripped your bodies as well as your brains. They investigated who you were, where you came from. They asked questions like "When did you last see your father?"

'Then we were all split up. I was sent to Glen Mill Camp, Oldham (Camp 176). It was an old cotton mill that had been a camp in the last war. I've seen Colditz on the television and, believe me, it was a holiday camp compared with Oldham. You see all those blokes walking round in uniform! There were 5000 of us in the camp and there was no garden – just one little street – and loads of barbed wire. No one dreamt of running away. We saw nothing of the outside world. All we could see was a graveyard. Funerals were the only excitement we had.

'We made a request for a football. The answer came back, "Sorry, no money!" This was the first bit of English I learned. We had an enormous number of professional people in that camp. You could take lessons in almost every subject: French, English, History, Chinese. All our teachers were professors; ordinary schoolteachers didn't get a look in there. You could go from morning to night taking lessons. If you were lucky you had a bit of a pencil and we used toilet paper to write on – there were great brown rolls of it. We would write down the English spelling of a word, how you pronounced it and the German equivalent on pieces of this paper and pull them out of our trouser pockets every so often when we needed to refer to them.

'We had an excellent theatre in Oldham; it was all made by the men from cardboard boxes. They were all professionals; there was not a single amateur on the stage. We had a professional orchestra, and the tenor from the Brunswick State Opera was in our camp. There were a lot of protected personnel (PPs) in our camp and they got a certain amount of money every week and they financed the instruments for the orchestra. They also had fags by the hundreds. We were given doughnuts every Sunday morning and we sold them to the PPs for fags. They put on plays and cabarets all the time. At Easter, they did *Dr Faustus* in German. For the rest, we played chess. I don't think there's a POW who can't play chess.

'In the morning, we had porridge with raisins in it. Then, every day for lunch, there was cabbage and frozen Australian mutton. Sunday was a bit better because we had mashed potatoes. In the evenings we had porridge again plus two bangers and a slice of bread. It wasn't too bad, except that there was nothing to do from morning to night. This diet went on till Christmas 1944. Then, all of a sudden, the food got very much better. It stayed good till the end of the war. We had no razor blades but they did give us a piece of soap.

'At Christmas we got £1 from the German Red Cross. It was a lot of money then. It could buy 200 fags. Whenever we got a fag, we cut it into four and shared it. We smoked the quarters on a needle. We also made our own lighters, because we didn't have matches or anything – we made them out of a piece of thread and a flint. We were very ingenious. All the wooden supports on our double bunks went on making toys and chess sets.'

Meanwhile Hans Reckel was continuing life as a POW in Britain.

'Our carriage was hitched onto a train for Carlisle in the inevitable Newcastle station. As the sky outside the carriage window darkened, our mood became correspondingly gloomier. We arrived at the well-known Camp 18 in the dark.

'For a change, we were put in D compound. There, only the kitchen and the camp administration offices ("writing room") were accommodated in barracks. The rest of it was tents, round army tents with duckboards and palliasses, in which a group of eleven men had to fit. The contents of our kitbags were most thoroughly searched beforehand, although this had only been done just before we were moved. We regarded this as deliberate aggravation.

'On the way to the tents, to the very primitive latrines, to the parade ground and to the dining room, we had to employ a certain amount of dexterity in order not to get stuck in the mud. As a last defence against the endless November rain, we dug trenches around the tent, and no one was allowed to touch the awning from the inside, otherwise it too began to drip.

'In this section of the camp, the German navy set the tone. This was particularly apparent in the morning, when someone went along behind the tents at reveille, practising his alarm whistle and filling the air with thoughtful dicta, designed to make it easier for us to get up. Many other encouragements followed the inevitable "Up! . . . up! . . . ", going as far as "Up, up, you weary lover. The camp is full of naked women!" But our inertia increased and one morning it came to pass that we were so late for roll-call that the porridge – in other words, breakfast – was cancelled as punishment.

'Having to lie around inside a tent all day soon led healthy men to devious thoughts. The pessimistic opinion of a nineteen-year-old, that we would remain imprisoned for the next twenty years, did, however, lead to long and animated discussion. One person even thought it would have been better if neither side had taken prisoners at all.

'It was more cheerful when everyone began to recount their memories of films which they had seen in some army cinema or other. But soon the accounts revolved around experiences at the Front, which had left such a deep impression on all our minds that one could hardly escape from them. In the evening, finally, we would sing again. Eleven voices filled the tent. Differences of opinion, memories and anxiety were temporarily unimportant.

'One unusually dry morning we, who were accommodated in the

muddiest corner of the camp, were taken down to the river. We had to carry stones from the edge of the riverbed to the camp in large wicker baskets, to make the roadway more passable. We did not work much but collected beechnuts on the way and rejoiced in the change and unexpected freedom of movement. Avid glances wandered up and down the hills, perhaps to spy out possibilities of escape.

'On 3 November it was suddenly announced that Camp 18 was going to be a base camp, as all "proper" base camps were fully occupied, and that we must stay there for an even longer period. This news was hardly calculated to give us pleasure. Conditions in the camp and our way of life could not be expected to change, except that we could hope for post from home.

'Still, perhaps there was some connection between this innovation and the fact that five days later we were moved out of the tents of D compound to the solid barracks of A camp. At first it was said that a commission from the International Red Cross had ordered this removal. Perhaps there was also some connection with the weather on the previous days. On 4 November the wind blew three kitchen tents down; on the 5th it was as cold as winter; on the 7th, it snowed and hailed; on the 8th we moved in streaming rain.

'The barracks were really already fully occupied, but we were simply stuffed inside. First thing on the following day, the whole body of men was newly divided up.

'Here, for the first time, the German camp organisation as a power in its own right came on the scene, representing the interests of the English rather than of the simple, non-privileged POWs. We had to wait for a good hour in the intense cold outside. Later, everyone was surprised to see how the camp leader in particular – a warrant officer of the "concrete navy" (coastal artillery), in appearance reminiscent of Napoleon – got fatter and fatter as the months went by, in complete contrast with the increasing thinness of the ordinary camp inmates.

'That our new barracks contained no beds and that the palliasses were empty, were only short-term transitional problems. A few days later an English officer tried to apologise to the barracks elders (hut leaders) for these and other inconveniences: England was only a poor country.

'In this section of the camp, English officers normally appeared in a somewhat different light. The morning and evening roll-call, not inaccurately known as the "cattle-count", was no longer a matter of

run-of-the-mill military routine, but was interpreted as a de-
monstration of hostile strength. Generally, we had to stand for a
very long time outside, with the barbed wire behind us, our eyes
turned towards the barracks, mostly with very empty bellies, often
freezing. In many cases, the count did not come up with the correct
result and then we had to wait while a second count was taken. On
11 November we had to "fall in" two extra times – once, the whole
camp had to march on the large meadow outside for a count.
Careful preparations were made whenever our very rare sojourns on
the meadow, already fenced in with barbed wire, took place:
machine guns at the ready were stationed at two corners and the
whole sentry staff were on their feet.

'In the evenings this camp admittedly offered an advantage
which I had not at first expected. Following its promotion to a base
camp, the large refectory barracks were opened up between supper
and lights out, as well as on Sunday mornings and frequently every
afternoon – for a series of productions, lectures, classes and light
entertainments. More important than the miserable equipment
available for this purpose was the readiness and surprising talents of
some of the men, who came forward with astonishing performances.
The inspiration for this probably came from the camp leadership,
which was supposed to offer distraction and diversion to the crowds
of men, which were becoming excessively large.

'On 10 November for the first time, I was able to go to a
performance of folksongs and poetry which bore the inviting name
of *Schatzkästlein* – "Treasure Chest". There was a great deal of
enthusiastic singing and recitation. A congenial atmosphere rapidly
developed, almost like an evening at a social club. The songs gave
vent to homesickness: the poems – by Goethe and Eichendorff,
Nietzsche and Rilke – to a certain pride in the cultural heights of our
own nation.

'On 11 November we even had the opportunity of seeing the first
night of an operetta, *Das blonde Glück*. Scenery and costumes, music
and performance were amazingly good – at least, so it appeared to
us. Women's parts – and not just in the nobler aspects of
characterisation – had obviously to be played by men, and the
sentiments of many of the audience were sorely tried. In the days
that followed, one heard rumours of ugly love affairs between
some of the performers. Camp gossip reached even greater heights
when the camp authorities openly warned all possible "loving
couples".

'The next theatrical performance, likewise "written" in the camp, was a drama with the beautiful title *Der Tanz ins Glück*, of a similar species to the operetta. Still, one could see that the drama group was making progress. The next performance, a simplified production of the famous operettas *Frau Luna* and *Der Graf von Luxemburg* was significantly better. On the other hand, the variety shows and cabaret evenings were no more than amusing and diverting. The high point of one of these entertainments was a radio commentary on an international car race in which – to the accompaniment of enthusiastic clapping – the English driver came in last. We gladly let ourselves wallow in this illusion as a substitute for what we generally did not have.

'Sober and without any illusions and very much liked despite or because of this fact, was a series of lectures on "Great Men in History", which ran from 13 November to the following January inclusive. A *Gefreiter* spoke very thoughtfully and impressively, first about Alexander the Great, Hannibal and Caesar. The long series of historical figures and events went as far as Bismarck and a portrayal of the Wilhelmine period. The dual themes "Men make history" and "Great men are the spirit of their nation" was not just an empty promise: the balanced structure they signified was really sustained – with the full approval of the audiences.

'Of at least as high a quality was a series of philosophical lectures: an expedition through the history of philosophy up to and including Marxism, delivered by the editor of a distinguished German newspaper. A lawyer talked about war injuries and marriage law. In addition, there were lessons in English, in German history, in geography and, from 11 December onwards, after a new intake, also in home-building (interior architecture), the building trade, musical theory, physics and mathematics.

'A flourishing high school could certainly have developed, especially as the listeners or participants were not only receptive but physically rested as well. But all too often the circle of participants was split asunder by transfers – frequently entirely arbitrary – from one sector of the camp to another. In addition, we were also hindered by the fact that we were denied almost all equipment: books in particular, but also writing paper and pencils, pens and ink. Out of these, only the lack of writing paper could be scantily made good, by requisitioning toilet paper and labels taken from empty milk cans, which were sought out in the kitchen rubbish dump. And, finally, the valuable time available to us for study was grievously shortened when on 18 November the evening parade was postponed to a later hour.

'Despite these difficulties, the greater part of the prisoners gratefully accepted the cultural arrangements. As I wrote home on 26 December, "I am lucky that so many lectures, entertainments and educational opportunities are offered here, so that one is not reduced to reflecting on one's own situation."

'The same purpose was served by an important part of all the other pursuits with which we filled our days. In the morning, after roll-call and breakfast, we had to wait for inspection before we were allowed to set foot in the barracks again. While we waited, innumerable groups or clusters of prisoners walked around the camp streets, whatever the weather, especially all along the fence. The view onto barbed wire was inevitable, and for this reason we mainly "took our turn" where there was the best possible view but passed the time mostly in animated conversation. At this time, too, many men went to the washroom to do their washing, either with the aid of their regulation hairbrush or simply by hand. Some people had providently manufactured special equipment out of pierced tins to scrub their washing. In any case, one had to reckon on it being very full in there at that time.

'Some people developed into positive cleanliness fanatics whom nothing could restrain. A few months later, some cases of note-worthy aversion to cleanliness also made their first appearance. If such cases became too bad, their friends sought professional assistance. And the water-shy could also not evade the weekly showers. Nevertheless, it did sometimes happen that a comrade was host to a head-louse – even in mid December. At roll-call, someone noticed one on the man falling in in front of him. As soon as our group was ready after the count, we crowded around this amazing, very active head, to get a glimpse of the dear little animals which were merrily running around behind the curly hair. Immediately after dismissal, the group leader saw to it that a hairdresser and a medical orderly dealt with the young man before he returned to our barracks.

'The afternoons were the time for individual activity in the barracks. This also included sleeping – in so far as the would-be sleeper had a bed in a quiet corner. But in most cases the bed was used for sitting on. Often several men would squat on the edge of the bed and one of them would hold forth, as had happened earlier, in the tents. Others played a German card game, or chess. In those days, the fashion for chess was spreading rapidly throughout the camp. Knock-out competitions for a championship were organised, champion and teacher were asked about rules and regulations, and a large audience crowded round the most important games.

'Chessmen were carved out of firewood and the experienced manufacturer burned patterns and markings on them with the red-hot point of a poker. The fashion for chess soon corresponded to a fashion for carving and burning, which had an unfortunate sequel in one case. On 8 December the inmates of one barracks were severely punished and moved to a tent camp because they had carved up bed-boards and whole bedsteads and worked them as carving materials. Many carvers had already lost their most important incentive to business on 24 November, when the commandant suddenly forbade all sales of carved objects to English soldiers. Until then, pipes (tobacco pipes) had been an important commodity, which, apart from anything else, brought a scanty trickle of cigarettes into the camp.

'A field day for all manufacturers was 30 November: the black-out was removed from all windows; all POW camps were meant to be brightly lit. The insignificance of the German Luftwaffe at this time could not have been more obviously demonstrated. The wooden frames were rapidly divided up and every last piece hidden under palliasses. Unfortunately, the nails which fell off in the process were fairly small and brittle, and therefore of little use for further manufacture. So in fact nothing had changed, in that we still had no tools, and the owner of a strong nail which could be used as a drill was regarded as rich. Typical of this situation was the very serious question occasionally heard: "Could you lend me your nail for a minute?"

'Anyone who could get along with a needle and thread to any degree, busied himself with avoidable and unavoidable repairs to his clothing. The quality of German wartime textiles became badly worn by the ravages of time and offered profitable means of passing the day. A few experts even undertook mending for other people, out of friendship or enthusiasm. And wash flannels, little holders for all possible utensils, shirt collars and even pocket handkerchiefs were produced, all from the original English palliasses.

'Of course, it was difficult to obtain the necessary supplies of sewing and darning thread. It was certainly possible to make do with threads pulled out of the palliases. But, when more substantial cotton was required, it was necessary to turn to the few dealers that there were in the camp, and who were widely recognised there. At appointed hours they were to be found on their beds, generally in the evening twilight, trafficking in the forbidden "black market". They knew who had what to offer, calculated their profits and haggled over a price. Cigarettes were employed as a means of currency. The largest part of these sales proceeds, as well as the profits, were very quickly consumed.

'Writing was another of the more popular afternoon activities. The few letters and postcards to the homeland could not fill up much time – except in anger over the fact that there were frequent occasions when we did not receive the wretched fixed minimum allowed us. But, amongst the 103 inmates of my barracks, there were always two who owned real exercise books and were beginning to set down their experiences on paper. Another wrote a long account and a series of poems on jam-tin paper. And, because we had no books to read, he read these out to us on many evenings.

'On 22 November we finally received our first book in the barracks: a Bible. Fourteen days later, a novel was also lent to each barracks, and by the dim light of one of our economy electric bulbs a *Feldwebel* read to us from it in a loud voice. Shortly before Christmas, a consignment of 500 books finally arrived in the camp. Again, these were only lent out for reading aloud.

'Sundays were spent somewhat differently. The morning inspection fell by the wayside, perhaps because it would have taken place at the time the religious services were held. The pattern of the day was more festive. The kitchen personnel strove to produce somewhat larger portions and a less prison-type menu, as well as taking pains with the preparation of the food.

'The wash-room was not as full, so that clever people postponed doing their washing till Sunday mornings. Sunday was also the day for writing letters and for thoughts of family and homeland. And the few men who were lucky enough to have saved some more and better items of clothing even dressed in a semi-Sunday fashion. But it should at the same time be mentioned that some of the inmates of this camp did not vary their normal routine for a Sunday or a festive occasion – in any case, not so that anyone would notice.

'At irregular intervals, certain events brought unexpected changes and provided subject matter for excited conversation.

'On 23 November "all Austrians, Sudeten Germans and Czechs" had to report to the Camp authorities. At the time there were no Czechs in the camp; it could only mean that Sudeten Germans should acknowledge themselves as Czechs if they ever wanted to see their homeland again – as was later attempted with the Masurians, who had to turn into Poles. A short time afterwards, the Austrians were actually moved into another camp. We were sad to be separated from them and on one hand pitied them, because they would certainly have an Austrian consciousness drummed into them in their new camp. On the other hand, we envied them, because they might go home earlier.

'On 29 November three men were summoned by name to collect post: the first letters from the homeland which everyone received in this camp.'

6 A Merry Christmas

Christmas 1944, and the spirit of peace and goodwill towards all men was sadly lacking in the war-weary world. On 15 December, Hitler launched his last attempt to swing the war in Germany's favour. Against all odds, he launched a massive attack on the Ardennes which was intended to precipitate another Dunkirk. Not until Christmas Eve could it be said with any certainty that the offensive had failed, and even then fighting did not cease for a further two weeks. To the POWs during this brief period, it seemed that at last the promised turn in the tide of German fortunes had arrived.

At home, the V2s continued to fall on London. The Ministry of Food allocated an extra ounce of tea for people over seventy years old. In a hospital near Newcastle, it was reported, oranges and nuts were distributed to German POWs on Christmas Day. The BBC's Christmas show that year was entitled 'Journey Home'. In the POW camps, with morale raised by the hopes of the Ardennes offensive, there were various attempts to accelerate the return.

A notable example occurred in the Marchant Camp, Devizes, Wilts (Camp 23), where under cover of the Christmas preparations such an attempt was made. The camp, like the majority of camps in the United Kingdom at that time, was full to capacity with freshly captured German prisoners recently brought over from the Continent. Early in December, an escape committee was formed and an elaborate plan drawn up. It involved commandeering lorries at the camp while Christmas festivities were in full swing; a link-up with a Sheffield camp where a similar mass-escape was scheduled; and the seizure of a radio station, from where a message would be flashed to Bremen requesting German warships to proceed to the east coast of England to pick up the escapees.

How far these ambitious plans would have succeeded will never be known. A chance word accidentally heard by a guard, and the project was exploded. A large-scale investigation was ordered. The prisoners whom the British authorities assumed to be the driving force behind the scheme were transferred to Camp 21, at Comrie in Perthshire. Before they left they applied their own retribution: a vicious thrashing was administered to the leader of the project, who, when confronted by the British authorities with their reconstruction of the plot, had admitted that it was correct. He had to be rescued by the camp commandant.

Less fortunate was a second prisoner, suspected by his compatriots of having betrayed the plot. Wolfgang Rosterg, a young *Feldwebel* who was already thought to cherish liberal tendencies, was amongst the group sent to Comrie. There, some 4000 prisoners, believed to have Nazi sympathies, were confined. Rosterg had a good knowledge of English and was asked to translate from British newspapers for his camp-mates. He was heard expressing satisfaction at Allied victories. One night his diary was stolen and his doubts about the Hitler regime read out for all to hear. This was evidence enough for the Nazi faction in the camp. A mock court was hastily created. Rosterg was dragged from his bed at midnight on 23 December 1944, forced to face a summary trial by his self-appointed judges, and found guilty of treason to the Third Reich. He was hanged in the camp wash-house.

When the body was discovered by the guards the next morning, an immense investigation got under way. The five men held to be primarily responsible for Rosterg's death were brought to trial at a British court martial, found guilty and in their turn sentenced to death.

However, the matter did not end there. The drama confirmed fears that had been voiced intermittently in past months: that Nazi elements were being permitted to gain dominance inside some of the camps and terrorising liberal-thinking or non-committed prisoners. There had even been reports that Nazi POWs were organising themselves into storm-troop units in captivity. The fact that German prisoners were allowed to salute British officers with the raised arm and Heil Hitler greeting current in their own forces did not allay anxiety.

A large part of the blame for this was placed on the type of men appointed as German camp leaders, the *Lagerführer*, and on the extent of the power they were able to exercise. Possibly they were chosen to represent their fellow prisoners in dealings with the British authorities because they were the best disciplinarians or the strongest personalities. They could be convinced Nazis. Once in office, their power to impose their convictions could be considerable. Despite government reiteration that camp leaders were not permitted to take any disciplinary action, they frequently sat in judgement on offences, in company with the British commandant; and repeatedly cases came to light of punishment, officially for insubordination to the camp leader, of camp inmates suspected by their peers of liberal tendencies.

To prevent such a situation arising, British government policy at this period had consistently concentrated on confining to separate camps those prisoners known to hold strong Nazi beliefs or with a history of strong affiliation to the Nazi Party. As 1944 drew to an end, this policy had patently broken down. With prisoners pouring into Britain in their hundreds, there was no time for the thorough screening required and no space to make the physical separation a practical proposition.

Camp 18, Featherstone Park, where Hans Reckel was continuing to keep his toilet-paper diary, was not immune from the unrest.

'On 3 December I noted, "Rain right through parade again, house search behind locked doors – in the night, someone tried to break out." My entry for 5 December should certainly be classified under the same heading: "Tommy forbade anyone to leave the barracks after seven o'clock in the evening because someone was said to have made fun of a guard." On 17 December we first heard to our delight that three Luftwaffe soldiers from B camp had successfully escaped – at least, from that camp. First, we had to turn out for an additional count in the evenings. Then, a few days later, I noted, "Commandant issues new restrictive measures: no more than two men are allowed to be outside together in the evening; walks are forbidden; no one can leave the huts from ten in the evening until ten in the morning. After another search, three men were arrested in a neighbouring barracks." As a consequence of this we could not get to the toilets at night, although both the English and German camp leaders knew that diarrhoea was going round the camp from time to time. An Elsan toilet, painfully reminiscent of the type we had in the tents, was placed in the hall of every barracks for really desperate cases. Obviously the commandant's reaction was connected with the general nervousness which was prevalent amongst the English. On 18 December the German camp police went through all the barracks reading out the news of the new German offensive in the Ardennes. A few days before, several people who had come out of hospital had told their friends that they had heard the news on the hospital radio that a revolution had broken out in Russia and that the Führer had announced the imminent end of terrorist attacks. After this, numerous rumours started buzzing round the camp again. Hopes and fears were aroused and our self-confidence increased.

'Even the German camp leaders reacted very quickly to the new situation – for example, by arranging an evening function called "Reflections on the Camp", at which they were unusually forthcoming. Anyone could ask questions. The post, current affairs, medical attention and care were discussed. Obviously the officials were trying to make contact with the mass of POWs.

'On 15 December all men over sixty were sent home under an exchange scheme carried out by the Red Cross. Amongst them was a fireman whom I had talked to many times. He had never been a soldier but had been sent to a French Atlantic port to modernise the fire equipment there. Many of the younger prisoners also had high hopes of being exchanged at some time.

'Without any warning rumour, everyone who had been in Camp 78 had to form ranks on the afternoon of 16 December. The lists were checked, and after that we discovered that we were going to get money for the time we had worked, which we could use to buy things in the canteen. Soon after, two groups from A camp were allowed to march out to the English canteen on two successive days. The choice was limited; everyone had forty cigarettes, matches and two razor blades. Toothpaste was much more important to me, since in the previous month I had had to limit myself to cleaning my teeth only twice a week. But toothpaste was not to be had.

'We had scarcely returned with the cigarettes before we became the centre of attention. People we had never spoken to before pushed towards us and offered their belongings for sale. One parachutist in particular owned for some inconceivable reason two uniforms, a German and a brown-coloured English one, and offered us his original parachutist's trousers for sale. The price was around thirty cigarettes. A dark blue woollen scarf could be purchased for twelve cigarettes. Non-smokers were undoubtedly the exploiters of every useful situation.

'I had a different sort of personal experience on 1 December. I was sent out on some work with a colleague. We had to drag one of the large rubbish bins from the kitchen across the main street of the camp and a little way down the river to the incinerator. The stink from them had annoyed us even in the camp. The bin was heavy, the distance was quite long and we were not very strong, because the food and way of life were not really particularly strengthening. On the corner of the steep slope which led down to the river we had to stop for a break and we took the opportunity of letting some of the pulpy contents run out of the dustbin down the grassy slope. Unfortunately an alert sergeant noticed this and warned us that fever could break out there. Then he ordered us to put all the rubbish back in the dustbin with our bare hands. On the way back, when we thought all our problems were over, he suddenly beckoned to us to leave the group and took us to a completely different part of the camp, where he shut us up in an empty detention cell. It was all we could do to restrain ourselves from swearing, while someone in the neighbouring cell was bawling out very loudly over and over again for a long time, "I am not guilty." A little later the sergeant came to fetch us, having found nothing on which he could or wanted to charge us. But he showed us to an empty tent, where we were supposed to stay until evening. Since no one was bothering about us and the sergeant was not to be seen anywhere, we ventured out of the tent after about half an hour, and of course went along the main road of the camp to the gate of A camp. A negro as tall as a tree stood on guard there and did not want to let us in, since we came from the "calaboose". It was only with a great deal of trouble that we partially convinced him that we had come from the sick-bay, and very dubiously he let us through. We were back just in time for lunch.

'Afterwards we thought we might have used this adventure to escape. But we quickly realised how stupid an unprepared escape in broad daylight would be.

'From the middle of December our thoughts began to turn towards Christmas. It had seemed inconceivable that we should be spending a long time in prison, but reality could not be changed either by wish or by self-deception. The disappointment was made easier to bear by the sudden announcement that the German Government was giving every POW £1 as a Christmas present, which was a significant amount of money at that time.

'So our preparations for Christmas began with the prospect of a substantial present. The camp choir practised carols, a few orators rehearsed a reading from *Faust*. The cooks prepared a festive meal, even making special Christmas pastries. A pine tree was put up in the Potsdamer Platz outside, as a Christmas tree. Somebody somehow managed to procure a small tree for our barracks. Someone else made candles out of discarded fat. Together we cleaned the floorboards and the beds in our barracks and finally one must mention the many small presents we had made ourselves, with a great deal of hard work. Despite and although a well-dressed Father Christmas appeared in our barracks and distributed a few small gifts from his sack, it was a sad occasion and our thoughts were with our homes in Germany.

'We celebrated the New Year in a very different way. On the one hand, we were in high spirits, because on New Year's Day we were allowed to spend our Christmas pound. But once again no toothpaste or biros – just hair oil! On the other hand, we looked forward to 1945 with fear. Those who were most frightened demonstrated the fact in the most obstreperous way by going out at midnight and singing the German national anthem until English soldiers dispersed them with truncheons.

Dr Harald Dreier spent the merry Christmas of 1944 in such a milieu.

'My next posting on English soil was the solid barracks camp in the county of Yorkshire [Camp 178, Ure Bank Camp, Ripon]. We arrived on the afternoon of 24 December, Christmas Eve. We were tired and hungry. We found empty barracks, no beds, no palliasses, but a most promising smell drifting over from the kitchen quarters. The prisoners who should have been responsible for camp management had been sent to the camp some time before. In the sick bay there were two doctors, a dentist and some medical orderlies comfortably settled in. In the evening, bales of straw, sacks and covers were delivered. Stuffing palliasses was certainly a significant occupation for the Holy Night. On Christmas Day itself, the food in the camp was very sparse: we were absolutely starving. But the "comrades" in the kitchen and the sick-bay lived under the protection of the English troops, like maggots in bacon. Obviously the English commandant had not been informed of our arrival in time. Over the holidays it was naturally impossible to order food. A lovely Christmas present!

'I did not understand the behaviour of the English military staff in appointing a goose-stepping Nazi soldier, who was even said to have been an SS man, as camp leader in this camp. Also inexplicable to us POWs was the order to greet English officers with the Hitler salute. There were still a large number of POWs, especially *Unteroffiziere* and *Feldwebel*, in the camp at this time before the capitulation, who believed in the wonder weapon and the "Führer's war to end wars". It actually gave them great pleasure to greet the English officers with outstretched arms and shoot back at them the retort "Heil Hitler!" '

Siegfried Bandelow had left Comrie before the serious trouble there.

'On 1 December I was transferred to Bridgend, Glamorgan, Camp 198. There were about fifty officers in each barracks. The German camp leader was Colonel Kaumann. We quickly organised the camp ourselves and got lessons, lectures, music and theatre groups going. I followed a course leading up to the *Abitur*. On Christmas Eve a celebration for everybody was held in the theatre and continued in the barracks later. Over Christmas there was a large exhibition of objects and artistic work made by POWs out of tin cans, wood, fabric and leather. They included chess sets, little boxes, cigarette holders, book covers, pictures, carvings and so on. The British commandant was Lieutenant Colonel Darling. It was at this camp that I heard the news about the Ardennes offensive.'

Only in one small area did the Christmas spirit retain something of its erstwhile sweetness. In Oaklands Hospital, Sister Scott went round and kissed every prisoner in Ward K on the brow and said, 'That's from your wife' to the married ones, and 'That's from your mother' to the young lads. 'An Austrian nursing sister who had a lovely voice sang "Silent Night" which was nice.'

For a Christmas present the inmates gave Sister Scott a book, which she still has, full of mementoes, signatures, drawings, photographs and poems by her prisoners.

'When this book was first started, I was with a patient at the end of the ward, when about thirty of the POWs walked down the ward to me. At first I didn't know what was to happen. Then they all bowed to me and Gustav was the spokesman for them. Then he explained about the book. This I treasure very much. I have so many happy yet sad memories of them.

'Gustav used to tell me that they all loved me, but I smiled and said maybe because they see in me a second mother.'

With the book came a poem:

> We would like to give you
> Pearls and precious things,
> Necklaces of amber
> Gold and silver rings.

There is no doubt about it,
In one way and another,
While we were convalescing,
You have nursed us like a mother.

We woke up every morning
To your cheerful, happy smile.
Our pain and our dejection
Were forgotten for a while.

No insult ever soiled your tongue,
Nor hate left any stain,
With love and kindness in your heart,
You soothed away our pain.

And so we offer you this book,
With wishes most sincere,
That God will keep you safe for us
For many and many a year.

May you live for long to come,
Have many hours of gladness,
Have pleasures, joy and happiness,
And never know life's sadness.

This is a Christmas present,
We give to you today,
Hoping that you'll remember us
When we are far away.

7 . . . and a Happy New Year

The Allied invasions pressed steadily forward in the early months of 1945. It was still not a story of undiluted success. The German POWs were not alone in regarding Germany as unbeaten. The Allied leaders too continued to consider German resistance as still formidable, and as late as February 1945 were carrying out massive air attacks on German cities, killing thousands of civilians. Neither the fears of the one nor the hopes of the other were entirely unfounded. In the first few days of the new year, the Germans launched an attack on Strasbourg, and the town was held for the Allies only by a determined effort on the part of General de Gaulle. On 11 February the Russian armies moving in from the east took Budapest, having already liberated Warsaw and Cracow, but in mid March were pushed back from the Austrian frontier by German resistance. From 4 to 11 February, Stalin, Churchill and Roosevelt held in Yalta the last of their great wartime meetings to decide how the postwar world was to be organised. Among other things, they considered the postwar division of Germany among the major Allies.

One thing the Allies were agreed on was that the situation of the 1930s, when a poverty-stricken Germany, humiliated by defeat in the First World War, crippled by reparations, in the grip of severe depression, had fallen victim to Hitler's promises, must never again be allowed to recur. A divided Germany was one aspect of their solution. But, equally, the question of the rebuilding of the country after the war gave food for thought. It was unthinkable that, when peace finally arrived, hundreds and thousands of German POWs, some still strongly permeated with Nazi beliefs, should be unleashed to restore the country in its old image.

It was on this basis that the idea of re-educating the POWs was born. The British Government espoused it as a policy as early as September 1944, when the Political Intelligence Department (PID) of the Foreign Office was made responsible, by a decision of the War Cabinet, for the segregation and re-education of German POWs. The general aims of the PID were, first, 'To eradicate from the minds of the prisoners belief in the German military tradition and the National Socialist ideology, of which the basis is that might is right and that the necessity of the state knows no law'; secondly, to impart to the prisoners 'an accurate understanding and a just appreciation of the principles of democratic government and their implications for the conduct of men and nations'; thirdly, 'to present the British Commonwealth of Nations as an example of a democratic community in action, while avoiding the projection of Britain as a model to be slavishly copied'; and, finally, 'to remove German misconceptions about European history of the last fifty years and especially about the origin, conduct and results of the two world wars'.

Herbert Sulzbach, a German Jewish refugee who fought in the German army in the First World War and on the British side in the second, became one of the most active and successful proponents of re-education. He was appointed interpreter officer at Comrie Camp in January 1945, shortly after the murder of Rosterg, and was almost immediately asked by several POWs for protection from their fellow prisoners.

This could be a key part of the British interpreter's role in the camp. It was through him that the prisoner who could not speak English (and the vast majority were in this position) could communicate with the British camp authorities. But British interpreters were in short supply and the quota in any case was one interpreter for a camp with fewer than 500 inmates, two when the number of prisoners was between 500 and 1500, and three for a camp with over 1500. In the absence of a British interpreter officer, a German interpreter was employed. If he happened to be a man with Nazi sympathies, he was able to distort the prisoner's request to suit his own purposes. He was particularly liable to do so if that request was for protection against intimidation.

And intimidation, in February 1945, was still rife. Following the incident at Comrie, an energetic screening operation had been carried out in the camp and all known anti-Nazis were sent to other camps for their own protection. At four or five other camps, however, fresh incidents of a similar nature were reported in the early months of the year. In Canning Town Camp in February 1945, for example, there were clashes between Nazis and other

German prisoners, resulting in injury to some of the latter. They required medical attention, but no serious damage was done.

A more unpleasant incident of a different nature occurred at Glen Mill Camp, Oldham. Siegfried Gabler recalls, 'In complete contrast to the treatment we received in general, something awful happened in Oldham. On 8 February 1945 the camp building was cleared for reasons unknown to us. The 5000 of us had to stand in the camp street for several hours and it drizzled with rain. We noticed that the camp was surrounded by armoured vehicles. To show that this wasn't getting us down, we started singing. Some men standing at the back started pushing (similar to a football crowd), and, I presume, one of the guards lost his nerve, pulled the trigger and shot a prisoner right through the neck. He was lying dead in the street only about six feet from where I stood. His name was Paul Hartmann, nineteen years old, from Posen. He died with his hands in his pockets. One of the rooms in Glen Mill was later named after him. You are about the first person I have talked to about this.'

Hans Reckel was still in Camp 18 as 1945 dawned.

'The sun shone in the early days of 1945, but the mild temperatures around Christmas were followed by genuine winter cold. On 8 January it began to snow. This made a pleasant change. The landscape reminded us much more of our homes or of picture postcards. And, remembering our childhood, we built snowmen, began snowball fights and some of us used a gently sloping path as a slide or ski run, until such activity was forbidden, because it wore out the soles of our shoes too quickly. It was unpleasant for members of the gang who did not possess coats: especially during roll-call, they stood and froze unmercifully. Only in the second half of January were we issued with brown woollen capes, but we did not like them, because they were not as warm as our coats and looked like postmen's capes. They did, however, protect us from the worst of the cold, and they were useful as blankets at night. And two days later everyone had to give up two blankets, which were replaced by a sleeping bag made up of two sheets sewn together; and so the capes were even more important.

'A casualty of the cold was the pump which supplied our water. This seized up on 18 January so that in the early morning, in the cold, we sometimes had to stand around the only tap which worked, with a lead bucket in order to wash ourselves.

'In January and February, cultural events became more frequent. In any case, that is how it seemed, because the preparations for them were so successful that the result became obvious. The musical events deserve particular mention. Besides concerts of requests held on Sundays, and of variable quality, there were the operettas which I have already described and, from the end of January, opera evenings, with excerpts from operas such as *The Magic Flute*. In addition, choirs and theatre groups grew up in individual barracks, so that even the apathetic were drawn in.

'What was even more important was the fact that, as the course of the war became more critical, the so-called *Zeitungsschau* ("newspaper show") became more significant. Few English newspapers penetrated the camp very regularly, and then they went only to the base personnel. So that the rest of the inmates could at least know some of the news, some of it was translated and read out from time to time at public gatherings, some was summarised and a small amount was commented upon. Because the man who organised the *Zeitungsschau* had spread undesirable propaganda, the camp commandant had him moved to B camp and the whole *Zeitungsschau* collapsed from 3 February.

'It was a period of ill tidings. Those who lived in East Germany were particularly nervous about news. They knew all too well how Russian troops had laid East Prussia waste in 1914, and how Polish guerrillas had ravaged Upper Schleswig in 1920. On 23 January I noted, "Evening *Zeitungsschau*: the Russians on the Oder; Beuthen, Posen and Insterburg fallen. Hauptmann (Captain) Willdie reported to have said soothingly that we must march against Russia again."

'I was friendly with a POW from Beuthen, who lived in the same barracks as I did. He was one of the first to receive a letter and so could breathe a sigh of relief. What he heard from his family was very reassuring, but the letter had taken a long time to reach him. Now he was worried whether his family was still alive, had been deported, had fled, and, if so, where they had been deported or fled to. He scarcely knew what to think – whether he should still write letters, and how he should direct his thoughts and his letters. That chap was relieved that we did not receive letter forms for weeks. But to everyone's surprise and envy he received two parcels from his parents at the beginning of February. This could only be regarded as an irony of fate.

'Those, like myself, who lived in the western third of Germany, in Göttingen to be exact, carefully followed all reports about the Allied bombing and the advance of the fronts, but events were not so overwhelming in West Germany. Those who had already received some post generally had good reason to be temporarily reassured.

'On January 29 I was one of the few who received signs of life from the homeland. Three names appeared on the noticeboard. We could collect the letters from the office. So that I should not have to answer curious or sympathetic questions, I read it out in public immediately: my family house was undamaged and my next of kin were in good health; but one of my cousins had been killed in Russia; another was in an American POW camp. My joy was not complete, but a feeling of great relief soon swamped everything else. I was generally congratulated and a few days later I had to report to the less fortunate in the *Lagerspiegel* (the camp news bulletin) on the condition of the letters, the length of time they had taken and their contents.

'Others received their first letters very much later, only after much suffering and increasing uncertainty. These included the married men, who were indeed objects of pity and probably knew that their grown-up or semi-grown-up sons were in special danger. Some heard absolutely nothing from their families, so that many months later they finally turned to the lost-relatives section of the Red Cross.'

Meanwhile, the number of prisoners in Britain continued to grow. Heavy fighting over the waterways of Holland in the early months of 1945 was yielding a new batch of arrivals, which included Lieutenants Kurt Bock and Egon Schormann.

'In Holland', writes Bock, 'I remember the basement of a textile factory, where the officers had a compound only separated by ordinary wire from the much larger room where the privates and petty officers were gathered. We spent several days there and it was there that I made the acquaintance of my friend Egon Schormann. I had nothing but my uniform. A habit which I still have today is of losing handkerchiefs, and, consequently, when I caught my first cold as a POW I did not have one. Through the wire, a soldier from my former company passed me a small red handkerchief. For many weeks it was my sole possession and for a long time I actually managed not to lose it.

'Our daily diet: tea with milk and sugar twice daily, poured into an empty corned-beef tin. If you had one! The first day this was difficult, as the ration was one tin of corned-beef for three men. Only one man could keep the tin. But, as the days went by, this problem was solved. With an empty tin to use as a cup, I now had my second piece of property as a POW. As well as the beef, we got some biscuits twice a day, and a teaspoon of jam once a day. It must have been sufficient calories but it was not enough really to satisfy us. As we had nothing to do but talk, this was an additional topic. However, there were enough other things to discuss at that time.

'Interrogations were going on all the time. As I had nothing to tell or to disclose, they seemed to be satisfied with one interview. There must have been frequent beatings of prisoners. I saw it myself in dim light and heard a lot of screaming for hours on end.

'There was a POW, a first lieutenant with quite a number of decorations for bravery who nevertheless openly criticised the German Government, especially Hitler. I had formerly heard many jokes but never, not even privately, experienced somebody talking like this. In these circumstances, with so many English soldiers around, it was of course no longer dangerous for him. It was a novelty for all of us and quite naturally he met strong opposition; but for the Englishmen, his life would have been in danger. I remember that I just listened, asking myself could it be possible that he was right – that things had happened which we did not know anything about? If his military record had been less good (it was far above average), I and others would have doubted his credibility. It was the first democratic discussion I heard.

'We were anxious to get news. What was the military situation? Who was advancing faster: the Western Allies from the West or the Russians from the East? What would become of Germany when there was an alliance? One older British officer also discussed these problems with us. He passed on information and showed photos: photos of people hanging in Warsaw, photos of Stalin, Churchill and Roosevelt at Yalta. We asked whether the Western Allies would get ahead fast enough to occupy the greater part of Germany. His reply: everything is already officially settled and agreed at Yalta. We laughed, telling him that this unity would not last long. I am sure that, if they had called for volunteers, they would have found enough to go on fighting against the Russians if only to keep them out of Western Europe. In the opinion of the British officer, the Russians were to occupy Germany up to the eastern banks of the River Elbe. I could not believe this and told him that in that case Hamburg too would become Russian-occupied territory and nobody could expect such stupidity actually to become fact, especially as it would not be necessary if only the English would advance fast enough.

'Everybody had received a thin cotton blanket. It served both as a sheet on the concrete floor and as a blanket to roll up in. One of the POWs had managed to bring a quilted blanket into captivity. I forget his name but I shall never forget him and what he looked like: bespectacled, dark brown hair. Enviously, I stared at him when he comfortably snuggled into his extra blanket. We talked about our future. About the Geneva Convention. We knew that this Convention existed, but what did it say? Some people claimed that they knew. Perhaps they did. Will they keep us long, once the war is over? Will they send us to England or to America? We listened to stories of the very few older German officers who had already had experience in the First World War.

'Ostend was the next camp after Tilburg, a former brick factory. However, it marked substantial progress as far as food was concerned. I remember we slept in a type of litter, but, again, only with our single blanket. Before we went to this camp or before we entered it, we had again been thoroughly searched. We had nothing, but this nothing had to be carefully screened. We could not anticipate that twenty years later screening would become almost a routine at all the airports of the world.

'The allocation of food at Ostend presented quite a problem. We got an excellent milk soup (for many of us, too little), and I remember having a serious bet that one person could drink the whole can if he could only get it for himself. As it was, the can served fourteen men. Apart from the milk soup, there was fine white bread, perhaps three loaves for fourteen; a small tin of herring in tomato sauce; a small chunk of cheese; and a piece of sausage or even two different types of sausage. All this had to be divided to serve fourteen men. Instead of this variety, it would have been better to have given us more of one type but in a large enough quantity to be cut into fourteen pieces. Of course, we did not have knives, and I forget how we finally managed the distribution. Anyhow, we survived, and I, with a severe cold, sneezing heavily, was frequently rinsing my handkerchief in cold water in the open air and then swinging the rag about whilst I walked around, to get it dry again. I did not dare hang it on the barbed wire.

'The weather was fair for early March. It was clear to everybody that the war could not go on for long. That we would be kept in custody for a long time was also certain. Therefore, we longed to be transferred to a permanent camp where we could settle down and do something useful, not just talk. We were anxious to be shipped to England.

'The Channel crossing was made on a transport ship which may have shipped armoured cars to the Continental battlefields. The fairly small number of officers was taken on one ship, and we had lots of room to settle down in small groups on riveted iron sheets. The huge, rectangular, steel-lined room was empty, but on one side, separated by a rope, stood the only visible guard. About 5 or 6 metres behind him, there was something which we could not immediately identify. We were hungry as we had had no food for a very long time. We were also thirsty. Where was the toilet? I am somewhat curious by nature – at least, even today I still have the urge to explore everything when I am on a ship. It was my handicap, shared with the great majority of my comrades then, that I could speak very little English. I told my comrades that I wanted to investigate the object behind the guard that had aroused my curiosity. We strolled over to the rope and I asked him where I could go to "wash my hands". I made it seem very urgent and after some difficulty he finally agreed. Another man kept up a discussion as far as he could, asking when supper would be served and other things. In the meantime, I not only washed my hands but also thoroughly investigated the hidden secrets and found cardboard boxes full of corned beef, our customary diet. It was not difficult to snatch a tin or two, hide them in my uniform and join my friends on the other side of the rope. Two tins for so many! But we developed a technique. The guard would permit only one at a time to go and wash his hands. These hands were then used to organise the tins. Not everybody dared take a tin, but, by the time we were summoned officially to line up for the distribution, we had swallowed the contents of quite a number of tins, though in fact it still only resulted in a small portion for each of us, and we had to take care that the guard did not become suspicious.

'A few more soldiers arrived to hand out the official ration. Two queues formed, but it was immediately obvious that nobody was counting us or noting who had received his share of one tin between two (instead of the one for three we had had on the Continent). After I had got my tin, I queued up again with another friend, and we tried and succeeded a third time. It was clear: navy rations were better!

'Nobody told us where we were going. In this completely closed steel box we could not even guess the direction. Maybe the guards did not know themselves. If they knew, how could they explain it? It was difficult to exchange more than the absolute essentials. The guards seemed to understand what we told them. We did not understand them, but just listened to a nearly unknown idiom.

'At least it was warm enough on board, and, having filled our bellies with corned beef, we settled down to sleep on the iron planks, the strange noise of the ship in our ears.

'Rattling of chains – anchor chains? – the sound of running feet, calls far away, made me wake up. A summons to do something. Always prepared to escape inactivity, I volunteered, and consequently was ordered to carry a bucket with dirt and refuse upstairs to the deck. Well, at least I was the first to see England: Gravesend.

'Hours later, a train took us elsewhere. It was not just an ordinary goods train, but we sat in comfortable compartments on upholstered seats. The railway men and women just looked at us. There was no screaming and even spitting at us like in Holland.

'Hampden Park: long rows of tables. Interrogation: your name, your rank, your company, your papers. I never got them back. Others did when they left the delousing station and the shower baths. Our uniforms had also undergone treatment. The leather visor of my cap was all crumpled up: the cap would not go on my head and had to be thrown away. I do not think I had any other headgear all the time I was a POW. I do not remember much about Hampden Park. I do not recall the room where we slept that night. The next day we were again put on a train as comfortable as the first. For breakfast we received our first portion of NAAFI cake and a nice cup of tea.

'Hours later: Nottingham. A huge camp consisting only of tents. Of course, this caused great disappointment. I remembered the castle shown on the Players Navy Cut cigarette packet. There were policemen on horseback riding alongside the barbed wire. The food rations here were more normal, though many prisoners still claimed they were hungry. The first distribution of cigarettes. The first attempts to organise some activity, but it amounted to nearly nothing, without any plan or material. It was still early spring, and, of course, not very warm for spending day and night in tents only. We tried to build a little stove just in front of the tent. We now had our first matches: Swan Vestas. One young officer, I remember, claiming to be hungry, bartered his ration of cigarettes for more food and the next day he tried to find someone to give him cigarettes for his food. This he repeated several times, as he apparently did not know which he needed or wanted more: food or cigarettes.

'Rumours spread about which camp we would finally be

transferred to – where we could at last feel at home. One day, after about a fortnight at Nottingham, it actually happened. But before this we received a bag and a white handkerchief – which made a great impression on me with only my small rag. But I already had one valuable extra possession: a second blanket. Before coming to Nottingham, I was so fed up with only having one blanket and freezing (and envious of the man with the quilt!) that I lied to the soldiers distributing the blankets and told them that I had pneumonia and if they did not want to be responsible for my death they should give me another blanket. This blanket, not registered, I considered as my personal property and kept for the next three years, only to be exchanged against a better one whenever there was an opportunity.

'The next camp was Crewe Hall, Crewe, Cheshire (Camp 191), with its enormous activity. But in my first days there I felt only relief at the narrow escape out of hell. And this hell was still going on on the other side of the Channel. My family did not know I was safe and I did not know if my parents were alive. Eight or ten weeks before, I had learned of the death of my younger brother, Martin, who was killed in action with the navy in the Channel at the end of August 1944. This news only reached me in December 1944. My elder brother had been seriously wounded, also at the end of 1944. I do not know when I received the news that he had lost a leg. What had happened in the last months in Hamburg we did not know. There were friends in the camp who had even more reason for their nightmares: their homes were in that part of Germany occupied by the Russians.'

8 Spring 1945

Little now stood between the Allies and victory in Europe. In March, British and American troops crossed the Rhine. On 11 April, American soldiers entered a place called Buchenwald near Weimar. On 13 April, Vienna was liberated. In the POW camp in Dunham Park, Altrincham, Cheshire (Camp 189) Austrian POWs made an Austrian flag and threw it over the branches of a tree to celebrate the event. Only the day before, President Roosevelt had died suddenly. Hitler momentarily thought that this was the miracle to save the German cause and bring about a compromise peace with the Allies. The illusion was short-lived. On 25 April, American and Russian troops, the Eastern and Western fronts, met at Torgau on the Elbe. Five days later, with the sound of Russian guns already audible in Berlin, Hitler and his new bride, Eva Braun, took their own lives.

In Camp 21 (Comrie), Herbert Sulzbach took active measures to communicate these news items to the prisoners, as a first step in his re-education programme. He frequently met flat disbelief. Elsewhere too, re-education was making slow progress, and reports of disturbances in the camps were still coming in. In March a serious incident was reported at a camp where one or two anti-Nazi German prisoners had been beaten up and severely injured by their Nazi compatriots. There was no British doctor in the camp. The Nazi German doctors refused to treat non-Nazis. One of the injured prisoners subsequently died.

In April, two prisoners in Pennylands Camp, Cumnock, Ayrshire (Camp 22), complained that they were threatened with hanging by their camp-mates for participating in anti-Nazi propaganda. One of them was assaulted and received minor injuries. Another prisoner in the same camp was beaten up because he was the foreman of a working gang. He was treated for head wounds caused by kicks and blows. The prisoners concerned in the attack were punished with detentions and transferred to a camp for Nazi prisoners. In addition, all prisoners considered likely to cause trouble were segregated in a newly constructed compound at the camp. Another 500 or so less ardent Nazis were transferred to other camps. The victims of the assault and any other prisoners who felt threatened were immediately given protection. In April 1945 the Secretary of State for War could report that 'ardent Nazis are segregated from other prisoners as soon as they are discovered and nearly a third of the German prisoners in our hands in this country have so far been removed from the rest as ardent Nazis'. There were, at that date, 196,000 German prisoners in Britain.

The German prisoners were causing their captors other problems. At four o'clock in the morning of 11 March 1945, sixty-seven German prisoners, all but two of them officers, escaped from Island Farm Camp, Bridgend, Glamorgan (Camp 198). Siegfried Bandelow was at Bridgend at the time.

'At the end of February, a tunnel we started from barracks 23 was discovered', he writes. 'It had been betrayed. The second tunnel we made was not discovered, in spite of thorough investigations. During the search of the barracks it led out of, the British officers in charge stood with the German camp leader and the barracks elder right at the entrance to the tunnel, while British soldiers tested the ground all round with iron rods.

'The escape was thoroughly prepared. We procured maps, equipment, provisions that would last, like rusks, etc. On 10 March the premiere of Heger's play *The Two Sons* took place in our theatre. At the same time, 9 p.m., the march out of the tunnel began. Everything went well until 3 a.m. Then the alarm was given. At the count which followed, Captain Gold assumed that a whole barracks must have overslept.'

There were 8000 German officers held in that particular camp, but only a small number were involved in the escape scheme, many of them experts in useful arts. An experienced civil engineer, for example, supervised the construction of the tunnel, which led the twenty yards from the prisoners' playing field to a corner of the living hut, where an eighteen-inch square of four-inch thick concrete had been cut out and carefully camouflaged. A feature of this tunnel was its ventilation system, designed by the same engineer and constructed from milk tins and the like.

The task of recapturing the sixty-seven was not light. They had scattered in stolen cars or hidden on goods trains or were tramping the countryside on foot. Four days later, nineteen of them were still at large, and they were only gradually brought back to the camp, some as they were trying to board a ship, others attempting to steal an aeroplane. On 20 March, Sir James Grigg announced in the House of Commons that 420 German prisoners had escaped from British camps since the war began. Only four to date had not been recaptured. The number of escapees could, he said, be reduced if more manpower were available to guard the prisoners and if the conditions in which they worked outside the camps were tightened up. Following the break-out at Bridgend, security regulations there were made more rigorous. Some of the escapees were very badly treated, according to Bandelow, and 'our camp was transferred as a punishment'.

'On 21 March 1945, I was sent to Carburton, near Worksop, Notts. (Camp 181). There a Captain Faulk had managed to obtain German personnel as informers, against promises of better treatment. We were told about this immediately we got there and got a great deal of fun out of the fact. The commandant threatened to hand us over to the Russians. There were a lot of political–military interrogations there. The result was that very many of us – approximately 300 – were regarded as "dangerous", because of our activities in the camp community. We were therefore transferred to Norton Park Camp, Nottingham (Camp 174). The choice was completely arbitrary: for example, the theatre group was chosen.

'At Norton the accommodation and the relationship with the English officers was good, except that the commandant was not liked by his officers. There, lessons, lectures, dramatics and so on, were continued. It was there that we learned of the end of the war, which we had been anticipating for a long time. On 15 April, by common consent, we all took off the *Hoheitsabzeichen* – that is to say, the eagle with the swastika. We unpicked the badges from our uniforms and caps. This was not a political decision. It had nothing to do with that (according to our opinion at that time). As we were going to another camp, we did not want to cause any split in the officer corps.'

Public sentiment towards the POWs was not at this juncture at its most charitable. The prosecution of a civilian in Rugby in March for obtaining food supplies from his local POW camp for his own consumption had given rise to renewed suspicions that the prisoners must be grossly over-supplied with food if they were in a position to open a black market. Anger was also aroused amongst the ration-weary British people at the information which gradually seeped out that the German prisoners who formed part of working parties were receiving larger rations of some foodstuffs than British civilians were. A statement by Sir James Grigg in the House of Commons in April that 45,000 Germans were already employed, mainly in agriculture and forestry work, unleashed a hostile question from Sir Alexander Knox: 'Surely it is possible to employ a much larger number of these prisoners instead of keeping them in camps, eating their heads off and doing nothing?'

There were British civilians who did love the German prisoners. In March some nurses faced legal proceedings for being too friendly towards them and suggesting marriage – in contravention of regulations prohibiting fraternisation.

The prisoners were finding other diversions. Re-education might be taking a little while to get off the ground, but education policies and programmes continued to be formulated within the camps, as a means of helping the prisoners to utilise their period of captivity to some advantage. The shortages – of teachers and textbooks, of pencils and paper – remained. Furthermore, the prisoners were often weary after a day at work and too tired to concentrate on study – particularly as the only place available for it was in a crowded hut where every sort of activity was simultaneously in progress. Dr Harald Dreier tells of one such education scheme as he reminisces about his life as a POW in April 1945.

'A barracks camp in the county of Yorkshire. Before the Allied invasion, soldiers from overseas probably had their quarters here. Now it is POW Camp 178 (Ure Bank Camp, Ripon). The date is 20 April 1945. It is bitterly cold outside. On the parade ground stand row upon row of large tables. In front of each table: a tommy. An English general with his entourage watches over proceedings from a raised place as if from a commanding height. We POWs are now directed individually, according to which barracks we belong, to a table. We have to undress. Each item of clothing is examined by the English soldier positioned in front of the table, and then spread out on the table. At the end, the order is given: about turn and trunk forward bend. Goethe's line "Ihr könnt mir mal . . ." is certainly applicable here; by the time all the POWs have shown that they have nothing to hide, it is evening. Lunch falls by the wayside. Back in the barracks we are not allowed to use anything which has not been searched, and, as previously mentioned, it is bitterly cold. The date of these events: 20 April.

'For me, 20 April 1941 had already been an occasion to apply that line from Goethe – in the case of one man who had been born on that day some years before. On that memorable day in 1941, I had received my call-up papers. When I had my last check-up, the examining medical officer summed up the situation: "Things must be very bad with the German Wehrmacht, if they're calling you up!" And my army book was stamped with "G-H" (only fit for home duty).

'That spring of 1945, I was giving instructions in German grammar to five English officers who were already considering some position or other in occupied Germany. The knowledge of the German language that these men possessed had still to be perfected. Then they went on leave. When they returned, we were hoping to move on to reading the works of a German author. But only one officer came back to Yorkshire after the leave, and he only for a few days. There was no question of continuing the lessons. He went to Germany and, when we parted, presented me with a pipe. It was no Dunhill, but a good pipe. I still have it today. There were teachers, assistant grammar-school masters and senior masters, amongst the camp inmates. Why the English interpreter came to me and offered me the chance to give the English officers these lessons, I do not know.

'At the instigation of the English interpreter, I then started various courses for the camp inmates with the help of one of the teachers and an assistant master: German grammar, English, Latin, history and arithmetic, including algebra. We naturally lacked textbooks. We also had no paper to write on. A couple of miserable pencils, some chalk and a blackboard were bought for us by the interpreter. The camp kitchen supplied us with a small quantity of paper in the shape of the wrappers from the milk tins. Interest in the courses died out when the POWs were moved nearer to their work on farms outside the camp.'

Hans Reckel, still in Camp 18, gives some idea of how re-education and segregation policies appeared to the ordinary prisoner.

'For a long time re-education was confined to negative measures. For example, from time to time all lessons were forbidden unless the democratic content of the teaching material had been thoroughly checked. Everyone was convinced that the frequent transfers from one part of the camp to another were also part and parcel of the re-education plan. On the one hand, the great mass of the inmates were to be protected from possible contagion from the views of the undesirable "black sheep". On the other hand, these dangerous elements were to be prevented from coming together in such large numbers that their ideas became even more extreme. But it was not very easy to distinguish the black from the white, and luckily they did not attempt to do so, either by asking questions or examining their consciences or by demanding that the prisoners in question denounce their ideas. All in all, it was left to the usual systematic examination by the unit to which the man belonged, and partly to the military authorities. For a few days and only for a few days, a very unusual method was employed. A barracks was filled half with members of the Free Germany movement and half with former SS members. Perhaps the idea was to force them to mix with each other and possibly after lively discussion discard their undemocratic views. However, contact between the two groups was not very close, although there was no friction. Despite everything, the changes in treatment undoubtedly had one good result: at the end of February all non-commissioned officers and sergeant majors were moved from camps A and B into camp C and discipline and morale rose considerably.

'Meanwhile in camp A transport groups were being made up in preparation for transfer to a work camp (which was better equipped and subject to fewer restrictions). To volunteer for this was a sign of a pacific and democratic attitude. But anyone who had been moved out of a work camp once without being given sufficient explanation did not see why he should volunteer a second time. Besides, further transports of prisoners came from other work camps at irregular intervals and they too had not been given convincing reasons for their removal.

'The new volunteers included a large number of somewhat less than reliable people. This primarily showed in their clothing and their behaviour, or, to put it more crudely, their oafishness and arrogance. The best example was a twenty-year-old sailor whose only items of clothing were a patched-up pair of denim trousers, a sweat shirt and a pair of home-made sandals. He had swapped everything else for cigarettes. He was completely re-equipped in the work camp. Unforgettable too was a young chap from Mecklenburg who had a few weeks previously all too self-confidently pronounced, "If the Russians ever reach Gustrow [his home town] then I shall be Germany's greatest supporter." But quickly, too quickly, he changed his mind, secretly applied to be moved to a work camp and disappeared without saying goodbye – also certainly not setting a very good example.

'Questionable also was the change in the way the English soldiers treated us. The strict ban on fraternisation only allowed them to talk to us about our work – apart from commands, to which we could not reply. From 7 March the implementation of orders was enforced in a new way. Every soldier on guard was equipped with a strong, beautifully made stick. The early abolition of caning was one of the advances which men in the German army had been particularly proud of for a long time. Because of that, no German POW could keep calm when a whole troop of Englishmen marched into the camp with these sticks and used them on the slightest pretext. The stick brigade became an especially hated part of camp life. There were no exceptions. Once, when I had been standing on the parade ground for hours, I was hit unexpectedly and sharply on my hand, which I had moved slightly behind my back instead of letting it hang motionless by my side.

'As the cane took over, many of the English soldiers grew less disciplined. This became evident after a few escape attempts. On 21 March I wrote, "Had to stay outside the whole afternoon whilst seventy tommies made a thorough search of the camp; my playing cards disappeared, other people lost cakes and cigarettes." Three days later, "Tommies have pinched 7000 cigarettes from the English mess." At the end of May, medals (Iron Crosses) were stolen during a search.

'In addition, the paltry space the prisoners were allowed to move around in was limited even further. At that time everyone was past feeling any surprise, but they could hardly be pleased. On 16 March extra barbed wire was placed around the outer path round the barracks and the parade ground. And on 18 April the parade ground was made one metre smaller with a new roll of barbed wire. Over a longer period, we were forbidden to speak through the inside fences to people who lived on the edge of the camp. Also in April the sick were no longer allowed to go from their own part of the camp to be examined in the fenced-off sick-bay and to be treated by a doctor. Instead, a treatment room was set up in every compound and the camp gates were opened only for medical personnel. And, finally, dogs trained to attack any prisoner trying to escape patrolled outside the main fence.

'The increasing roughness of the treatment also became apparent when work duty was extended to Sundays. We first began carting stones on Sunday mornings as early as the beginning of March. And, so that no one should be able to relax in any time that remained to him, the commandant, Lieutenant King, already known for his occasional vexatious whims, ordered that the prisoners must always appear "as if they were on parade".

'On the other hand, it never became entirely clear if the shortage of food should be regarded as deliberate policy on the part of the retaining power. POWs are always hungry and unemployed POWs even more so. Every third conversation centred on the three Fs: Freedom, Females and Food. In the course of time, the last mentioned became all important for most of us, because the quality and quantity of our diet was frequently variable and it was in addition unbalanced. It was probably the camp doctor who saw to it that everyone received a fresh cauliflower stalk to nibble on two occasions in the spring, so that the evil effects of vitamin deficiency were kept within bounds. As an additional source of vitamins, I picked myself some young sorrel leaves when we went out onto the meadow, but this was possible only once every six weeks or so.

'In the second half of March the quantity of food was noticeably reduced: for example, in the mornings and evenings there were only two instead of three slices of white bread. To begin with, it was said that the winter supplementary food ration had lapsed; later it was attributed to a German attack on Newcastle. In April the food at first improved again. But every suspicion obviously returned when on 1 May, at the same time as a commission from the International Red Cross was inspecting the camp, we were served with extraordinarily large portions of exceptionally good-quality food. This was followed by several days of correspondingly meagre portions.

'Nevertheless, the list of the exact food rations due to every prisoner of war was scrupulously tabulated, down to the last grain of salt, and generally pinned up in the kitchen barracks. Only no one could check how much of it reached his plate. A factor in the general mismanagement was the system of "second helpings". The leftovers, or, more accurately, the remainder of the midday meal held in reserve, were distributed in turn to the personnel of each barracks. But the quantity and food value of these second helpings were entirely different things. In the worst cases, a voice might be heard from the depths of the kitchen shouting, "The barracks want second helpings. Another bucket of water!" Then the result could only be described as water-soup.

'The smallness of the dining room led to further disadvantages. As in a boarding-house, every place in it had to be occupied several times in succession. But the guests did not arrive at reasonable intervals. Instead, they pressed inside, barracks by barracks, driven forward by the hungriest. Only the last, therefore, were able to eat wholesomely and in peace.

'Side by side with all restrictions, limitations, aggravations and depression, re-education in a positive sense was also pursued – but, unfortunately, only for a small circle. Thus, the "Free Germany" people received generous allocations of cigarettes from the English clerk. The privileged also included the base personnel, who were always paid for their work, and the most inferior of them was looked after as well as in a work camp. The more desperate the situation in Germany, the happier most of them became.

'I felt that a high point of their "democratisation" came when, on the evening of 28 April, in the kitchen barracks of C camp, the personnel, inspired by one of their abundant banquets, roared out the "Internationale" together with other "red"songs. The extent of the protection the English gave these people emerged quite clearly on 11 June, when someone was put in the "calaboose" because he had dared to complain about the kitchen personnel. These methods certainly did nothing to advance the understanding of the great mass of POWs.

'Of course, there were also bright spots which made life in the camp somewhat more tolerable – the fact that they were few fixed them all the more firmly in our memories.

'At the end of January, for example, a guard assigned to watch while we hauled stones chatted to us in quite a human and friendly manner, despite the ban on fraternisation, about his experiences in Pomerania, where he had been a prisoner in the First World War. On another occasion, in mid March, we had to fetch wood from the strip of woodland on the slope. For a while we no longer saw the camp, and the trees and the flowering snowdrops reminded everyone of home.

'Once, in the middle of April, there was a break in the routine and we were allowed out onto the large meadow to watch a football match in beautiful sunshine. But most eyes were fixed less on the game than on the castle and the green valley: on a picture of freedom.

'To this context too belongs a memory of the period of the first evil wave of guilt propaganda. The commandant made a personal inspection of the barracks at this time, and praised us with the verdict "very good". At all events, tidiness and cleanliness were still appreciated, and this common ground of understanding restored our self-respect for a while. An event on 27 April must have affected us in a stronger if also somewhat questionable way. I noted at the time, "Hauptmann Willdie talks as if all good Germans are concentrated in C camp".

'On many occasions our life was also relieved from quite a different direction. Miserable but moving were the remnants of the "forces comforts" which the German Red Cross sent from a Germany that was almost completely beaten. On 17 March everyone received some rose-hip drops, which were then regarded as the sweets with the greatest vitamin content. On 28 March it was two slices of black bread – a delicacy in the land of white bread – as well as some bonbons and dried plums. Another time it was six to ten cigarettes per man, which had to be separated with a razor blade. The last consignment contained some games and useful articles which we raffled. That was the last to reach the expectant recipients. But a few months later I heard from camp mates who had been in Camp 18 longer that our splendid camp leader had had abundant packets of tobacco from the German Red Cross piled up in his own room.

'Among the normal mortals in the camp, there were also a few who were able to unpack a quantity of delightful and fortifying delicacies from parcels from their families: cakes and sausages, fat and cigarettes, and other proofs of love and solicitude. Once, on 29 March, I too was among the fortunate and could go across to the clerk, where I untied and unpacked such a parcel under the eyes of a sergeant. It was only sad that I was the only person at the time to bring such riches back to the barracks. When I allowed one or two of my close friends to share the sausage, the bad feeling amongst the many others was clearly perceptible. And it was not exactly surprising though decidedly annoying when one day I found that the last of the few boxes in my kitbag, which had still been half full, was nearly empty.

'The Commission of the International Red Cross must indubitably also be mentioned here. Although in fact it only appeared in the camp very seldom, it gave everyone, even in the saddest situation, the feeling of not being entirely abandoned to foreign despotism. Many wrote the address of the Geneva office on some secret note or other and carefully kept it with them during the whole period of captivity.

'Even more important almost than the bright patches and relaxations outlined above was the comradeship which, under the

influence of common misfortune, bound men together who otherwise might not have bothered with one another. Out of this
friendships had grown up which had already survived and grown
stronger over many changes of place as we moved from camp to
camp.

'I still remember well how the circle of my friends and comrades
sat down together on the night before my birthday. The best artist
designed a greetings card with clover leaves and horseshoes as good-
luck symbols. Five signatures were affixed in the middle and the
result was handed to me at midnight together with five of the
friendliest handshakes, when obviously I was still blinking my eyes.

'Anyone who was at least halfway secure, like this, could also
experience and utilise from time to time the pleasures which the
camp and the barracks at least in theory could offer.

'The most important of these were the walks, the "turns" spent as
far as possible in friendly conversation. Some particularly lively
people even fastened their newly washed handkerchiefs or other
small pieces of laundry onto their uniforms with safety-pins or
home-made pegs and, decked in this way, walked along the barbed
wire until everything was dry. The games of cards played round the
stove were another source of social pleasure.

'Less pleasant than soothing was a special English custom which
many of us soon recognised as genuine progress compared with
homely German practices. This was the pleasure of the famous
English tea. It was, to be honest, not exactly the most famous brand
that was served us. But in between meals, almost at any time of day,
a bucket of left-over tea stood in the kitchen barracks and invited us
to test the truth of the beautiful German phrase "Wait – drink tea."

'Despite this, our mental state did not improve with the passage of
time, and a few people certainly showed serious symptoms of
incipient "camp madness". On 24 May an old man who up till then
had attracted little attention had to be taken to the sick-bay. For
several days before that, his glazed eyes had scarcely seemed to
recognise anyone; he no longer answered when spoken to; and he
only mumbled to himself. And we had already heard the horrible
news from B camp in April that a man who had just been moved
there from a less austere camp had hanged himself in the night.

'Specially prone to depression were the many smokers, who found
the enforced weaning away from their habit extraordinarily
painful. Gone were the days of the desperate experiments when
they attempted to take tea-leaves from the kitchen rubbish bins, dry

them and smoke them. The most addicted had also long since sold their wedding rings to English soldiers – that is to say, swapped them for cigarettes. It was in the first place forbidden to swap cigarettes for bread; secondly, hunger was painful; thirdly, it was an uncertain transaction. In A camp, where the black market had been brought to a state of particular perfection, someone was palmed off with a cigarette which had tobacco only at the ends and grass in the middle. That black-market cigarettes were actually offered by the base personnel and the medical staff – as well as people who were not actively employed by the medical services but could produce a certificate from the Red Cross – made their standing even more dubious.

'The situation was such that the greater number of camp inmates could only gnash their teeth and try to carry on from one day to the next. The barracks elders had the thankless task of looking after the necessary tidiness and cleanliness, so that no one let himself go too much or ran to seed. Just because there was no regular or meaningful work, this danger was very great. Anyone who lay down on his bed again immediately after breakfast had to be thrown out. Anyone who was not punctual for meals was cautioned and then had to wait for an hour the next time. In several cases the barracks elders decreed evening room-arrest. Some of the men involved regarded the discipline the barracks elders exercised merely as an additional evil, of the same ilk as the restraint of being a POW.

'The only possibility of speedy release from this situation was escape. But the trouble was, this camp did not exactly offer good opportunities for escape. And the fact remained that, even if a break-out from the camp succeeded, it was still difficult to reach a port, to catch the right ship, to land on the Continent unobserved, and to arrive in a neutral country. An anecdote which, it is true, was first told a year later, demonstrated the extent of the problem quite impressively. A POW succeeded in escaping. He reached a port and smuggled himself onto a ship. Shortly before it put out to sea, he was discovered and taken before the captain, who very boldly announced that he was prepared to take him back to his home port. But this home port was Leningrad and the escaper preferred to be handed back to the English authorities.

'Nevertheless, eight men risked an escape to freedom from C camp on Easter night. Thereafter, all the men in the camp had to stand outside in the pouring rain the whole morning and a further hour in the afternoon. The result of this collective retaliatory measure appeared the next day in general colds and headaches, but not in the apprehension of the escapers, who despite everything were able to roam around outside as free men for three days. After their recapture, they were brought back to camp, tried, together with an accomplice who had provided them with a map of the country, imprisoned, and finally moved to another camp.'

9 Peace in Europe (I)

On 2 May the commander of the Berlin garrison surrendered with 70,000 men. On the same day the unconditional surrender of the German forces in Italy came into effect. In Camp 21, Herbert Sulzbach undauntedly pursuing his re-education programme, invited a group of POWs to listen to the news on his wireless. Shortly afterwards, the German NCO who had switched on the set returned to his office to request protection. His fellow POWs were accusing him of collaboration and claiming that the BBC announcement was propaganda.

Over the following five days, Allied generals were receiving unconditional surrenders from all sides of Germany. On 4 May the German forces in the north surrendered to Montgomery on Lüneberg Heath. On 7 May, Jodl signed an unconditional surrender to Eisenhower at Rheims. On 8 May, at Zhukov's headquarters in Berlin, another surrender was signed.

On 8 May the British public flooded the London Streets, singing 'There'll always be an England' and dancing under the streams of ticker-tape descending from Admiralty Arch, cheering and shouting outside Buckingham Palace as the Royal family, King George VI, Queen Elizabeth and the Princesses Elizabeth and Margaret Rose, in company with the hero of the hour, Prime Minister Winston Churchill, appeared again and again on the balcony.

The total defeat of Germany could no longer be doubted. Henry Blunden at Oaklands Hospital, Co. Durham, could say, 'when the war ended everyone was pleased because they thought that then they would get home. They were not political animals. There was a general feeling of relief and rejoicing that the war had ended. Actually, many of them had become pro-English by that time. They really liked it here', but it was a time of traumatic readjustment for many of the German prisoners. As Kurt Bock put it, 'In April and May and also afterwards not only Germany collapsed but also the *Weltanschauung* of the majority, who sincerely had been sacrificing their lives.'

The destruction of Germany would of itself have been sufficient of a disaster to the members of the defeated Wehrmacht. But the blow was twofold: to the humiliation of the loss of the war and the annihilation of the ideal of Nazi invincibility was added the discovery of the nefarious practices within the concentration camps – practices perpetrated in the name of the German people and for which, therefore, every German might be expected to bear some degree of responsibility. These were vast, long-lasting problems which the prisoners were to live with for many years, if not for the rest of their lives.

Reports of the German concentration camps, first entered by Allied troops in the latter days of April 1945, were uncovered in the British press, filling its readers with horror and disgust. Days after the troops had opened the camps, a British parliamentary delegation set out to investigate the situation. They found evidence of bestiality, inhumanity and torture carried out over a period of time and on so vast a scale as almost to defy belief. Films and photos of the concentration camps were shown to the British public. On 8 May the Secretary of State for War was asked in the House of Commons whether he would arrange for the film of German concentration-camp atrocities to be shown to German POWs. The films were duly shown in the POW camps. The reactions they aroused were mixed. Some prisoners regarded them with open cynicism as further examples of British propaganda. After consideration, Sulzbach came to the conclusion that this disbelief was a positive sign. The prisoners simply could not believe that such cruelties could possibly have been committed – let alone in the name of Germany.

Henry Blunden said, 'Quite a few of the prisoners said it was not true. They all, without exception, said they didn't know all this was going on. I think this was true. We chatted to individual prisoners about the film. They thought we'd invented it. The argument was that the English had had concentration camps during the Boer War.'

To others the truth was all too apparent and the guilt and shame were almost intolerable. The columns of *Wochenpost* reflect the mental anguish aroused amongst this sector.

It is with revulsion that the inmates of Camp 31 [Ettington Park, Newbold-upon-Stour, Stratford-on-Avon] have through press, radio and films received the information of the inhuman cruelty which has been perpetrated in the concentration camps of

Buchenwald and elsewhere. We share the opinion of the ten English MPs who have visited these unheard of abominations that the system of exterminating whole groups with inhuman bestiality represents the lowest level to which mankind has ever fallen.

We do not want to be mentioned in the same breath with creatures such as these who have sinned against human rights so grievously. We will eliminate this cancerous growth from the German people. They are not a part of Germany but an evil minority which has dragged the image of Germany into the mire in the eyes of the world. [12 May 1945]

A sermon preached in Camp 180 (Trumpington, Cambridgeshire) on 6 May and reprinted in *Wochenpost* was even stronger:

With horror and disgust we Christian Germans have heard of the crimes which have taken place in concentration camps in our homeland for years. The worst injustices have been wrought on the people in these camps. Without proper courts or without the natural opportunity usual in a constitutional state of protecting themselves, they were robbed of their freedom and their families, stamped as criminals and at the mercy of despotic action and contempt . . . .

We declare as honourable Germans that we despise from the bottom of our hearts these horrific crimes carried out in the concentration camps and in no way can we have any fellowship of feeling with those responsible for the crimes. But we remain duty-bound to our people and exactly for that reason we renounce those who have destroyed justice, the basis of the life of the people . . . .

We Christians confess our guilt before God that our love of Jesus could not have prevented the outbreak of hate and genocide. We bear willingly with our people the consequences of these crimes. We admit with a great sense of grief that hatred and murderous lust could have broken out to such a great degree in our homeland. We bow before God's judgement in communal guilt with our people and pray: 'Save us God from our Crimes of murder . . . .' [19 May 1945]

Kurt Bock, explaining his own personal reactions says, 'For me, Bergen was an army training camp, though I have never been there.

KZs [concentration camps] had existed since 1933 and everybody knew about them, though at that time the only KZs mentioned in the papers were Dachau and Oranjenburg. All the other names, such as Auschwitz, Theresienstadt, even Neuengamme, which is a village in the Hamburg region, only became known after the war. That camps existed was common knowledge. Even the illustrated papers in 1933 printed pages and pages of photographs of "Enemies of the people" detained in KZs. This therefore, was no secret – at least, not completely. I remember those photos and to me, a boy of fifteen, those men looked like criminals (I know now that most people will look like criminals if photographed *en face* and in profile with their number shown on the snap). I do not know if we were told anything further about these men, though I vaguely remember stories about company directors enjoying champagne and caviare while several million were living on the dole. I did not know anyone personally who was detained in a KZ, but after the war a lot of people turned up who claimed to have been KZ inmates for a longer or shorter time.

'Though the KZs were talked about openly, I do not remember there being any discussion about whether these men were officially convicted. Today I would ask these questions, but the problem did not exist for me then, and apparently not for the grown-ups either. The fact was accepted and we believed that these people were endangering the war effort. Also during the war, I never knew anybody who disappeared there. On the other hand, there were stories of prominent men outside the political scene: a famous submarine captain and the tennis champion von Cramm and the like, who according to rumours were detained in such camps.

'Their existence therefore was no surprise and the cruelties of which we were given official information in Crewe Hall Camp were received with many doubts. After all, we had been told about the First World War, when Allied propaganda reported that German soldiers had chopped off the hands and arms of Belgian children in 1914. Could we now believe these stories in 1945? I do not think that we were too shocked, as we simply thought that the stories, if at all true, were very much exaggerated.

'Many of us had terrible experiences during the war. Some of us had been encircled at Stalingrad and only narrowly escaped. For us, what did it mean to hear that KZs existed? I had been wounded six times in Russia, one of my brothers only twice but he had lost a leg, and my younger brother also twice, but he had died the second time. Cousins, brothers-in-law, uncles had not survived. War was a horror, the KZs only part of it; and, we on the Russian front, could we be greatly impressed after having lost so many friends and comrades, so many of them mutilated and us with the horrible sight of corpses collected before being buried quite fresh and dominating?

'The horrible facts about camps where Jewish people were killed were not disclosed at the same time, but a few months later, I think. This was something completely new and, as I remember, I was stunned and also doubtful. This simply could not be true! We were forced to attend a film and we asked ourselves, "Is this true or just propaganda?" This was so exceedingly abominable, it was simply too much to believe immediately.

'By no means all of us agreed with actions (as far as they were known) taken against the Jews. I think many of us felt it was unnecessary to deal with them any differently from us. We knew that there were Jews who had fought in the First World War and had been decorated. We did not think it was correct to treat them as they were treated, but we did not know what actually happened to them later in the war.'

Hans Reckel records his memories of the last days of the war in Europe: 'A new series of almost unbearable news reports started coming in in April. On 6 April I noted, "Have obtained an Italian prison newspaper of 31 March according to which the Allies are not even over the Rhine yet." But the harsher treatment the English guards accorded us made it clear to us that our reserves in Germany were quickly running out. Added to that, on 10 April a German pilot was brought into C camp and completely verified everything the British had told us. On the same day I read the news from the Front in a London paper. My own town was reported to have been conquered by American troops. When, shortly after that, I received a letter and a postcard from there, I had a sick feeling in my stomach that this might be the last time I ever heard from my family.

'After this, on 20 April, the German camp leader forbade all frivolous activities, in view of the inhuman deaths in German concentration camps which had been made public. On 26 April, closely guarded like criminals, we had to march into A camp, where a barracks had been arranged as an exhibition room. Pictures and cards of the Allies' advance were displayed to convince us of the conclusive nature of the German defeat, and at the back of the hall there were dreadful pictures which had been taken in German concentration camps of piles of corpses and mass graves to demonstrate German vileness. No one could look at these pictures without being deeply shocked. However, the desired effect was delayed for a long time, because one of us who had seen the mass graves at Katyn being uncovered convinced us that, although the pictures displayed were authentic, the captions were false. They belonged to the victims of that Soviet massacre of Polish officers. Our re-education was therefore under a cloud from the beginning.

'On 3 May the last remaining doubters were convinced that Germany's final resistance was coming to an end. A picture of the corpses of Mussolini and his mistress was pinned up on the noticeboard. The death of Hitler, on the other hand, was only a rumour at that time. At this period, a loudspeaker was set up in one of the refectory barracks and the German-speaking broadcasts of the BBC henceforth crackled continuously, like well-aimed arrows bound to annihilate the last residual intellectual resistance in the camp. They often included a few incomprehensible reports, something on the lines of the statement that at one time "the German doctors were not able to give blood transfusions". More important was the information, absolutely impossible to misunderstand, contained in Churchill's impressive speech to the House of Commons on 8 May. From the village came the sound of church bells softly ringing; some shots were fired below the river; in front of the camp, the Union Jack was hoisted. Less soberly, the German theatre group put on a variety show that evening in which the chorus "As beautiful as today, so it must stay" constituted the high point.'

10 Peace in Europe (II)

The British public was certainly not yet ready to forgive and forget. The days following the celebration of victory over the Germans saw the fires of their resentment stocked by other fuels. British soldiers who had been held as POWs in Germany were coming home. 'Is the Minister aware', came a question in the House of Commons, 'of the very great indignation felt by the people of this country about the way the German prisoners are being fed, in view of the fact that our own prisoners have stated that, but for the Red Cross parcels, they would have been allowed to starve?' What action did he propose to take, ran a second question, in response to a petition submitted to him by the Hon. Member for Wallasey on behalf of 650 women protesting against excessive rations being issued to German POWs in this country?

At the end of May the Government, which had hitherto turned a deaf ear to all such pleas, succumbed. In the face of a world food shortage and with a war-ravaged Europe to be fed, an all-round reduction in food rations was imposed. British civilians received lower rations, but German prisoners of war received even less. Non-working POWs were cut back to 2000 calories a day; POWs employed in working parties were given extra quantities of bread and potatoes to bring their daily intake up to about 2900 calories. In view of the fact that the normal diet, according to the British Medical Association's Committee on Nutrition, for men carrying out very heavy work is 4250 calories daily, it can be understood that employed prisoners were often reduced to unorthodox measures to satisfy their hunger.

And more and more prisoners, in these first months of peace, were being employed. By the middle of June 1945, 70,000 of the 207,000 German POWs in Britain at this time were engaged in agricultural and other useful work (side by side with some 118,000 Italian co-operators). Moreover, they were being used for more varied work. In addition to the 50,000 engaged in agriculture and forestry, some of the remainder were now involved in the preparation of housing sites, road-making, sewer constructions and other civil engineering works. But there was no satisfying the British public. They did not want the prisoners to be sitting around doing nothing and 'eating their heads off'. Equally, they did not want them to be taking jobs away from the British boys who were gradually being released from work of national importance and drifting back onto the job market. At the end of May the Minister of Labour was asked in Parliament if he were aware that the workers of Newcastle-on-Tyne refused to work with Germans. He was requested to note that there were sufficient local unemployed to cover the situation and in view of this to issue instructions that 'no German prisoners of the late war' would be drafted into that city. R. A. Butler gave his assurance that there would be no deviation from the principle that POWs were only employed on work of urgent national importance when British labour was not available. Yet the question came up again in early June: Was the Minister of Health aware that the unemployed in the Spennymoor area would deeply resent German POWs being engaged on the preparation of housing sites? Would he obtain all the labour required for this work from the local labour exchange?

There were other minor symptoms of inhospitability in a Britain which was finding that peace did not mean the return of plenty. The prisoners, it was said, were responsible for a shortage of cigarettes in British shops. The prisoners were occupying train seats at the expense of British passengers. On the Kendal section of the 10.25 a.m. from Euston on 1 May 1945, all the first-class accommodation was reserved on War Office instructions for German POWs, who travelled three a side of each carriage. Ordinary passengers, including several travelling on important national business and at least one recovering from a major operation, did not enjoy such comfort.

Transport of prisoners was a recurring problem. Trains were not the only bone of contention. The public was no happier about a fleet of buses and lorries which, in a town that had suffered heavy bombing, collected a party of some 500–600 prisoners from their station of arrival in order to drive them a mere mile or so to their camp. 'Nothing,' the spokesman of the furious townsfolk told the Secretary for War, 'nothing would have given greater delight to the inhabitants of the anonymous town than to have seen these men marched through the streets to their prison.' Sir James Grigg explained patiently that 'there was always the possibility that the delight of the anonymous town referred to might have taken the form of contumely and under the Geneva Convention the detaining power is under obligation to protect prisoners against contumely'.

Another questioner gave Grigg the chance to get his own back. When asked why it was considered impracticable to take POWs to democratic institutions to encourage them when they went back to Germany, he could retort, 'I get into enough trouble for taking them about in railway trains . . . .'

But the question shows that the idea of educating, or rather re-educating, the POWs was coming to the forefront of the political scene. It found expression in fears that the government might be planning to release upon a Germany beset with monumental difficulties prisoners who were still aggressively Nazi in their sentiments. These fears were groundless. There was no thought at this juncture of repatriating any prisoners – let alone those who remained confirmed Nazis.

On the contrary, prisoners were still being brought into Britain in considerable numbers. The Channel Islands, which had been occupied by the Germans since 1940, were not liberated until three days after VE (Victory in Europe) day. Alf Eiserbeck was one of the Germans brought to England as a result.

'I volunteered for the navy in 1941 and had the usual training: infantry training first. I was in the Hitler Youth. You had to be. If you weren't, you wouldn't get a job. It was more or less compulsory. I was at navy school for six to nine months in Berlin (Neustrelitz, which was a brand new school). After that I spent a couple of months in a "holding company" until I got a job on a ship. Then it was minesweepers, stationed at Antwerp. We went all the way round the North Sea, the Baltic, Norway up to the Arctic. We escorted convoys right round Europe and the North Cape of Norway. I was also given U-boat training.

'In March 1943 I was back in Germany and then posted on to the second *Vorposten* [outpost] flotilla at St Malo. We stayed most of the time there doing convoy escort. We used to go convoying escorts from St Malo to the Channel Islands, Cherbourg, Brest, Bordeaux and back again.

'On D-Day we were in Granville [a small port on the French coast between St Malo and the Channel Islands], lying outside at 8 a.m. waiting to go to Jersey. We were attacked by twenty-four Hurricanes with bombs and broad guns all directed at one small ship (they had come back from bombing France). They came right from the sun so that we couldn't see them and attacked. They never hit us once and we never lost one man. After the Americans advanced, we left St Malo and went to the Channel Islands and stayed there. We couldn't go anywhere else then.

'At the end of 1944 we tied our ships up at a small port in Guernsey, left them there and moved off. We took over some houses and moved in. We just did guard duties and nothing else till the end of the war. At that time, I weighed about 160 pounds. When I came to England as a POW, I weighed 98 pounds. There was plenty of food on Guernsey, but the German command wouldn't release it.

'Two days after the war ended, the British troops came. The Germans wouldn't fight; they couldn't stand up. I was guard commander twice a week and I had ten to twelve men for the duty. I would watch them, with their white steel helmets on, carrying their rifles and dressed in full uniform standing to attention. After a few minutes they would start to sway and then fall over. They were then taken to hospital.

'I was taken to Kempton Park from Southampton by special train. We stayed there for two days of interrogation, medical check-up, delousing. They took everything we had: watches, lighters, etc. They left us nothing, just what we were wearing. Everything else was put in a heap and burnt. I had a service watch, which was taken. They were all Jewish soldiers in Kempton Park and they didn't like us too much. We had no razor, no nothing left. The moment we reached our first camp, we were issued with razor and razor blades! And we had to pay for them! In Kempton Park they gave us very good food and lots of tinned meat. Quite a few of our chaps died there from overeating.

'On the following day we were on the way to Driffield in Yorkshire in a special train. We arrived at 8 p.m. and had the longest march I've ever had – eighteen to twenty miles – to the camp [Butterwick Camp, No. 159]. I thought I'd never get there. There were 4000 men there in four pens. It was a mixed camp with both officers and men. Some of the men were working. We were pretty short of food there. It was a tent camp with twelve men to a tent. We were there only three weeks. No issue of clothes there – only a razor.

'Then 500 men were moved to Didcot, Berks (Camp 652). We still lived in tents there but these were big marquee tents with thirty men per tent. There we were issued with clothing. We cleaned the camp up and pitched new tents, because the old ones were filthy. The Italians had been there before us and we refused to live there until it was cleaned. After three weeks, we started work in a depot in small groups. I started in a small group of eight to ten men, working in the army camp in the messes: washing up, cleaning, potato peeling. This was just the job for us, as we could eat as much as we liked. After a short while, five to six weeks, I went to work in the depot itself in the sheds, unloading and loading trucks, lorries, etc. – anything that came along. The civilians refused to work with us and threatened to strike. After a few weeks, everyone wanted POWs to work for them. They were fighting to have us.

'The German camp leader, a staff sergeant, came from near my home and knew my parents. Through knowing him, I got a job as a driver, driving the camp commandant about and also 10-hundred-weight trucks. This meant driving outside the camp and I went all over the south of England. I couldn't read or speak much English then. I didn't learn much in the camp, except for words we needed, like "cigarettes" or "bread" – the essential words. We started evening classes in English in the camp but I didn't go. I wasn't interested.

'After I'd been in Didcot a couple of months, we all had to attend a cinema in the camp. They had an escort all round the cinema so that no one could get out. Everyone had to watch. The film they were showing was one of the Belsen concentration camp. As we didn't know anything about Belsen, we were all laughing at the film. We thought it was British propaganda, specially made by the British to show to us. Surprising we didn't wreck the cinema tent, we were fooling about so much. Later on we would have wrecked it, because later we learned not to stand any nonsense. We had to stand on the parade ground for eight hours as a punishment for fooling around.'

Siegfried Gabler was one of the prisoners detailed to swell the POW agricultural working force.

'The day war finished, everything changed. They split us into little groups. I ended up at Mortimer, outside Reading, Berks (Camp 88). There were 500 of us in the camp, which was an army barracks, where we had more space than in Oldham. There we were split up into little working groups with one of our own corporals or sergeants as gang leaders. We went out to work with a guard – mangel-hoeing – acres and acres of it. There were about twelve of us in a gang. Well, it often happened that when it was time to go home, we had to wake our "guard" and then help him look for his rifle, as he had forgotten where he put it. The first sign of rain, any bit of drizzle: right! We were finished for the day. They didn't expect us to work in the rain.

'In these early days, when we made the first contacts with civilians, people expected us to be a load of savages, because of what they had heard and read about the German army. On one of my first farms, I was shifting hay when I found a nest of little rabbits. "Go on! kill them!" the farmer said. I couldn't. "Weren't you in the German army then?", he asked. British people found, rather to their surprise, that (at least some of us) looked and behaved like human beings.'

The end of the war obviously meant changes of circumstances for many prisoners. Even Dr Harald Dreier found himself engaged in manual labour.

'In late summer various transports were mustered. I belonged to a transport which was moved to the "Garden of England" in Kent. There I was appointed as a medical orderly to the sick-bay. It was a tent camp in a large park. The German doctor at this camp was a Bavarian. Although the sick bay was abundantly supplied with medicaments by the English, our camp doctor prescribed aspirin for any pain above the navel, castor oil for pain below. People he could tolerate – and there were always notorious shirkers to be found – received medicinal showers and rest cures in the sick-bay. The doctor very soon noticed that this type of medical attention did not exactly earn my respect. I was therefore dismissed from my post as medical orderly. Because of my profession, I should certainly not have been allotted to work outside the camp. Notwithstanding, I and a medical orderly comrade who had also been released from the sick-bay were ordered to shovel coal out of a truck. As a result of our refusal, the English camp commandant sentenced us to fourteen days' confinement for failure to obey an order. Those fourteen days were very pleasant. Our prison was an extra tent, cut off from the world around us by high barbed-wire fences. At mealtimes we were served from the English camp kitchens. This food was considerably better than in the POW camp. According to the terms of our punishment we still had to shovel coal out of waggons – under the supervision of an English guard. But the English commandant found our Red Cross sleeve badges disturbing. They were taken away from us and never again returned.'

Hans Reckel was still at Camp 18 at that juncture.

'A few days after the end of the war, lists were already being drawn up on a large scale in preparation for the division into future work groups. Theological and medical students, as well as men who wanted to train as primary school teachers, were put on special lists, ostensibly for study camps. In addition, all miners were collected up and soon afterwards transported to Germany – to the Ruhr and Saar areas. They were replaced by the garrison from the island of Jersey, who came into D camp on 21 May.

'Amidst all this administrative work and change, the "Intelligence" people, for the most part Jews, were active to a high degree. One could not ignore the fact that their attitude and conduct towards the prisoners had changed in the course of time. There was nothing left of the laughing manner with which an intelligence officer had turned towards a young POW in Camp 16: "What, so young and already SS? We'll send you home as a monarchist yet!" On the other hand, hardly any of the camp inmates were so fanatical or so stupid that they had not gained some understanding of the change.

'There were exceptions on both sides. On 10 May a lieutenant from B camp had to take up a position in front of the calaboose entrance, stand at attention for several hours on end, and salute every English soldier that passed. And on the following day all POWs had to stand at attention on the parade ground for four hours, because one or two English officers had not been saluted by a few prisoners.

'The reduction in food rations imposed in June also met some understanding, although everyone grumbled about it and everyone was worried about further reductions. For we were certainly aware from the wireless news bulletins that rations for English civilians had also been cut. In addition, at Camp 18 the situation had not yet been reached where almost every parade was punctuated by several prisoners toppling over from hunger.

'That first happened at the next, and far worse, camp. Only there too did we meet cold hatred in person, in the form of a French officer.

'A few days before leaving Camp 18, we had to whitewash the inside of the barracks and make them beautifully clean (for the first time). The first barracks had to be completely cleared by 14 June. A considerable number of the bedsteads were moved out completely, so that our successors would have more room than us. Furthermore, one of the refectory barracks was closed to us and fitted up for a completely different type of use, which we found almost unimaginable: it was going to be a cinema. A rumour which had been in circulation for a long time, was confirmed: Camp 18 was to become an officers' camp.

'Early on 15 June, the camp gate opened for a large group of men on the march who were finally leaving the camp. I was amongst the marchers. Some weeks before, I had had a dream: I could raise myself up into the air by a skilful leap and an equally skilful and inimitable placing of my legs and movement of my arms. Watched with astonishment by a few bystanders, completely unnoticed by most of the others, I could fly at will far out into the twilight. I often had this dream again after that. This remarkable memento of Camp 18 did not fade until over ten years later.'

11 Re-education

Hostilities had ended in Europe. They began in Britain itself. The country was in the grips of the first election campaign since war had begun, five years before. On polling day, 5 July 1945, the electorate swept the hero of the war, Conservative Premier Winston Churchill, out of office. They brought in a Labour government with an overwhelming majority.

Hostilities against Japan still continued. On 6 August the Americans dropped the first atomic bomb on Hiroshima, causing untold damage and suffering and profoundly shocking the whole world. Three days later a second bomb was unleashed, on Nagasaki. On 14 August the Japanese surrendered. The world was at peace.

The problems of the peace in Europe were already being tackled. On 5 June the Allied Control Commission, meeting for the first time, announced that it had taken over all powers of government in Germany. The Commission consisted of the Allied commanders-in-chief, Eisenhower, Montgomery, Zhukov and the Frenchman de Lattre de Tassigny. The Germany it was to govern was divided into four zones of occupation, roughly in accordance with the territory conquered by their respective armies.

In July the policy they were to follow was decided at a high-level conference at Potsdam attended by President Truman (who had replaced Roosevelt), Joseph Stalin, Churchill and the new British Labour Prime Minister, Clement Attlee. The main points emerging from their discussion, embodied in the Potsdam Agreement, included the decentralisation of the political and economic life of Germany.

The country was to be completely disarmed and demilitarised and kept in that condition. All clubs and associations were to be abolished, for fear that they would nourish any military tradition. Most specifically, the National Socialist Party and all organisations and institutions connected with it were to be dissolved. All Nazi laws which had provided the basis of the regime or established discrimination on grounds of race, creed or political opinion were to be cancelled. All members of the Nazi Party who had been more than nominal participants in its activities were to be removed from office, while its leaders and high officials were to be interned, and war criminals were to be brought to judgement. At Nuremberg, Herman Goering and twenty-two members of the Nazi hierarchy were tried. After a hearing lasting ten months, eleven were condemned to death, seven imprisoned, and three acquitted.

The Potsdam Agreement included an injunction that German production of metals, chemicals and other items essential to a wartime economy should be restricted to her peacetime needs. The whole economy should be decartelised and decentralised. There was also general agreement that the victorious Allies should obtain reparations by 'removals' of industrial plant.

On the positive side, preparations were to be made for the eventual reconstruction of German political life on a democratic basis, particularly by the encouragement of democratic political parties and the introduction of self-government from local councils upwards. Subject to considerations of security, freedom of speech, the press and religion and the formation of trade unions were to be permitted. No central government was to be established for the time being. One of the objects of the occupation was declared to be the convincing of the German people that they had suffered total military defeat and could not escape responsibility for the inevitable suffering and chaos which they had brought on themselves.

For the new Germany to arise from the ruins, trustworthy, liberal-minded Germans were desperately required. Before the end of the war, plans had already been formulated by the re-education section and the British military authorities to repatriate specialists amongst the German POWs for posts which demanded particularly reliable and responsible men. The specialists had to be men who had an 'A' screening rating and who normally lived in the British zone of Germany. Known as Operation Oberon, the scheme was under way by August 1945, when the new Labour Secretary of State for War, J. J. Lawson, told the House of Commons that, although the general repatriation of German POWs had not yet been considered, a small number of non-Nazi specialists had, at the request of the Control Commission, been returned to Germany to assist in the country's rehabilitation. It was anticipated, he said, that the number of these would increase. In addition, a number of sick and wounded had been sent back for further treatment, but a great effort had been made to ensure that these did not include former members of the SS.

The political affiliations of prisoners sent back to Germany obviously had to be carefully screened. But both the selection of reliable experts to serve under the Commission and the need to ensure that the repatriated sick were not ardent Nazis were only part of the purpose served by the screening system. It was also essential for the camps in Britain to be able to distinguish 'white' prisoners, who could be of use in providing positive leadership in the camps, from the camp leader downwards; for the damage that could be done by the appointment of a Nazi-indoctrinated camp leader was fast being recognised. In addition, screening could help to pinpoint prisoners who were potentially disruptive influences on re-education programmes within the camp, influencing the less convinced, easily swayed majority to resist the efforts of the re-educators or actually terrorising those who participated in the work of re-education.

For re-education was proceeding apace. Kurt Bock was sent to Crewe Hall (Camp 191) in March 1945, and stayed there for some seventeen months. He recalls, 'we had lectures on democracy, so-called re-education, and we could if we wished attend these lectures in the big dining room. Of course, there were still a lot of men, especially in the first year, who mistrusted the lectures and considered the lecturers, if they were obviously emigrants, as traitors. Later, this feeling disappeared. One most prominent lecturer was an elegant and still quite young man, Mr Rossiter, who was nevertheless not accepted by all POWs. He was constantly accompanied by a big, beautiful dog. He smoked a pipe and sat, relaxed, on the edge of the table when talking to the audience. Though it was supposed to be a secret, it was already well known in the camp that his real name was Rosenthal and that he was the heir to the world-famous chinaware factory in Selb, Bavaria. When talking about Rosenthal/Rossiter, I found that one of my friends did not remember the man at all. We found out that this friend was at the time opposed to re-education and never participated in the lectures. This may be the reason why he did not remember what in my opinion was a rather outstanding fact.

'In spring and summer 1945 there was always a vast audience for the daily press review, read aloud after it had been translated, and commented upon. This was a purely German affair, except that the man in charge got the newspapers from the camp authorities. Some of these "lecturers" did an excellent job, in my opinion. It was also very difficult to find the right tone. By the middle of 1945, we also received an English newspaper for each hut – that is, for about sixty – but the majority were not interested, because they could not understand it. I could not understand it either, but nevertheless had to fight every day to get the paper from the five or so other men in our hut who also wanted it. Someone even had a dictionary, but he was reluctant to let it out of his sight. At that time it was enormously valuable. The newspaper was of course also used for vocabulary in our English lessons, and we asked our "teachers" to explain the incomprehensible phrases.

'Later, loudspeakers were installed in the open air, where German news was broadcast twice a day – even the official broadcasts from Hamburg, I think. Those who were interested in the English language also had the opportunity to listen to English news and the English-language course on the BBC. It was a job for men who really wanted to learn, as we had no shelter from rain or wind, and in winter, of course, the audience melted to rather a small number.

'Information via newspapers became very slowly better at the end of 1945 and during 1946, but it was still far too little for those who were really keen on it.'

Herbert Sulzbach was scoring notable successes in the erstwhile 'black' camp at Comrie. In September he arranged a debate amongst the prisoners on the theme 'Will this House accept the proposal that all POWs should be sent home immediately?' In his report on this event to the camp commandant and the Political Intelligence Department he could write,

Most impressive was what was obvious in every speech: Full confidence in the decisions and administration the Allies are setting up in Germany, trusting their conquerors as if they were their friends. . . .

They are fully convinced of the catastrophic defeat and speak openly about the fact. They emphasised the chaos the 'criminal Nazi leaders' had left behind; they know – and they speak about it – that Germany is utterly destroyed. . . .

We have the chance of a lifetime to re-educate all POWs. They are willing to learn, willing to abandon all Nazi and even Prussian ideologies; the speakers were middle-aged men and also included some not more than 22 years old . . . . The soil is prepared for the

adoption of a new way of German life. If we organize re-
education all over this country and wherever POW camps exist,
we can turn the Germans into a peace-loving people.

Sulzbach's final coup at Comrie occurred on Armistice Day 1945.
He had previously sent a circular to the inmates of the camp:

Never again shall such murder take place! It is the last time that
we will allow ourselves to be deceived and betrayed. It is not true
that we Germans are a superior race; we have no right to believe
that we are a superior race; we are equal before God, whatever
our race or religion. Endless misery has come to us, and we have
realized where arrogance leads. In this minute of silence, at 11
a.m. on this November 11, 1945, we swear to return to Germany
as good Europeans, and to take part as long as we live in the
reconciliation of all people and the maintenance of peace.

Nearly all the 4000 prisoners in Camp 21 responded to this call,
turned out and stood to attention on the football pitch as the Last
Post ended the two minutes of silence that Armistice Day.

Eugene Rolfe was also entering the periphery of the re-education
field at this juncture.

'I was sergeant interpreter at German POW camp 661, Eynsham
Park Camp, near Oxford', he told me. 'It was a working camp – all
the men were out at work except the doctor. I went there in about
November 1945. The only thing I had to do there was take *Appell*. I
took turns with the other sergeant and officers. The prisoners would
be standing in threes and I had to walk up and down the line
counting them.

'The only thing I was really left doing was political re-education.
The British Army people were sceptical about this work but they
couldn't do anything to sabotage it. I started a camp newspaper
there, *Unsere Stimme*. The Foreign Office provided the paper and
stencils. The Germans illustrated it and did all the work. It was not
very seriously censored. I contributed one or two articles.

'One thing I did do as an interpreter. One day a chap was killed.
He was sitting against the backboard of a 15-hundredweight lorry.
The lorry skidded and he was thrown off. There was an inquest and
I had to go along as an interpreter. I was grateful that no one in the
British lines knew what terrible German I was speaking! I wrote to
the dead prisoner's family in Germany expressing my sorrow.

'One chap put on a one-man exhibition of fossils and geological things he'd collected. It was absolutely beautiful. He was a soft-spoken young man who was definitely a Nazi. The Belsen film was shown in the camp when I was there. He said, "No German would have done such a thing." There was a door in his mind which just remained shut.

'On Monday nights we had hops for the British company, and the Germans supplied the band. Siegfried Adolph, a brilliant and democratic person, one of the prisoners, would come along dressed in black with a concertina and would move among the dancers. Two British girls – they were sisters – used to come along. Siegfried appropriated the attractive one (her name was Peggy) and I was assigned the plain one. He got too friendly with his girl and was put in the calaboose for this. It meant solitary confinement in a Nissen hut. In his words, he was discovered putting international under-standing on too direct a basis. He wrote an article about it for *Unsere Stimme*.

'One night the Germans were having an *Abschiedskonzert* round a fire – one of the comrades was going home. I was allowed to bring my mother along. She didn't speak a word of German but she was very fond of music and she got this through to the prisoners. Then I took her along to the chapel. They had the use of it alternately. My mother simply stood there and said, "Here, in front of the altar of our saviour Jesus Christ, I think we are all equal." My mother was a real natural. She had a great success with the Germans.

'I remember at Eynsham a young chap looking at the *Daily Mirror* in the Information Room and saying, "You know, this paper is criticising the government!" He couldn't believe it.'

In December 1945, possibly to help to answer the reluctance of the camp authorities to encourage re-education programmes, the Political Intelligence Department of the Foreign Office clarified the aims of its programme in a booklet entitled *The Re-education of German Prisoners of War*. It was addressed primarily to the com-mandants of camps and placed great emphasis on the need for the co-operation and support of them and their staff if any scheme were to be successful. It took special pains to reassure them that re-education would in no way interfere with discipline. 'On the contrary,' it said, 'in the British conception of discipline, with its lesson of firmness, fairness and justice, and its emphasis on *self*-control, there is positive educative value.' The importance of *self*-control was in fact paramount. While opposing any schemes of self-government and self administration by the prisoners in the camps, the booklet stressed that participation in all the media of re-education – lectures, English lessons, films – must be voluntary. 'This in itself can be a lesson in democracy', it stated.

The booklet also laid down guidelines for the classification of prisoners as 'whites' ('anti-Nazis with democratic convictions. They must be firmly opposed to aggressive nationalism, racial intolerance and dictatorship of any kind'); 'greys' ('those with no deep political convictions, who have never been deeply implicated with the Nazi Party or connected with Nazi crimes or other atrocities'); and 'blacks' ('ardent Nazis . . . with a clear Nazi record in the past, or . . . still very much under the influence of Nazi ideals').

12 A Bleak Future

November 1945 saw the emergence of Richard Stokes, MP for Ipswich, as spokesman for the prisoners' cause – 'our MP', one of the prisoners calls him. On 6 November he voiced questions in the House of Commons which he was to repeat in varying terms on different occasions throughout the next two years. On learning that the Minister of Works had 27,700 German POWs at his disposal, he asked whether prisoners who were employed were 'paid a full and proper wage' or whether they were being 'used as slaves'? When, he continued, would they be sent home?

This, needless to say, was the equally burning question in the minds of all prisoners. All too soon they realised that no rapid return to home and family was in prospect. Kurt Bock writes, 'In August 1945 the official representative of the International Red Cross Organisation, Mr Forell [the Revd Birger Forell of Sweden], paid a first visit to Crewe Hall Camp (Camp 191). His arrival had been announced a week before and there were many rumours as to what we could expect from his visit. I think the German *Lagerleitung* had the opportunity to talk to him. What I remember, though, is that Mr Forell told us that he could not give us any hope that we would be able to return to Germany in the near future. As apparently no plans for immediate repatriation existed, the Red Cross calculated that they would be looking after us for the next *two years*. This news was received like a blow from a sledgehammer and it was certainly lucky that Mr Forell did not know the full truth, as it turned out to be two and a half years from that date for the majority of us.'

This was a hard future to look forward to, particularly for the younger prisoners who had barely experienced life as adults before entering the armed services and to whom the years of imprisonment seemed like an eternity. Low morale was exacerbated by constant intense anxiety about their families and friends at home. Normal life in Germany was completely disrupted.

Homes had been damaged and destroyed during the bombing and fighting of the last months. Supplies, accommodation, transport,

finance and ideas were in total disarray. Above all, the country was
in a turmoil of population movements. 7 million members of the
defeated German armed forces had to be dealt with. Allied POWs
and some 3 million foreign workers employed in Germany had to be
repatriated. Approximately 10 million Germans who had eva-
cuated the bombed cities were seeking to return to their homes.
Members of German minority groups in liberated countries – for
instance, the Sudeten Germans in Czechoslovakia – were now
evicted and returned to Germany.

Where, in this milling throng, the individual prisoner asked, were
his own individual family, loved ones, home? Postal services had
almost completely ceased and his question remained unanswered,
leaving the way open to every type of morbid fancy – too often,
unfortunately, justified.

In September the British authorities made a determined effort to
put prisoners in touch with their dispersed families. They were
invited to send postcards stating 'Ein Mitglied der geschlagenen
Wehrmacht sucht seinen nächsten Angehörigen' ('A member of the
defeated Wehrmacht seeks his next of kin'). But this was not met
with any great degree of gratitude. 'The phrase', writes Kurt Bock,
'was a topic of discussion for weeks and months and certainly not
forgotten by anybody. The German army had laid down arms.
However, nearly everybody thought that the phrase was un-
necessarily insulting and there were quite a lot in our officers' camp
who solely for this reason refused to send such cards. Many of these
had to be convinced that by not sending the card they would keep
their relatives ignorant of their fate for many more months. There
might in the end have been 5 or 10 per cent who did not send the
card. I did not like the phrase either, but I was not too particular
and did not hesitate to send the card, and I remember that I made a
number of friends send it as well, against their initial objections.'

The lack of mail from home at this period was one of the most
depressing and demoralising factors. The importance of letters to
the prisoner cannot be overestimated. They were the slender
placenta binding him to his family and home; the sole basis he had
of reconstructing in his imagination the scene to which he would one
day return. Kurt Bock writes, 'We were allowed to write one
postcard every week in November 1945. One of my friends was from
that part of Germany which is now in Poland. He had no contact
and nobody else to write to. Therefore I wrote a second postcard to
my mother in his name, addressing her as "Dear Sister". I did so

every week for some time. Later we were permitted to write letters; these, however, could only be on prepared paper. There were POWs who spent hours and hours writing their cards, once the limitation on words had been cancelled. They wrote very long stories in microscopically small characters, counting the number of words and boasting how many they had managed to get on the small letter-card.'

Postal services between Britain and the American and British zones of Germany did not begin to flow again until the end of 1945 – and then only slowly and irregularly. To the Russian zone of Germany and Berlin, they only began in February 1946.

'On 1 December 1945 I received the first mail from my mother!', writes Siegfried Bandelow. 'After a year and a half, the first news from home! A little later, at Christmas, I received news that my fiancée had been able to fight her way from southern Germany to my mother at Göttingen.'

In March 1946 Mr Bellenger, Financial Secretary to the War Office, could report that officers were permitted to send three letters and four postcards monthly, other ranks two letters and four postcards.

The general sense of futility and claustrophobia was particularly pronounced amongst the officer POWs, who, according to the terms of the Geneva Convention, could not be made to work against their will. A booklet written by the prisoners themselves and presented to their interpreter officer, Captain Sulzbach, tells of the really oppressive mental boredom that afflicted every one of the 4000 officers held in Camp 18, Featherstone Park, in the summer of 1945.

About 80 men lodged in each hut: apart from the beds, the only furniture consisted of two tables and four benches. Prisoners squatted on the edge of the bed, or lay on the two-tiered bunks. There was not a single moment of real peace to be obtained anywhere because one was continuously surrounded by games of cards, stories, discussions, lessons and other noises. There was also the summer heat. . . . After roll-call in the morning, no-one was allowed to set foot in the huts until 11.45, and during this period, the crowds of POWs loafed around the huts and inside the narrow circle of barbed wire fence. Singly or in groups the POWs crowded past each other in a permanent circuit round the huts – nothing but men, always the same faces, the same voices, the same conversation, the same environment . . . .

In autumn 1945, Lt Col. Vickers was appointed camp commandant of Featherstone Park. Vickers, a former POW himself, immediately grasped the situation. By October 1945 he had persuaded a fair proportion of his officer POWs to engage in voluntary agriculture. The experience of going outside the camp, of doing physical work in the open air, went a long way towards making captivity more tolerable.

Siegfried Bandelow was moved to Featherstone Park on 16 June 1945.

'Here we were divided up into separate camps', he writes. 'The "blacks", i.e. those graded "C" – the so-called Nazis – were placed in camp A; they were all officers whose names began with A to K. The "whites", those graded "A", were put in camp C; officers whose names began with L to Z. Officers taken prisoner at the time of the capitulation were put in camp B. It seemed a very strange political division to us.

'In about July a new commandant took over, a Colonel Vickers. He had been in German captivity twice himself and he saw to it that we were very well treated. He said he wanted to treat us as he himself would want to be treated. In January 1946 Colonel Vickers took on himself the responsibility of taking down the barbed wire in Camp 18, after we had given our word of honour that we would not try and escape. As far as I know, no German officer broke his word during the whole time, although the IRA tried to persuade some officers to flee to Ireland.

'Here too we immediately built up a cultural life. We established a school, a university, a library, theatre, orchestra, and so on. I worked in the theatre group and produced a musical-literary matinée every Sunday, *Schatzkästlein*. Our cultural division tried to make life in captivity easier for everybody. We did a great deal of acting: Schiller's *Piccolomini* (*Wallenstein*, part II) and *Don Carlos*; Shakespeare's *Julius Caesar*; and some plays written by members of the group.'

The educational services the camps provided certainly helped to alleviate the depression which tended to grip many of the prisoners during this immediate postwar period. At the lowest level, they could reduce boredom and the time left for gloomy brooding. At the best, they offered the prisoner the opportunity to feel that he was utilising the 'wasted years' to effect by preparing himself for a useful life when he did eventually return to Germany. Here again it was the younger prisoner, who may not even have begun training for a career before he was called up, who had the most to gain. But all, as Oberst (Colonel) von Viebahn pointed out at the opening of the academic session in Featherstone Park in September 1945, owed it to themselves, their families and their country to make themselves as highly qualified as they were able.

Several camps at this period were giving their inmates a chance to pursue courses and gain certificates which would eventually be valid and useful in the new Germany. Three camps moved away from the mainstream and specialised in specific branches of training. At Devizes, in the notorious Camp 23, a doctors' training scheme was brought into being early in 1945. There POWs whose medical training had been interrupted by war service were enabled to continue with their studies. At Norton Park Camp in Nottingham (Camp 174), a scheme for training primary-school teachers was already in operation by August 1945. The project was run by the YMCA and owed its foundation to the fact that the YMCA, feeling the German prisoners' resentment of the Government's re-education policy, thought that some other method of training the POWs for their future role in Germany was required. The YMCA claims that, all in all at this camp, 600 elementary-school teachers were trained for schools in Germany, 130 prisoners received basic theological training, 125 youth workers were prepared and 200 students took their matriculation (*Abitur*) for the universities. Finally, there was a Catholic seminary for theological students in Camp 186.

Crewe Hall (Camp 191) could claim to offer a prime example of the standard educational courses when Lieutenant Egon Schormann joined Kurt Bock there in April 1945. He was twenty years old. By the end of the year he was fully involved. Though originally a law student, Schormann broadened his options by taking a five-month course of instruction in the hotel and catering industry and religiously went to classes on 'Organisation', 'Occupation within the trade', 'Knowledge of laws and decrees', 'Knowledge of foodstuffs and nourishments', 'Knowledge of wine, spirits and beverages', and the like. The creation of specimen menus for the hypothetical 'Hotel-Restaurant Wildermann', proprietor Egon Schormann, must have been a strange, fantastical task to be engaged in in a POW camp in the months following the war. Such items as 'blue trout' and 'venison' must have been as remote as a dream from camp fare, and even the 'cheese dish' was a figment of imagination to appetites geared to the $\frac{2}{7}$ ounce of cheese a day which was all that postwar Britain could spare its German prisoners.

At the end of the course, Schormann dutifully sat the examinations in these and other subjects and obtained professional qualifications which would be accepted in Germany – if he wished to utilise them.

On 3 March 1946, he wrote to his parents,

My dear ones,

The three-day examination in the hotel and catering trade finished yesterday. I passed with the comment 'nearly good' [*sic*]. It covered twelve theoretical branches of the subject, as well as a practical examination. The examination stuck closely to the professional rules of the hotel and catering industry, and the five-month course was taught by eleven masters according to professional rules. The professional diploma was endorsed by the English commandant.

I truly hope that I shall never need to make use of this certificate, but who can tell? There was rather a lot of teaching towards the end, but I can now give all my attention to preparing for the *Abitur* and to my law studies. It can never be a bad thing to acquire a practical trade as well. It is just good that we can work all day; otherwise we should have been in straightjackets long ago.

The training in an alternative career was doubly necessary for prisoners whose education had been interrupted by the war, because of the uncertainty of the possibility of returning to university. Schormann wrote on 13 February,

Dear Parents,

At last we can talk about my career in a bit more detail, although it will certainly be completely different. I have almost completed three terms of Law, but the time will not be counted at university in Germany. This would not be so bad. When I come home, I shall have to take my *Abitur* again. After that, I do not know whether I shall be able to start university immediately. I shall be at least twenty-three when I am released. I shall not find it easy to go back to school for another six months. However, I would do so if I were certain I could begin my studies right away. According to the news about German universities, this does not appear to be so. I must therefore look at other openings. What about the police? The *Abitur* will be useful even if I do not study. This would be the only career that comes anywhere near the one I have lost. I do not want to be a waiter. I only followed the course of instruction so that I could work as an under-waiter if times were bad. Certificates are always useful. If you could only write more details. All we know about life in Germany comes from the newspapers, and the picture they give is very incomplete. Rest assured that I am using all my time for learning, and that I know that nothing is in vain. Nevertheless, I do not want to depend too much on studies, for there are thousands who have been waiting longer than I to begin their studies and for a place at university.

Theatrical and musical activities also provided diversions and aided morale, and here again Crewe Hall excelled. The *Schlosstheater*, with a stage built by the prisoners themselves from old chests, tin cans, bottles, old iron, straw and the like began operation in January 1945. It began humbly with variety evenings and poetry readings. By November the prisoners had the opportunity of seeing *Was ihr wollt* (*Twelfth Night*) by William Shakespeare and of hearing a song recital of works by Beethoven, Mozart and Brahms. On Christmas Eve 1945, Bach's Christmas Oratorio was performed, and in February 1946 the group actually held a Theatre and Music Week, which included three symphony concerts. They had come a long way from the early days when every note of music had had to be written out from memory, when scenery was made from bits of wood and old sacks, and costumes from black-out material. As the months went by, not only did actors and technical staff become more skilled, but in addition costumes could be hired from Manchester, and musical instruments and scores were provided by the YMCA.

'I remember a number of these plays quite well', writes Kurt Bock, 'and I managed to see some of them twice, though the tickets (free of charge, of course) were limited and allotted to the huts. I also tried and succeeded in getting seats in the front rows, pretending that my eyesight and hearing were far below average.

'Herbert Klomser from Austria, a baritone, was, I think, the only full professional.

'Apart from classical plays by Shakespeare and Kleist, there were also productions both the text and music of which were written in the camp: for instance, *Der falsche Kalif*, music by Fritz Heller (a rather quiet man, a teacher by profession; he was living in my hut and I really do not know how he managed to compose the music so successfully under these circumstances). Remarkable too was the decor. The scene demanded oriental carpets and what we saw really looked like original Isfahans, Keshans and Ghoums. The man in charge, H. Zechel, was an outstanding expert who had written some well-known books on oriental carpets before the war. L. Amrein produced the impressive jewellery for the Khalif, his ministers and the belly dancers. It was all made from empty tin cans.'

All these factors combined to make his stay at Crewe a not unpleasant time for Bock. He still recalls the daily routine when he was there in 1945.

'I vaguely remember a trumpet signal to tell us to get up. Who blew it? A POW or a guard? I did not sleep so long at that time, and therefore the signal did not disturb me. I remember some of us getting up as early as 6 a.m., running around the camp, taking cold showerbaths, even in winter, hanging out our blankets to air them every day. The majority (I was among them) got up at about 7 a.m., washing in the special hut lavatory about 100 or 150 metres away. Breakfast was eaten in the dining hall and this consisted of porridge, tea, bread and butter. A teaspoonful of jam was handed out only on Sundays.

'Roll call at 8 a.m. We had to line up five rows deep and we were counted and recounted until the officer responsible was convinced that nobody was missing. It could take thirty minutes or even an hour, and in cold weather and with rainy spells it was not too agreeable. When this ceremony was over I usually ran back into the hut at high speed (though there was no reason to do so) and one of my friends reproached me for not doing as he did, i.e. walking back to the hut in a dignified manner after the signal had been given.

'Each hut had a nominal chief, but I do not know whether he was appointed (in the beginning it could have been the eldest or the highest rank) or elected by us. The job was without any importance anyhow.

'The voluntary courses started at about 9 a.m. Lunchtime was in shifts according to subcamps A, B and C and hut number. I was in C5 at first, and then, after a few months, in C3, but I do not remember why I had to change.

'In the afternoon there were more courses or sports activities or helping level the soccer pitch, rig up the posts for basketball, etc. Others just did things they liked – if they found the material to do them. My friend Joachim very early on made himself a slide rule out of the black enamelled steel strips on our bedframes. He polished these and cut in the marks and figures, calculating everything carefully and exactly by himself so that it worked with logarithms. He was an engineer and this slide rule is still in his possession.

'Taking part in courses and reading were some of my activities, and in addition I played a lot of sports, especially handball and basketball. Walking for hours and hours around the camp premises in the beautiful park was also quite enjoyable; and in spring, when the rhododendrons, which seemed to be hundreds of years old, were in flower, it was extraordinary.

'Talking to friends, talking and talking round and round. Have we ever again had time for these discussions? I certainly have not and I regret it. Everybody had his own life story and there was also the present and even more important the problems to come: what would happen to us and when? There was nothing hectic about it, and we had to lead an extremely moderate or rather poor life, with nothing to entertain us (from the present point of view). It could be compared to monastic life (though monks, I think, brewed beer or distilled fine liquors) or to prison life (in one way better, in another worse, for we did not know for how many years we had been condemned).

'But I do not think this time was lost; I even think of it as a nice time. It is unreasonable to think of it as a nice time, but I cannot help thinking of it this way.'

Obviously none of the stimuli, however creative or time-consuming, could do more than deaden the homesickness and the anxiety about events at home, as well as the sense of hopelessness about time lost and uncertainty about the future in a defeated Germany. Not the least demoralising factor for the prisoners was the lack of information about the probable length of their detention in Britain. Pleading for their rapid release, Richard Stokes in the House of Commons on 27 March 1946 graphically summed up the situation: 'there can be nothing more dreadful – nothing more degrading, than finding oneself as a one-time fighting soldier, detained for an indefinite period, under conditions which at best cannot be agreeable, as a result of capture by the enemy . . . . One of the worst features of the present situation . . . is the uncertainty about their future, the lack of definition as to what is to happen to them, how long they are to be detained, when they are to be sent back to their own country.'

Part of Stokes's argument for an immediate start to repatriation was based on the Geneva Convention, which laid down that repatriation should be effected as soon as possible after the conclusion of peace. Unfortunately, as Mr Bellenger, Financial Secretary to the War Office, pointed out, a treaty of peace had to be concluded between governments, and there was no government in Germany with whom a treaty could be concluded. 'I imagine', he said, 'that at some time one will be concluded with Germany. When that time comes arrangements will doubtless be made for the repatriation of POWs held by us.'

With this meagre promise, the prisoners had to be content.

Christmas under these circumstances could not be an entirely joyful occasion, but the prisoners were determined to make the best of it. 'The second celebration of Christmas in captivity: I was in Featherstone Park', writes Siegfried Bandelow. 'We had been given fir trees, had made some cards ourselves and prepared little presents so that everyone received a token gift.'

'It began', Egon Schormann wrote to his parents from Crewe Hall Camp, 'with a festive meal off white tablecloths, and closed with the lullaby "Sleep, little one, sleep." When we had got back from the dining room we found a small tree awaiting us. It had been decorated with a great deal of love, with seven white candles, and it was just like when mother used to light our tree at home. A barracks choir, not exactly beautiful but loud, sang old Christmas songs. Our hut sheikh said a few appropriate and a few inappropriate words about the homecoming next year, which we did not believe. A Christmas story was read out and a thick cloud of English cigarette smoke lay over everything and enfolded our thoughts, which on the whole were not confined to the barracks. At twelve o'clock, the resounding choir rang out through the starry night with the old German Christmas song *Stille Nacht*. It was absolutely quiet all around us, and it was as if the heavens were our German heavens, and the night our Christmas night, and we expressed our homesickness in the words "Damned shit!" English jazz sounded from the castle: a great ball with women shrieking. All in all, a very successful evening, as the newspapers would say. The food was so good and plentiful that it took us a long time to get to sleep. My portion could have fed a whole family.

'And that is how we celebrated our festival, and, if anyone showed signs of depression for five minutes, we immediately helped to chivvy him out of it with our mirth. We have become ever-ready for such situations.'

Poems written by Egon Schormann during his sojourn at Crewe Hall and which won him various awards in literary competitions held at the camp crystallise the variety of emotions that dominated the POWs' life at this period. They have been translated from the German by Sheila Wright.

Lament

If I could only say your name just once,
And hold your hands in mine and touch your face,
And if I could ask of Heaven when I'll be home –
How easy things would be – but still I can't.

If I could only get some news to you –
A little greeting breaking through the dark,
If I could know your heart still beats for me
How happy I would be – but I don't know.

If I were certain of the time to come,
The days when life will shine on us again,
You'd never hear a murmur from my lips,
If I were certain – but I am not sure.

Do you count time?

Do you count up the hours, the days, the years –
Do you count time? Then prove your vision now!
Do you hold fast the only thing that's real –
Our youth? – Oh no, you cannot hold it now.

And doubly now, here in the fears of war.
Are you accounted not to be a man?
Who counts you now, when you're a prisoner
Here in this foreign land? – now time counts you.

Monotonously, the days and nights return –
Autumn and spring – you hardly notice them.
You sadly brood on human justice now,
And lose the concept of both place and time.

You still look for the laughter you once knew –
The grin of scorn, the only smile you see –
In sleep you look for it, you seek it waking

Do you count time? oh no – but time counts you!

Farewell and homecoming

Your heart says 'yes' and you have smiling eyes –
Oh, if there were no waking from this hour,
From such a joy, that drowns our very being.
A hundred thousand fires would blaze up then,
And all our lives would be one recognition
In that same dream that loving gives to us.

You give, and then your rosy lips do kiss
As if they could know nothing of farewells:
From your full hands you give us every joy
Ours is the time, the hour before we wake –
Your heart says 'yes' and you have smiling eyes –
When we awake, there's no going back.

And when I have to go, you'll say so bravely,
'I will not ask when we shall meet again.'
You comfort me, smile as you give me up:
'Good-bye' you say, 'and go: for duty calls you . . . .'

Your heart cries 'no!' – and oh, your eyes, they weep.

Four weeks

It's four weeks now, since you last wrote to me –
My child, I swear you've really gone too far!
Amazed, you wonder where time has gone –
Ask Time, my child, ask Time – that cruel Time.

You promise it's the last time it will happen,
And on the paper there's the mark of tears –
Page after page you give me now to read –
But you are *there* – *there's* not the same as *here*.

You live your life – the hours go fleeting by;
And time to you is like a quick-drawn breath –
And so I can forgive you your misdeeds,
Your idleness as well, my dearest child.

What do you know of every deadly minute,
Of hours like days, like never-ending days?
And how we try to get away from *now* –
For, deep within our hearts, we're sick for home.

You say that it's the last time it will happen,
The very last time you'll forget to write,
And on the last page, here I see it written,
My dearest love, you say you still love me . . . .

What have I left? – your gentle, quiet smile –
But it's as well you shouldn't know it all;
And yet, dearest child (and yet you are so wise),
I love you just because you're what you are.

First greeting

And one day was a day like every other
And then I held your letter in my hand,
A certainty about Fate's hardest questions –
The first dear greeting that I had from home.

A year of loving on in fears and sorrows –
O Time, how cruelly you can mock us so!
Torments of waiting! Nothing's left me now
But some faint hope, and still my trust in God.

After this waiting comes a deeper calm,
And now a mountain's lifted off my heart:
And like an act of grace I hold your lines,
This sentence, like a treasure, 'I am well.'

In silence and in peace the heart can trust
I see a faint gleam from the light to come:
You are alive: and our tomorrow lives
In you and me . . . . one day I'll be with you.

13 No Burden

The year 1946 marks the turning point in the British attitude towards the German POWs. 'The Honourable Member's suggestion that the POWs in this country are a burden to us is wholly misconceived', said the Right Hon. Herbert Morrison in the House of Commons in February 1946. 'The great majority of these prisoners are engaged in work of the highest importance for which suitable British labour is not available. No arrangements have been made or are at present in contemplation for the repatriation of the German prisoners. On the contrary, arrangements are in hand to bring further German prisoners to this country from other areas in considerable numbers to make good the loss of Italians and to supplement the POW labour force.' Repatriation of Italian POWs had begun after the 1945 harvest.

Demand for the services of the German prisoners came not only from British industry and agriculture. There were also demands for the repatriation of non-Nazis to assist the Allied Control Commission in its task of reconstructing Germany. The Commission had signified willingness to accept any number of anti-Nazi miners, bank officials, lawyers, factory managers, police, as well as experienced workers in agriculture and food-processing, transport, port and telegraph services and public utilities. In February 1946 the Chancellor of the Duchy of Lancaster reported that so far 650 such POWs had been repatriated under the Oberon scheme. Some 2200 had been selected as suitable candidates, but there were 'physical difficulties in transporting large bodies of men to Germany'.

'In January 1946 the first 137 men were repatriated from Featherstone Park', writes Siegfried Bandelow, 'including a lieutenant who wore the *Ritterkreuz* [a military decoration] and was repatriated as an active anti-fascist. Later it turned out that he had lied to everyone. He was a medical orderly – not an officer, no *Ritterkreuz*. Mementos which he had said he wanted to take to relatives in Germany he had exchanged for cigarettes in the camp.'

More and more German prisoners were indeed working in Britain. In March, 100,800 were engaged in agriculture, while 30,000 were employed by the Ministry of Works on housing sites, in building-materials manufacture and in civil engineering, 4800 by the Board of Trade in timber production, the fertiliser industry, tyre production, salvage, and so on, 2000 by the Ministry of War Transport on the railways and roads, in quarries, on canals, and so forth, and smaller numbers by the Ministry of Food (800) and the Ministry of Fuel and Power (200).

The Government, grappling with the problem of bringing the productivity of the prisoners to its maximum without upsetting British labour by arousing fears of cheap competition, decided that as from 1 April 1946 farmers should be required to pay the minimum wage rate fixed by the Agricultural Wages Board, for their prisoner-labourers, as opposed to the 1s. 3d. per hour previously paid. Of this, the prisoner himself received 6d. or 1s. a day according to the nature of the work he did. In addition, he was given free accommodation, food, clothing, and all necessary medical and hospital treatment.

The discrepancy between the two rates was the subject of one of Mr Stokes's tirades in the House of Commons in March. 'Here, we have a very large body of able-bodied people virtually treated as slaves', he thundered. 'I had some of these people sent to me. In the firm with which I am connected, we had some work that we wanted done. . . . I think I am right in saying that we had to pay something like 66 shillings a week to the Government. It is nonsense for the Government to suggest that it costs 66 shillings a week to keep a POW. . . . If POWs are employed, they should be paid wages, or credited with wages, with which, when they go home, they can start life again in their own countries. Do not let us forget that the slavery charge is one that is levelled against the so-called war criminals on trial at Nuremberg. . . .'

For the Government, Mr Bellenger explained that the prisoners' own country paid them or credited them with, or should credit them with, soldiers' earnings, and that they would receive these when they returned home. Prisoners in Britain got working pay in addition to that. 'Those who are prisoners of war in our hands . . . are treated far better than their compatriots are in Germany. They are better fed, they are better clothed and they are better housed.'

'That', Stokes retorted, 'only means we are better slavemasters.'

The attitude of the British public towards the POWs was also changing. The ban on fraternisation was still in existence. Members of the public could be prosecuted (and some were), under the Prisoner of War and Internees (Access and Communications) Order 1940, which made it an offence to do, in any place in the United Kingdom where POWs were detained, any act likely to prejudice the discipline of any prisoner. The German prisoners, for their part, were forbidden to fraternise with members of the public or to hold any conversation with them except in so far as might be strictly necessary for the efficient performance of the work allotted to them.

But, inevitably, with so many German POWs working outside the camps – some of them even billetted on the farms where they were employed – the barriers were illicitly crumbling. 'Fratting' was the word commonly used to describe such behaviour, particularly on the part of young English girls.

An Edinburgh lady recalls how just after the war four German POWs came to work at the market gardens near the shop where she was employed. The manageress of the shop was sorry for them, because they looked pretty bedraggled. She put some buns into a bag and took a packet of Woodbines down from a shelf and handed them to the shop assistant with instructions to give them to the prisoners. 'I wasn't too keen,' writes Mrs Brown, 'but I picked on the nicest looking one, stuck the bag in his hand and fled. That night he left me a bunch of flowers on the milk barrow with a note which said, "Talk is forbidden, it is not a wit, say it with flowers, so I say it with it." When they finished their job there, I got another bunch of flowers and a letter which I still have.'

Griselda Fyfe remembers a group of German POWs repairing the tramlines in front of her house in Edinburgh shortly after the war ended. 'There seemed to be a constant stream of housewives taking them cups of tea, etc.', she recalls.

Dr B. M. Steen, when working in the EMS Hospital at Ballochmyle, Ayrshire, in 1946, also found a change: not only in the British (or, more precisely, Scottish) attitude, but also in that of the prisoners.

'I was again working on the medical side and almost exclusively with civilians, but I assisted with POWs who were entirely German. I saw POWs in the out-patients clinic. They were mostly men in their thirties and forties. I found them always co-operative, though there were a few lead-swingers – although communication was limited. There were no interpreters, and I could just get by with routine questions in English: cough? headache? pain? appetite?

'As, at that time, I was specially interested in diseases of the blood, I frequently visited the medical ward for POWs, to investigate special cases. These were mostly myeloid leukaemia between the ages of thirty and fifty. It was difficult to assess the mental state in people suffering from such a disease. Nevertheless, there was no doubt that the German ward earned the praise of the sisters and nurses because of the co-operation and willingness to help on the part of the POWs. There was much fraternisation, to what extent in the night one can only guess. The men of course generally, but especially the family men, longed to be home and were worried about wives and children. The Scots probably accept foreigners more readily than the English, especially when they are clean and tidy, as the Germans were, and there was no antipathy towards them. They were accepted not as guilty people but simply as pawns in the hands of the powers that be, as perhaps the Scots themselves are inclined to feel when fighting on behalf of the English.'

Alf Eiserbeck too was fortunate in his attempts at fraternisation.

'At the end of 1945, thirty 3-ton lorries were brought up from Oxford. There were thirty drivers from the POW camp needed and I volunteered. I gave up my other job and drove the lorry internally from shed to shed within the camp. We would pick up soldiers from the camp in Didcot and take them to work, back for lunch and home in the evenings: four journeys in one day.

'In May 1946, suddenly one Friday evening, all drivers had to report back to the office and get loaded up with tents, equipment, etc., for the army. We were filled up with petrol and told to be ready to move off at 6 a.m. on Saturday. We drove in convoy to Dover with British dispatch drivers escorting us and every fifth lorry had an escort with a rifle in his cab to stop him running away. We had our break in Maidstone in the town square to eat our sandwiches and drink our tea from canisters. All the drivers got out and escorts with rifles sat all round us to stop us getting away. The British officers sat down and had tea with us while the Pioneer Corps guarded us. The officers told them to put their bloody rifles down and come and join us – which they did. When we got to Dover, there was no one there to unload the lorries, therefore British army leave was stopped and the British army had to unload our lorries. You should have heard their language! We spent the night in huts in Dover. There was a dance in the camp that night, as it was the weekend. Our escorts looked the other way and we all went to the dance. After a quarter of an hour, we had a fight with the army and had to go back to our huts. That was the end. Next day we went back to Didcot. The commandant of Didcot Camp stood by the gate as we drove in and saluted every driver – every POW. (We never believed in the Hitler salute – particularly the navy. On board we never gave it – even after the assassination attempt, when it was compulsory. We only used it on land, and certainly never in POW camp.)

'After that they sent us out one morning to pick up ATS [Auxiliary Territorial Service] girls and take them in to work. After two days, the civilian drivers in the camp complained that this was not right, so we were stopped. As a protest the ATS wouldn't travel in the lorries and walked to work. POWs were put back driving them.

'The camp itself at night was like a workshop. Everyone worked like mad, making toys. It was like a factory. They were then sold for cigarettes. The most impossible things were made there: dachshunds on wheels, with rubber in the middle so that when they were pulled along they wiggled; chickens on wooden boards who pecked when elastic was pulled. We also made suitcases out of plywood. We took tools from the depot. One tent even had a complete dentist's outfit, which it used for engraving. Unfortunately this was missed and had to be returned. I didn't do much. I did the selling and got commission. As I was driving, it was easy to get the stuff out of the camp. Even the police at the gate bought toys from us. After that, they couldn't stop us any more. We had the free run of the depot and could take out anything we wanted.

'The weekends were mostly spent on sports. We did them amongst ourselves to keep fit. A lot of the equipment we made ourselves. We acquired axles from the depot for weight-lifting. We used a steel bar to make a high bar for the gymnasium and fitted it up ourselves. We used the parade ground as a football pitch. There were evening classes every evening: English, languages, building, engineering – all organised by POWs. We had lots of young chaps in our camps, so these classes were very popular. I gave instruction in motor engineering. When we arrived at Didcot Camp it was empty. There was nothing there and we had to start everything ourselves. We had a big band. The German camp leader was a musician and used to play in a band at home. We bought instruments with the camp allowances. There were fifteen to eighteen men in the band, It used to play in officers' messes, dances, etc., all over the south of England. It was a well-known band. We drove them all round.

'In March 1946, 1000 men were brought back from the US to the camp. Now there was football every weekend, with matches between one camp and another.

'Wherever you looked in Didcot, there were notices saying "Fraternisation with POWs is strictly forbidden." You couldn't miss them. Even then, at night times, about four of us always managed to get out of camp over the barbed wire and through the depot fence. We went to meet people: sometimes ATS girls, sometimes civilians. We went to a pub and had a drink. One pub landlord put his living room at our disposal and only allowed POWs into it (the landlord worked at the depot).

'1946: in the national papers there was a big article "POW's Living in Tents Outside Camp." That was us. We took small tents and pitched them outside the camp, and when we went out at night the ATS girls met us there. One night a civilian girl from Appleford missed her bus and was walking home over the fields when she saw our tents and reported it. Military and civilian police came over, saw us and had us. We only got a warning, no trouble.

'In Didcot we once had a spot of trouble, when some people escaped and they counted us and we wouldn't stand still and lots of us went to the toilets. These were great long things with corrugated buckets and they got full with everyone standing there, smoking. The guards came in with bayonets and put one through a tin and just missed one of our men, so we took their bayonets away, so that the POWs had the bayonets and the guards had nothing.

'When we used to go out at night, we would sometimes tap the guard on the shoulder and say "boo!" and he'd be scared stiff and run a mile.

'At the end of 1946, one of our chaps committed suicide. He came from East Prussia and he had just heard that he'd lost all his family. He got so depressed, he went out at night and hanged himself on a tree in the village. We had to go out and fetch him back. There was tremendous propaganda in the press. They said he was due for repatriation and didn't want to go back.

'In the same year, two POWs escaped at the same time from my tent. They got into the back of one of the lorries. I told them not to get into my lorry. They got a free trip to Dover. They put a mark on the tailboard so that I'd know which lorry they were in. They got to the docks and one of the chaps asked somebody how certain football teams had got on that day. The man said that those particular teams hadn't played that day. He got suspicious and the prisoners were taken in. They were back in Didcot two days later and given twentyone days' solitary. They were supposed to have all their hair cut off, but they wouldn't keep still, so the POW barber refused to cut it. The British captain also tried and failed. They were marched all round the depot to show that they didn't get away. They were the only two who tried to escape, the whole time I was at Didcot.

'In the depot in Didcot, one shed was used for storing alcohol for medical use. We went at night and took one can. We mixed it up with Camp coffee, custard powder, anything we could find and drank it in tin cups. We had two little cups each and were so drunk! Every time our can was empty, we took another 5 gallons. We had some really good times in that camp.

'Soap was still rationed at that time. The ATS girls we drove were searched every night, because they worked with the soap. We said to them, "How much do you want?" We took a case of 144 slabs for them. It went on like this, for some time.

'One of our chaps met his aunt in Didcot. She had come over after the First War. We went there a couple of times for a cup of coffee or tea. She had nothing much in the house. Her husband drank a lot and didn't get much money. We took officers' mess chairs for them, knives and forks, plates, crockery – not just half a dozen, but everything in boxes. They had enough to last them for fifteen years. The husband was a farmworker. They were quite nice people.

'At the end of 1946 we had an inspection of our platoon. We had to go to Slade Camp, where a general from Southern Command inspected us. About two weeks before this, we had taken fifty cans full of paint, and the POWs who were spraying the sheds sprayed our lorries inside and out with green paint. We went there in the evenings and at the weekends to do this. As the inspection came up, the whole platoon went to Oxford and lined up, and when the general came round he checked the vehicles, their engines and gearboxes, looking for oil and dirt. After he'd finished, our platoon in Didcot was pronounced the best in the whole company. As a result, we got a transfer to Bulford Camp, Salisbury Plain. The lorry-drivers were the pride of Didcot Camp, and when we left we had a farewell party, drinking our special brew as well as beer, which we could buy (it was specially brewed for POWs). When we left the next morning, we each had a gallon of our alcohol in our bags.

'Before that, on Christmas Eve 1946, POWs were coming into Didcot by train. Three lorries had to go down and pick them up. We had two escorts with us six drivers. The train was over two hours late. While we were waiting, some of the ATS girls came past who knew us, so we all went into the pubs drinking.'

Another enthusiastic fraterniser was Siegfried Gabler, still at his agricultural camp at Mortimer.

'Gradually, we began to go out on our own, in ones and twos. We went all over the place to work: Reading, Basingstoke, Newbury. We liked that because we came into touch with people outside. We were not supposed to talk to anybody but we began to get to know people, mainly through other people who worked on the farm. One of them had a daughter, a lovely blonde called Freda. Later our barbed wire came down foot by foot, until it was only 2 feet high. Every night we had to line up and be counted, and as long as the number was right it was OK. From the Saturday evening count until the Sunday evening count, no one bothered about you. So, after the count, over the fence we went. I generally went to the farmer's house.

'There was one escape attempt from Mortimer. He got as far as Southampton and, the funny thing was, he couldn't speak a word of English. He got done for stealing a bicycle and a suit, and got twenty-eight days. He was a real celebrity when he was brought back, sitting in the sun in something like a chicken run. Even the English soldiers celebrated him. He got better food than anyone else.

'But pinching from one's mates was punished terribly. No one had much. There were cases of this. They made them wear a sign round their necks saying, "I pinched from my mates" – or something – and then they had to walk round the camp. They also had to stand in the dinner queue and everyone sloshed a spoonful of stew in their face.

'At Mortimer there was table-tennis, boxing and football, but no classes. We had a football team but only played matches amongst ourselves. We spent our spare time making slippers and toys. Our favourite thing was slippers. We made a lovely slipper. We used to nick sacks from farms, and weave them and sell them in Newbury at a hairdresser's. I'd take them in, three or four pairs at a time and take orders for the next batch. We had a film every Saturday night, one week in English, the next in German. I didn't see any of them. I had to meet Freda.

'We used to buy cakes, socks etc. at the canteen with camp money and sell them to the blokes on the farm for real money. We had 6*d*. between us and we used to knock on doors – any doors – and say, "Could you sell us a loaf of bread?" We knew the answer we'd get: "You can have a loaf. Keep the money." Our 6*d*. lasted us for weeks. Our tanner did about a hundred loaves. We also managed to subsidise our food in other ways. Chaps who were working on market gardens flogged stuff. Half of everything they found went home – like eggs. We had great big greatcoats with half linings. These made lovely bags when we carried the coat over our arms.'

14 A Change of Scene

In May 1945, the month when the war ended, there were 199,550 German POWs in Great Britain. In the first half of 1946 their numbers rose dramatically (despite repatriation of the sick and the specialist), until in September they had reached a high point of 402,200. The Government had been true to its word: large consignments of POWs from overseas were being brought into Britain to swell the POW working force.

The reverse movement is reflected in the POW figures for Canada. They had reached a maximum of 33,800 in June 1945. By December 1946 they had fallen to zero.

Many of these German prisoners shipped to Britain from Canada seem to have been under the impression that they had been told that they were actually going home when they embarked. This 'deception' later gave Richard Stokes, MP, a good opportunity for protest in the House.

The emotions of one of them are succinctly described in a letter written to Sister Scott at Christmas 1946:

Time passed on, and in July 1946 we were to be shipped home [from Canada], as they told us. I myself was rushed back to camp one day by a special 'plane, which had taken me a hundred miles deep into the forest a few days ago to fight a bush fire. I just arrived in time. All the belongings went head over heels into the kit bag. Life was bright again! Really, we started off from Halifax just on Mother's birthday, July 2. I could hardly believe it. To be home?

Well, the first shock was the disembarkation in Southampton and not in Cuxhaven, as rumours were saying. And here followed aplenty. I'll save you from telling them all. Right now I am working in a brickworks in London. Instead of Ontario's resinous air I am now breathing a lot of brick dust. The work is hard, but I still can stand it. Almost every night when I return to camp a letter from my wife is waiting for me. My wife fled from East

Prussia to the Danish peninsula, where she is now with my mother in Schleswig. We've lost everything because of the Russians: house, my things, and my job. But wife and child are safe and I could thank the Lord on my knees for it. They are waiting for me to return, and so providence wills it, I shall be home one day. Next year probably, provided everything is running to schedule. . . .

However, it was not only from Canada that prisoners were being brought into Britain. They were also arriving from camps in Western Europe. K. E. was captured in the Ardennes in February 1945 by Americans 'who came down in gliders'. ('The American soldiers were the least humane. They stripped us of everything. They didn't even leave us a hankie.') He was nineteen years old.

'Obviously from an early age we were all part of Hitler Youth, though I can't remember if we were conscripted. I was a Hitler Youth leader – but how can you be a Hitler Youth leader at the age of sixteen? I particularly benefited from the flying corps under Hitler Youth. Every year we were sent off for three weeks into the mountains, where we were given gliding instruction as well as flying.

'My parents were far from being behind Hitler. My father was a complete non-joiner: he belonged to absolutely nothing. He was a carpenter by trade but in 1940 he was conscripted into the airforce, though he was rather old for this. His duties were airforce maintenance and he was stationed on Alderney in 1941–2. He wrote home that he was coming on leave in 1942, but he never arrived: "missing presumed killed in action" crossing to Cherbourg.'

K. E. was handed over to the British shortly after capture and subsequently spent periods of time in camps near Brussels and in Holland (where he was a member of a labour detail). In February 1946 he was brought to England.

'We were put on a covered goods wagon on a train at night. We thought we were going home, but the direction was a bit odd. We soon discovered that we were going the wrong way. We went to Ostend and were then bundled on a ship and landed at Tilbury – still at night. We were put on a train; it was a passenger train and we hadn't experienced such luxury for a very long time. I shall never forget the sight of the lights of London and the feeling of being totally lost in space, in a strange country where I didn't belong. I was utterly dismayed.

'It was still night when I arrived at Moreton-in-Marsh, Glos, a few miles from the camp. I was billeted there. There were lots of German POWs there who had been sent back from Canada. The next day we came before a medical board, because we were in such an undernourished condition. Our weight was so low that they thought we had come out of concentration camp and were rather surprised when we said we hadn't. We were examined and put on a strict diet. We were not given the full diet and not allowed to work for four weeks. We were all sent to different camps. There were lots of POWs from the French zone and we were all lumped together with people we didn't know. Whilst I had been in the main camp near Brussels, we had all been classified according to the zone we lived in. I came from what was then the Russian zone. But rumour had it that you would never be let free if you came from the Russian zone. I had a good friend who came from the French zone and he suggested that I give his address as my own. This I did. Unfortunately, in Moreton-in-Marsh we were parted.

'From there, we were sorted out and I eventually landed up at Besselsleigh, Berks. Small units of 100–120 POWs were made up. One of the work details was at Harwell, putting down foundations for prefabs. I also worked on the land at Littlemore, Oxford, on a farm. There the people were extremely nice. I was the only POW there and I always got biscuits and a can of coffee with lots of milk. I sat in the barn by myself drinking it. I did enjoy it. We were all taken to work by an army truck and dropped off at various places. There was no hate relationship, even with the guards. We got on quite well with them. We were also used on building works – on the Bayswater Road Estate, Oxford. I drove a dumper shifting earth. We helped build roads and sewer systems. What firms did, which they were not supposed to do, was give us a couple of pounds, which provided incentive to work harder. There was a little shop I used to go to with a fellow POW who spoke English and buy cotton, safety pins and needles to send home, because these things were in short supply there. The shopkeepers were very good to us, though you'd get one or two who were less friendly. We wore army uniforms with patches (green, yellow, red), so that we were distinguishable (otherwise they were standard British army uniforms). There were holes cut under the patches so that we couldn't take the patches off. However, friends had given us old raincoats, so we slipped them over our uniforms when we went into a shop (the friends were people who worked on the building site). We always supplemented our food. There was a canteen but we were not allowed to buy there because we were not supposed to have any money. Therefore, we sent an English pal in to buy for us. We could slip into shops in our raincoats. The shopkeepers knew we were POWs, but they were not vindictive.

'The camp was pretty good and the food was pretty sound. We made toys and produced slippers, etc., and took them to farms and factories to sell. About six of us worked at the cement works at Kidlington. I had a job with another English tradesman, repairing huge boilers. Old Bert was a very good chap. At the canteen they used to make beautiful cheese sandwiches with fresh bread and lots of butter. I always remember them. I used some of the money which we made from selling toys to buy the sandwiches. There was a canteen in the camp as well. It supplied cigarettes: Players No Name Cigarettes, which we thought were absolutely awful and reckoned they made them specially for us. While working, we were paid in camp money, which we spent at the canteen. I remember great slabs of fruit cake.'

George Weiser was also captured in February 1945 in the Ardennes campaign, and also by American troops. After that, temporarily at least, his fate differed from K. E.'s. Apart from the fact that he was in the medical corps of the Luftwaffe and therefore classified as 'protected personnel', he remained in American hands and spent the remainder of the war in the United States. He did get a brief glimpse of England *en route*, though. After a few weeks in a couple of camps on the Continent, 'We went onto a landing craft and came all the way across the Channel to Southampton and into another transit camp. We were there for about a fortnight to three weeks. There was no interrogation. Then we were put on a Liberty boat and shipped over to New York harbour. On the way over, the convoy was attacked by German U-boats.

'I came back to England in June 1946, in a big troop ship. We were first taken to Belgium. We were told we were going home, back to Germany. We landed at Antwerp and were put into a transit camp. We stayed there for about two or three weeks. Then the British army took us over. The food was lousy. I lost about 3 or 4 stone in weight. It was our own cookhouse staff who sold food to civilians: we got what was left. A few of us escaped, some to East Germany. One sent us a postcard saying "I've made it."

'At the end of June we were all put back on a train. We thought we were going back to Germany. We went back to the coast and were taken to Le Havre. They marched us onto one of those landing craft – about 150 to 200 of us like, you know. They took us all over the Channel to Southampton. It was like a long box inside. The American personnel were more frightened of us than anyone. They wouldn't let us on deck, though there were rough seas and everyone was seasick. We went into a camp just outside Southampton. We got there in the middle of the night and stayed there for two or three days. Then they put us on to lorries and we went to Wales. It was a small camp outside Cardiff and close to the coast on an inlet. We were there for three or four weeks. The food down there was good and we made up our loss of weight. We collected shellfish whenever the tide went out, got a great basketful every day.

'Then they took us to Shrewsbury. This was another transit camp and we were there for one month doing nothing, just odd jobs for British officers. Then they took eighteen or twenty of us to Whittington barracks to the officers' mess. I worked there eighteen months, first of all as a cleaner and washing up. One day the cook wasn't feeling very well when he got up in the morning. He didn't feel like making breakfast. Well, I've always been interested in cooking so I said, "I'll do it." After having done this for two or three days, he let me do some of the dinners. After a bit, I asked Captain Dobson, who was in charge of the officers' mess, if I could be allowed to do some cooking, so he enquired of the cook if that would be all right and then he said OK, but I'd have to be prepared to take turns with the early breakfast. I got a small room of my own over the mess. I had to get up at 5 a.m. to get everything ready. Gradually, I was allowed to do bits of cooking, like small cakes.

'The cook and I were good friends. He had a girlfriend living $2\frac{1}{2}$ miles away and one night he says to me, "How would you like to come with me?" I said, "You're joking. I can't get out of here, not with a POW uniform on." He says, "Don't worry about that. We'll get you a jacket. There's a push-bike out here, you can have that. Lets go." By then I spoke reasonably good English, with a Staffordshire accent, like they did. We went out of the back, where there were lots of trees. He said, "If anyone stops us, let me do the talking." But no one ever stopped us. We got out to Mary's place, a cottage in the country. She introduced me to her parents and I got on very well with them and was accepted as one of the family. I often went down after that, even without him. I went to her brother's place too.'

15 Summer 1946

That summer of 1946 was indeed a question of all hands on deck. All the prisoners available were being brought to England. All the prisoners in England who could be persuaded to work were employed. In many cases too, officers who could not be compelled to work under the terms of the Geneva Convention had volunteered. A noted example was in Featherstone Park (Camp 18), where, under the inspiration of Colonel Vickers, voluntary work had already begun in October 1945. In that summer of 1946, the camp opened hostels within a 50 miles radius of the camp for prisoners doing agricultural work. With only an English sergeant and two privates to act as guards, the atmosphere was immeasurably pleasanter for the prisoner. But this was not the object of the exercise. The main purpose that summer was increased production.

And, with this in mind, it was not difficult for the Government to turn a deaf ear to requests for a positive move in the direction of repatriating its prisoners.

Though Richard Stokes continued to thunder in the House of Commons demanding their speedy return, under his interpretation of the terms of the Geneva Convention, Government policy remained firm. It was summed up by Philip Noel-Baker, Minister of State, in a statement in a debate on Germany that took place on 29 July 1946: 'I think it is certain', he said, 'that since the Geneva Convention was made, there has never been any war in which such enormous numbers of people were taken by one belligerent state virtually as slaves to work on its territory for many years while the war continued. Therefore it is not unreasonable that when the war is over some prisoners of war may be held for a certain time longer than the Convention may have contemplated originally, as some form of reparation. Certainly there has never been a war in which there has been such a great physical destruction in the territories of other countries for which reparation was required . . . .'

There were more substantial arguments for the retention of the

POWs. Noel-Baker used them all. First and foremost, there was a great shortage of food in the British zone of Germany. Britain had been making sacrifices to send food there and might be required to make more. 'Belsen Rations for Germans – Or Less for Us' ran the headline of an article in the *Observer* on 11 March 1946, which interpreter officer Eugene Rolfe translated into German and pinned up on the noticeboard of Eynsham Park Camp, Oxon (Camp 661). 'Unless the British and American people are prepared to make sacrifices . . . the German ration will probably have to go down to 700 calories a day by the end of April. The Belsen inmates never had fewer than 800.' The 200,000 or so POWs engaged in agriculture in Britain were producing food for the Ministry of Agriculture. It was therefore not unfair to say that they were in reality producing food for Germany itself.

Such reasoning was in conformity with the atmosphere of the time, when voices in England were being raised to ask why the country was sacrificing scarce foreign exchange, why the people were forgoing increases in their own rations to help the nation that had been responsible for all the trouble in the first place. And in truth the population of the American and British zones of Germany were being kept alive at subsistence level – the level necessary to prevent 'disease and unrest' – by $1\frac{1}{2}$ million tons of food imports at the expense of the British and American taxpayers.

The Minister's second argument in favour of retaining the German prisoners in Britain was therefore all too valid: if they had been sent back to Germany *en masse* there and then, they would indeed have been considerably worse off than they were in British camps. At the end of March 1946, the Economic Directorate of the Control Commission had finally agreed on the shape German industry should thenceforth assume under the terms of Potsdam. It involved the dismantling of 1636 factories in the British and American zones and a reduction in the German standard of living to 74 per cent of its prewar average.

Furthermore, the prisoners needed to be screened and re-educated before repatriation was possible. All this took time . . . .

All in all, although he agreed that the policy of His Majesty's Government was that German POWs were not to be kept as slaves in Britain indefinitely and would be repatriated in what might be called a reasonable period, it envisaged a monthly repatriation rate of 2000 for the country's 388,000 prisoners.

This statement must have received considerable publicity in the

German press, which may have given undue prominence to the magical figure 2000. His parents' optimistic reaction to the 'good news' elicited an inevitable response from Egon Schormann:

Crewe Hall, 23 August 1946

My loved ones,

I find it inexplicable that after I have now been writing for a year, you are still time and time again disappointed at irresponsible newspaper reports and other rumours about our return. According to an official communication in the Lower House, some 20,000 repatriates will be sent back to Germany up to July '47, 2000 of whom have already been released. There are 388,000 here at the moment. The German newspapers must have made such a story out of those 2000 repatriates that everybody's relatives are writing, 'He is coming.' Believe us, this is not so. As soon as something official is known, you will obviously be told immediately. And as long as we write, 'We are not coming', it unfortunately is more true than all newspaper or wireless reports – and you must believe it.

Back to repatriation: the release of the POWs is a political concern, dependent on the shortage of workers in England, for the 388,000 are all working – except we few officers (some 10,000) – and, if the situation stays as it is, then I shall still be here when I am twenty-three, and I have come to terms with this. Compared with the situation of our comrades in Russia, things with us are really good and we ought not to complain. But, after all, England is not Russia. Please forgive me if this letter is all higgledy-piggledy, but no one can stay absolutely normal in these circumstances. If we were given the slightest knowledge of the approximate length of our stay, then we could accept it, but this not knowing, which has already gone on for fifteen months, is now making the strongest nerves come near to breaking point.

Meanwhile, screening and re-education of prisoners was proceeding apace. Dr Harald Dreier must have emerged from the screening process with flying colours, undoubtedly assisted by his earlier involvement with education programmes in the camps. In any event, in July 1946 he was considered 'white' enough to be sent to Wilton Park Camp, Beaconsfield, Bucks (Camp 300). Wilton Park, the 'training centre', had been opened in January 1946 to supplement and crown the general work of re-education. It was established to meet the need for a more individual approach in addition to the mass approach already made in the camps, to encourage educational self-help by training prisoners to stimulate re-education in the camps; and to supply the demand of the Control Commission for specially trained ex-prisoners with high vocational qualifications. In the event, it took mainly 'A' category prisoners from all the British camps and provided some 300 of them with courses lasting six to eight weeks.

A small permanent educational staff, supplemented by outside lecturers, was engaged in projecting the British way of life, providing an impartial view of German social and political development and showing the political necessity of the United Nations Organisation, in which it would be in Germany's interest to co-operate.

Godfrey Scheele was involved in Wilton Park from its opening in January 1946.

'I was asked by Dr Koeppler to join his staff at Wilton Park. I was in the army and had done a bit of teaching before the war. I was a resident tutor there and also lectured on the Weimar Republic. The object was to help the German POWs to get a more genuine understanding of the true history of their country than they had obtained from Nazi teaching. Some of them, the very young ones, had never heard of any other viewpoint than the Nazi one. They also had lectures on the British background and law. I also gave them some lectures on the British dominions overseas.

'They came for six-week periods. They had already been screened by this time and in any case most of them were already disillusioned with Hitler. I think that the development of the German Federal Republic speaks for itself. Its development was even better than could have been hoped and immeasurably better than that of Germany after the First World War.

'The prisoners were definitely very interested to hear the new view, and the very different view, of how things had developed as they did. We had all ranks on the course – we even had a general on one course.'

Dr Harald Dreier is more caustic on the subject.

'I must in some way have been an embarrassment to the English commandant at my previous camp. I was suddenly moved to an education camp in the vicinity of London.

'Re-education was a very ambitious undertaking – one might even say a presumptuous scheme. In my eyes it was totally superfluous. The lectures and discussions could have made no lasting impression on POWs who were camp followers whom the English authorities had screened as more or less harmless. Camp followers are just camp followers: yesterday of the Nazis; today of the democracy; tomorrow of the Communists. For these, the course was a pleasant change from the dreariness of camp life.

'The anti-Nazis needed no re-education. The appeal was in the main really to the trade-union and Marxist-Communist oriented participants, who took the lead in the discussions. All that remained for the democratically-minded POWs was to exchange information and opinions in private groups during breaks.

'The colours red and brown in politics symbolise the same terrorising of conscience. In addition, it came to light during the course that one of the tutors had collaborated with the so-called *Rote Kapelle*, an espionage organisation in the pay of Moscow.

'The communal expedition by a single group to London in civilian dress was the sole pleasant thing at this camp.'

Siegfried Bandelow, still at Featherstone Park in that summer of 1946, is no kinder about re-education. He was more at home on the cultural scene.

'In order to make life easier for the other POWs at Featherstone Park Camp, we carried out a very intensive cultural programme, with theatrical productions (for example, in May 1946 we gave sixteen performances of *Troilus and Cressida*), as well as school and university courses, musical presentations and so on. In our officers' camp, we had enough teachers, professors, and artists to offer a considerable degree of choice. Sometimes we had the opportunity to work on farms in the country. In June our theatre gave *Danton's Death* by Büchner.

'It was at this point that the so-called "re-education" began. This was done in a very clumsy way. Very many of the speakers were unable to put themselves into the state of mind of the German officers they were dealing with. From my notes it emerges that most of the lecturers did not understand that the German POWs regarded themselves first and foremost as German officers and that political questions – National Socialism, anti-semitism, etc. – were for them only something with which they did not or could not identify. I personally well remember a talk with a Dr Wolf (from the Dresden State Theatre), who lectured at Camp 18 at that time. It was on the occasion of a farewell party for a number of us who were to be moved to another camp, after the last performance of our *Schatzkästlein* in Camp 18. Dr Wolf was a very intelligent man and one of the few exceptions who showed great understanding of our position.

'Lt Col. Vickers accompanied us to Camp 17 [Lodge Moor Camp, Sheffield]. His wife with her three youngest children bid us farewell at the railway station. This positive and humane attitude made a great impression on us. When Lt Col. Vickers saw the condition of Camp 17, he said, "I'm sorry, so sorry, but I can't help."

'At camp 17 the conditions were very much worse than at Camp 18: bad barracks, too many men in all the rooms, bad food, etc. I continued my work in the cultural department, with matinées, theatre performances and so on. A good side of the change for me personally was that I met up with old comrades.'

16 Repatriation at Last

Repatriation was of course the burning question in the mind of every prisoner: when would he get home to wife and children, parents and sweetheart? When could he begin to live a normal life as a full and free man?

In September 1946 he received a partial answer. It was then that British Government policy towards its prisoners and towards Germany generally jolted into a new phase. Whereas previously the prisoners had as far as possible been retained (to supplement the country's diminished manpower as much as anything else), and in fact their numbers had been augmented by the addition of shiploads from overseas, now the new Financial Secretary to the War Office, John Freeman, announced, 'The people are needed in Germany far more urgently than they are needed in this country and the Government is determined to get them back there as quickly as possible, taking account of all the circumstances, according to the most orderly scheme and in the most orderly manner that could be devised.' Repatriation had become a positive policy.

Freeman's announcement was made on 12 September. Only three days earlier, US Secretary of State James Byrnes, speaking at Stuttgart, had evinced a change in attitude towards Germany in general. 'Germany', he said, 'must be given a chance to export goods in order to import enough to make her economy self-sufficient. Germany is part of Europe and recovery in Europe, and particularly in the states adjoining Germany, will be slow indeed if Germany with her great resources of iron and coal is turned into a poorhouse.'

How near to a poorhouse it already was can be gathered from a letter a repatriated prisoner wrote to Sister Scott at Oaklands Hospital on 25 November 1946 from Hanover Vinnhorst:

A week ago I arrived at home, thus we were on the way to Germany for a month. You can imagine how lucky I was when I saw my home after such a long time. But I was very disappointed for it is here very sad and bad. Nearly the whole of the town is destroyed and we have just a bit room to live in. But the worst is to get food and other things for what we get our rations is very small. I wondered how my wife could stand it. I hope that I shall succeed in getting a bit more food. Food is the worst of all. From other small things we get just a few cigarettes, no coffee, no cocoa, no tea. Soap and other toilet articles are very scarce sometimes not at all to get. Yes, we had it much better in the hospital but rather I am at home and can take care of my wife . . . .

'You know my farmer, I have written to him and asked him to help me a bit for my wife. I hope he will do so as the parcel mail to Germany is open. . . .'

It was letters such as these that prompted Sister Scott at Oaklands Hospital to spend most of her 'salary on parcels of clothing etc. for the different POWs that asked for help' in the years immediately after the war. 'I got the prisoners', she recounts, 'to make dolls with different cottons, and then I bought large tins of ascorbic acid tablets and sugar-substitute tablets. These we put in little bags in the body and feet of the dolls and then sent them off, and a letter would follow later telling them to open up the dolls. These tablets were much appreciated.

'When Werner Fischer got home, his sister got twins and they had no clothes or food for the babies. I sent two sets of everything for a child and two or three large tins of Cow and Gate baby food.'

Organisations such as 'Save Europe Now' were formed and reports of their activities filtered through to the prisoner of war camps in Britain.

'In November 1946 I was at Crookham Common Camp, near Newbury in Berkshire', Eugene Rolfe told me. 'It was on a former American air base. Victor Gollancz lived nearby and he came over one Sunday and gave a talk to some intelligent young prisoners. He was the most literally Christian person you could meet. He had a group called "Save Europe Now" concerned with starving Germany.'

It made a tremendous impact on the Germans that a Jew could have done this for Germans. Under the impact of Gollancz's address, Rolfe participated in a campaign to persuade the Government to allow private individuals to send rationed foodstuffs abroad. He pinned the letter he wrote to Prime Minister Clement

Attlee on 20 November 1946 to the camp noticeboard. Great was his delight when on 3 December the sending of such parcels was made legal. 'I put a notice on the board of the camp saying that we could send some of our personal rations to Europe and we did actually send some rations', he told me.

By the new repatriation law, no further prisoners would be brought into Britain. On the contrary, from the end of September 15,000 prisoners a month would leave Britain for their homes. They would be selected according to four categories. The first two covered classes of prisoners eligible under the previous scheme: POWs graded 'white', and those chosen on economic grounds as urgently needed for the rehabilitation of Germany. The other two categories marked innovations. The first introduced a scheme for repatriation on compassionate grounds. The other envisaged gradual repatriation on the basis of length of imprisonment. At the same time the Government announced that it was increasing opportunities for rehabilitating and re-educating younger POWs on the lines of the scheme already well known at Wilton Park. 'We are alive to the difficulties of re-educating younger Germans to a sense of social duty and democratic politics', said John Freeman on 8 October. Walking a precarious tightrope between Germano-phobes and -philes he explained, 'We cannot – and the House and the country would not wish us to – treat the German prisoners of war with such consideration or with such softness as to deprive the people of this country of what they need, or hamper the reconstruction of this country. But we do believe that they should be treated with humanity and with the dignity and decency which they deserve as human beings and which we Socialists on this side of the House at any rate have always striven for and hold in the greatest respect.'

It is from this point, from the autumn of 1946, that screening and repatriation become inextricably interdependent. There is no question but that screening posed an impossible task. To place hundreds of thousands of men into categories – white, grey or black, or A, B or C – according to their ideological beliefs, was a Herculean undertaking. And inevitably few found it satisfactory. 'I was screened in Didcot', says Alf Eiserbeck. 'How could a man who didn't know you and who saw you for three or four minutes tell what you were?' Kurt Bock writes, 'It would be interesting to meet somebody who did this screening and discuss with him what he thinks about it now. At that time, it seemed to all of us absolutely ridiculous, though some people certainly took advantage of it, just telling the officers what they wanted to hear. Some of them were repatriated at an early date, as being classed "A", they would be able to boost re-education in Germany. I do not remember a single question I was asked, though there can only have been two or three of them I was supposed to answer. In my case, the questions were reasonable and could be answered without twisting my mind or feelings at the time. Others were asked (several told me), "Hitler, was he a genius or a culprit?" Anyhow, I was classed "B—". There were rather few "As" and, again, few "B—s" and "Bs". The greater part were still "C" and some of them were immediately transferred to a special camp far north in Scotland. They were considered to be completely unripe for re-education, but when they returned to our camps later in 1947 nobody talked about this any more and they got home in the same lot and under the same terms as we did.'

Some of the questions reported to have been asked by screening officers were not so routine. Stokes, for example, cited cases at an East Anglian camp where a prisoner who intended to become a Roman Catholic priest was asked whether he had 'had sex relations with women before', while another man was faced with the question, 'How often do you masturbate yourself every day?'

Eugene Rolfe was given the job of rescreening some of the prisoners at Crookham Common Camp:

'I was told, "grade up the blacks into grey if you can." The general idea was to try and upgrade them and get them home. I was given about twenty to grade. They were mostly agricultural labourers and had no idea of politics. The prisoners in that camp were mostly grey, though a minority were white.

'There was a puffy-looking young chap who worked in the kitchen. When I asked him, "What do you think of Hitler?", he said, "Hitler died at the head of his troops." He was obviously one of those who was loyal to the Führer!

'A chap at Eynsham said to me, "Grade me what you like, but 89 per cent of the German intelligentsia are Nazis. You'll never be able to run the schools there without them."

'There was another chap, a big blond man. He was my idea of a good German. You felt that you had the same European background as he had. I'd have trusted him with my life. There were three things in his mind and they weren't incompatible. Firstly, he was proud of being German; then, he was proud of being a worker (he was a miner); and, finally, he was proud of being Roman Catholic.

'These war relationships had something quite extraordinary about them which was akin to love. There were very, very close bonds.'

Herbert Sulzbach – by autumn 1946 Captain Herbert Sulzbach – merely felt that the screening teams 'had no idea of the German mentality. They asked silly questions and received silly answers.' In view of this, he obtained permission to do the grading himself in his own camp (he had by this time moved to Camp 18, Featherstone Park) and in others in the vicinity. In this capacity he was able to help many prisoners be repatriated sooner than expected, owing to what they told him of their problems at home. Repatriation on compassionate grounds was a fairly fluid concept. Not all cases were as self-evident as the one quoted in the Commons on 5 February 1947, of Paul Becker, a POW at Loxley, whose wife had been injured in a street accident in June 1946, had had both legs amputated and was still in hospital. One of his children had died of starvation in February 1945. The other was seven years old. Becker was graded 'B'. He returned to Germany with the first batch of prisoners repatriated under the compassionate-grounds scheme, in February 1947.

Despite its defects, the September repatriation announcement had a 'tremendous effect on the morale of the prisoners. Merely the knowledge that their imprisonment would not continue indefinitely, that it had a fixed term, gave birth to a spirit of optimism. Knowing that one day it would end (the end of 1948 was the final date mentioned at this stage) made a calm acceptance of the present easier. There were still odd unhappy incidents. One unfortunate, Otto Jankowick, was shot by a Polish guard while attempting to escape from a camp at Sudbury, near Derby, in October. He was spotted by the guard outside the barbed wire at 1.30 in the morning and challenged four times, but he continued to run. He died in hospital at 6 a.m. the same morning. The following January, Obergefreiter Alfred Ruf of Stuttgart was found hanged at Grange Farm, Colesdon, Beds, where he was engaged in agricultural work. He was a good worker, enjoyed good health and was normally a cheerful man. On 17 January he disappeared during a meal break and was found hanged by the tapes of his cape. His friends had no idea why he should have committed suicide. The inquest found that he took his own life while of unsound mind.

But these were isolated cases. Life generally had assumed a calmer, more cheerful aspect. Siegfried Bandelow, in yet another camp, writes, 'In August, we changed again, this time to Camp 184, Llanmartin, Monmouthshire. The camp commandant, Lt Col. Clarke, gave us the impression that his attitude towards us was very negative. Here again, we immediately founded a cultural division and a theatrical group and started work. We performed Shakespeare's *Tempest*. Together with another officer, I also took up the task of building up a library. In this camp, there was again political interrogation and re-education. A Mr Rossiter was very active in this respect, but he also helped us with our work. The first people were being repatriated. At this time, we had regular postal contact with our relatives if they lived in the British zone of Germany.'

The satisfactory state of the mail services, at least with the Western zones, is attested by Egon Schormann's letters at this period. They too reflect the new, happier attitude. He had by then been transferred to a new camp, Llanover Park, near Abergavenny, Monmouthshire (Camp 200).

22 September 1946

My dear ones,

The first post in our new camp has arrived. . . . This camp is called Llanover Park. There is nothing to be seen but barbed wire. Crewe was idyllic by comparison. The countryside is glorious. South Wales. The mountains here are like Solling. Not as many woods. Forestry is not an important factor in England [*sic*]. The area is more beautiful than flat Crewe. But scenery by itself is not enough for us. More to the point, cigarettes have again climbed to twenty-five (during the war, there were weeks when we got 100). At the end of the month, the first 15,000 of the new repatriation quota which the Government has announced are leaving. Three men from our camp are already included in it. Everything is moving. I am going to give one of the men who is going to Brunswick a letter for you.

Musical preparations for Christmas have begun slowly. There are no provisions for a Christmas tree here as there were in Crewe. All in all, every second word now is Crewe. Education is absolutely dormant. We have no energy for self-education. But as soon as the food improves I shall start working again. With what we get here, I could just as well die of hunger in Germany. Of course, I immediately attribute this defect to the new camp. For in Crewe (Crewe again, already!) things were better and our diet should not have changed so much.

On 22 October 1946 he gave vent to some of his exasperation at the non-arrival of a letter from his girl-friend:

Dear Mother,
   Do not say anything to Marga about the eight weeks. Do you hear? I don't want you to. The girl is charming in her innocence. There will soon be a letter with a thousand apologies and then one cannot be angry with her. Perhaps it is a good thing that she doesn't know how we wait for the post here. It is our only distraction from the monotony. I do not know how we filled the day before we began working, and here talking about the post helps pass the waiting period. Let me add that we have become ungrateful and we are, in any case, irritable – but after sixty days I am already banging my fist on the table. If I were an older man, I should say, 'Ah yes, women!' I am too unsentimental to be jealous – and too young. So I am left with a middle course: she can wait until she is black in the face. . . . I am only afraid that I am not really prepared to do it. Ah yes, men! Now you are having it at its hardest, Mother. . . .

14 November 1946
Dear Parents,
   Here, after the break caused by the move, teaching goes on. I could come to Germany now as a woodcutter . . . but you have to sign on for too long a period. In addition, heavy work is not for me.
   When one has a lot of time on one's hands, one is glad to seize on any foolish ideas. The latest is POW statistics. According to them, I have written 1700 sides of paper, 600 of which are law notes, 500 for the waiters' course and book-keeping (shorthand), 600 in literary efforts. But these figures are meaningless if one thinks of the time. 268 books read. You probably have been shaking your head about my reading too much already. We have time to read a book a day. Unfortunately there are not enough books here. 160 hours of *Doppelkopf* [a card game] played. Our day begins at seven o'clock and ends at 22.30. Twenty four films have been shown and the curtain of our theatre has risen and

fallen fifty-one times (we have seen and heard mainly chamber music; one opera, two operettas, all first performances, equally good; two musical comedies, dramas, comedies and others, and, as a high point, just one orchestral concert of German, Italian and English masters as well as Bach's *Christmas Oratorio*. This is the good side of our captivity. On New Year's Eve we heard a recital ranging from the Prologue to the *Pagliacci* to the *Cavatina di Figaro*, and, when the clock struck twelve, the immortal overture from *Fledermaus* rang out. The baritone from the Vienna *Volksoper* was in our camp, but (and here one can say, sadly) he left us half a year ago. At the beginning of November, he sang in the Alpenland programme and sent us greetings from Graz. That was a small sample of our statistics. Added to that there is the women's work, with ninety-four hours of washing washed, and don't ask me about the sock-darning: I become ferocious. But, when the washing is hanging on the line, then I understand the joys of a housewife; but I do not want to exchange these pleasures with you – I remember the hen-pecked husband.

20 November 1946

. . . Today I can give you some pleasant information. We can write five letters and three cards a month. This letter is already opening the ball. The post is as good now in eight weeks as it used to be in six months. Cases of divorce in our ranks are increasing. It is quite simple: the woman gets pregnant and then writes, 'Prepare yourself for a shock. I've had a bit of bad luck. . . .' It is terrible for the husbands. Only yesterday they were still building their dreams on the loyalty of their wives and now today they are holding letters like this in their hands – and this often happens with marriages which are five or more years old. Why am I writing all this? My friend (I shall tell you about him later) is amongst the unfortunate. Still, enough about that. Captivity is a small school of life (something which it basically can not be). Have you received my second photo? In the background on the right is one of our living barracks, left is the church (to which I must admit I do not go). On the picture you have almost half our hut community. The one in the coat is the aforesaid friend (a law student). The little one on the bench with the spectacles is Dr Stephan. The one in the foreground with his hands over his knees is the man who has slept below me since the beginning of captivity (an engineering student). He is a doctor's son from the Rhineland, a nice fellow whom I have not quarrelled with all this time (and this is a rarity in double bunks in our nerve-wracking situation). We turn our bunks into a sofa in the daytime and live on them. Here I sit at the window where there is adequate light. Over the bed hangs a picture of Bodenfelde in a frame which I made myself with a kitchen knife. Yes, we have learned something. . . .

1 December 1946

My dear ones,

I wish you a merry Christmas – and perhaps next year we shall be able to clink glasses and say, 'Happy Christmas!' The pattern over the years is as follows: 1942, I was at home; '43, in Posen; '44 in Reichswald; '45, in Crewe; '46 in Abergavenny; and '47 at home again. A small free Christmas journey round Europe.

3 December 1946

My dear Mother,

You have not really understood the way the groups are divided. Group 26 includes prisoners who were captured in February 1945. It is therefore not a political division – nor yet according to rank. Because I was taken prisoner late in the war, I am amongst the last. If repatriation continues, I can be with you next Christmas, but I shall still celebrate my twenty-third birthday in England. Please don't worry about me. I am well. Parcels from the Western zone have already been arriving here for the last month – but very irregularly. It is a matter of luck and somehow depends on the regional post offices. Here, I am organising the newspaper stand for our camp, so I receive additional food (as a camp worker) and therefore things are better for me. This means three slices of bread and two potatoes a day. I lose time because of this work, but on the other hand I do have newspapers from Germany, Switzerland, Belgium, France, England of course – and more food. Therefore please don't worry. Today they are showing the film *Hallo Janine* with a thousand naked female legs. Somewhat risky for our camp – but the extreme interest shows that they are still very much in demand. The oldest family men are queuing up – a fine affair! The wife of a comrade writes, 'Your young son . . . (he is six years old and his Daddy has still never seen him) – Your young son asked me today, "Tell me, Mummy, do you really know Daddy personally?"' Until I marry one day, dearest Mother – which will not be for another eight years yet – we shall sit together you and I on many more evenings. And I have become such a quiet person that I can scarcely imagine that I was once a wild youth and a restless sort of fellow. Who knows which was better? And now I am going to test the beauty of a thousand naked female legs.

7 December 1946

Dear Father,

If you could see me now – even the writing of this letter shows the solemnity of the occasion (as someone in the neighbouring bed has just established), for an hour ago I received a new suit. I shall spend the next few days with a crease in my trousers. I am generally envied. They have done everything but tell me that clothes do not make the man (an hour and a minute ago, I still looked like a rag-picker). They also said that I must have looked really elegant in a civilian suit – especially in the eyes of a pretty girl. The first I have proved to you; the second is far from apparent to me. When I have worn these trousers out, I shall be on the brink of repatriation. The money which I receive here amounts to 750 gross in German currency. Hopefully it will be paid out to me in Germany. When I am discharged, I will also receive 80 in discharge money. More simply, I cannot earn money merely by sitting around. But I would gladly work, believe me. We have just finished our Sunday morning frolic. It has again cost a third of a cigarette. Now we are waiting for lunch, which, with its pudding, marks the high-point of the week. The YMCA, which is theoretically supposed to attend to us (the Red Cross has completely refused), now sends us books. I already own a small classical collection of university textbooks. If we are allowed to send any more parcels, I shall send them home to you. By now they weigh more than my clothes.

21 December 1946

My dear birthday Mummy,

It almost seems as if I will really be with you on your next birthday. Four years certainly ought to be long enough for me to have to send you my greetings by letter. But, of course, it is not arranged on that criterion – which is morally indefensible. The POW question is an economic and political one and is not influenced by whether a thousand German mothers are crying for their sons, women anxious about their husbands, and children saying 'Daddy' without ever having seen him. If you have grasped this, then you will know that we are still not coming. My dear Mother, I will not depress you: one day I shall be standing in front of you, and then we shall go along together for many, many years and forget about this time, which will seem like a bad dream. You just tire yourself out if you go on hoping from one month to the next. Ask me again next year. Count as I do, from 1948. The coming twelve months will pass as this year has passed. And, if I am not with you at your next birthday, then we can begin to count the weeks.

The relaxed atmosphere of the period is equally reflected in the memories of a British soldier who worked with the prisoners. Corporal Henry Posner remembers, 'I first met the German POWs at the end of 1946 and the beginning of 1947. At Harcourt Hill POW camp [Camp 43, North Hinksey, Berks], where Westminster College now stands, I was acting as pay clerk for the small British contingent in charge of the camp. The contingent of about thirty had 600–700 POWs in the camp, with 500 in another section: 1100 altogether. It was a mixed camp, with a very few Italians, and both officers and men.

'By this time, the war having been over for some time, one was in the grey period where the prisoners were obviously going to be repatriated, so that the intensity of feeling had really gone out of people's minds, the fire had really gone out of people's bellies. Let's face it: even today, thirty-odd years after, people whose families were affected still have a desire for retribution – feelings of hate. In most people's minds, even as a Jew amongst these German POWs, the hate didn't seem to be there – not that burning hate.

'All our prisoners had been screened and there weren't any known ardent Nazis amongst them. In actual fact, it had got to the stage in 1946 when the POWs were driving their comrades out to work in trucks and driving themselves home in trucks. They were practically self-sufficient within the camp. They attended to their own internal social law and economy. They were given their rations and had their own kitchens and cooks to cater for themselves and they could be relied on to share out their food in a fair-minded way and attend in most ways to their own rules and regulations. We were only called upon to attend to misdemeanours and infringements. The camp was wired all round, though the amount of barbed wire was minimal. There was no point. If anyone wanted to get away, he could just walk off when he was working if he wanted to go. We sent agricultural parties out every day.

'They were allowed out for certain periods over the weekend, only on Sunday afternoons and certainly not at night. Fraternisation was forbidden but it was still taking place. They would go out the back, where a couple of females had set up an establishment in a tent not far from the back of the camp. The going rate was a shilling a time.

'The guard became very lax at this time. Everyone was fed up by then. If they wanted to clear off, they could. If we wanted decent food, we got them to come in and cook for us. It was the best food I ever had in the army. They baked fresh bread every day.

'The guard got so lax that, when the lights went out in the British officers' quarters, our guard went to sleep too. One night we had a corporal in charge of the guard, and at about 12.30, when the lights went out in the officers' quarters, he left a trusty German in charge of the guard. When we got up in the morning, we found that a German in detention in a cell had picked the lock (he was a locksmith!) with a bit of bent wire taken from his bedstead. He had just picked up an ignition key from where it was hanging on the wall in the guard room, and just drove off in a lorry. Two prisoners actually got away that night. One was picked up on Ascot racecourse: he had his washing hanging up on a hedge. The other chappie was picked up at Tilbury docks.

'But the one thing was that there was this great camaraderie between soldiers, even if they were on opposite sides. This chap wouldn't answer questions about the guard on duty until he got back and was told what story to tell. Then he just stuck to this story. Soldiers on either side were allying themselves as soldiers. It was the beginning of the feeling amongst people that, although they had been on opposite sides during the war, they were getting together on the lower rungs of society as opposed to the establishment.

'There had been a little time since the war and a feeling of relief had set in and the fire in the belly had been dampened down, but there had not been enough time to get friendly. There had been enough time to carry on a friendly conversation as opposed to friendship. You then found it difficult to believe and to understand that people who carried pictures of their wives, children, grandchildren around with them could be the same people that we had been killing off.

'Most of them by this time were speaking English. It always seems that more people on the Continent speak English as well as their own language. Many of them quickly found out that, if they were going to be human when they got out, they had to do something. Classes were organised in the camp, doing all sorts of things. They had their own tailor's shop, their own boot-repair shop. They did practically everything possible in that camp to make it self-sufficient. They had concerts, plays and films. I had a suit made in the camp: it was the finest tailored suit I've ever had (and my father is a tailor), then or since. It was just fantastic. The tailor's shop was just supposed to do repairs for inmates, but they made my suit for 300 cigarettes. It started as 200 cigarettes, but they made it clear after a while that they had lost interest unless another 100 cigarettes were forthcoming.

'Some of the prisoners adapted, others brooded. One chap had been a wireless operator. Because we had a particularly good wireless receiver, he used to come into the orderly room and ask permission to turn it on and get Morse code and practice taking it down. He would sit and do this for hours. It was simply pitiful to watch it. He was one of a few who were very young and obviously broken persons. They just couldn't really believe how things had turned out. In the main, the people there at this time were just waiting and hoping for the time when they would go back and pick up what was to be picked up. You'd get one or two cases of people breaking down. Though the war was over and they would eventually get back, the strain became intolerable. We had a subsidiary hospital camp near the Bury Barn. We had a chap who had gone berserk and we had to take him out there. It was just before or just after Xmas 1946.

'I do not remember any re-education. We got very little trouble from people doing reasonable work. This method contributed to re-education – showing how reasonable we were. We got something out of it too.'

1a. Sister Bessie Scott   1b. Egon Schormann

1c. Egon Schormann and a fellow POW

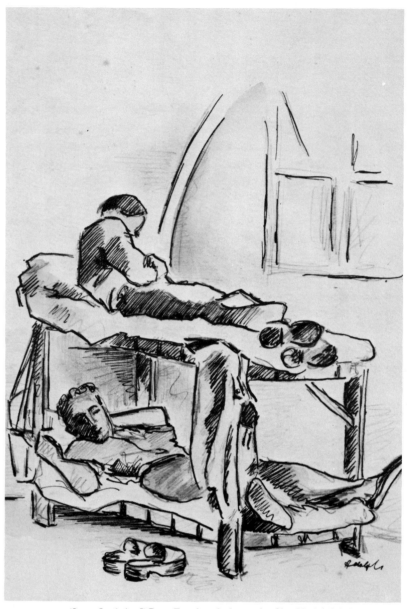

2. 'Lazy Lads in C.B. at Eynsham', drawn by Siegfried Adolph

3a.   Eugene Rolfe

3b.   Henry Posner

3c.   Siegfried Gabler

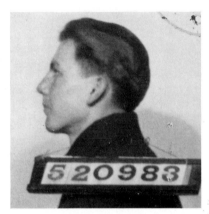

3d.   Hans Reckel

3e.   Siegfried Bandelow

3f.   Kurt Bock

4/5 (top). Card given to Sister Scott by K. H. Willig, 1 June 1947

4b. Crewe Hall POW Camp, provided by Egon Schormann

5b.   From Sister Scott's book, drawn by Arthur Schulz

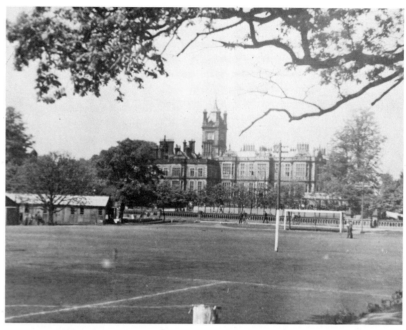

6a.   POW Camp, Crewe Hall, Crewe, Cheshire, provided by Kurt Bock

6b.   POW Camp No. 278 Clapham, Bedford, 1948

Army Form W3054 (German)

PRISONERS OF WAR POST CARD.

Kriegsgefangenensendung.

NUR FÜR DIE ADRESSE.

Zur Beachtung.

Nichts hinzufügen

Widrigenfalls wird

die Karte

vernichtet.

An _Wilhelm Bock_

Hamburg-Sasel

Alte Mühle II/12

Zur Beachtung. Nichts hinzufügen. Widrigenfalls wird die Karte
vernichtet. Nichtbezügliches durchstreichen.

Ich bin in englische Gefangenschaft geraten.

Bin gesund.

~~Bin leicht verwundet.~~

Feste Adresse folgt.

Absender _Oblt. Kurt Bock_

Regiment _Heer_

Datum _19. März 1945_

1500m 11/43 [87564] 33811/1571 1,485 500 3/44 M&C Ltd. 47-211

7a and b. POW postcard from Kurt Bock to his father, March 1945

II. TEIL

Letzte bekannte
Anschrift des
nächsten Angehörigen
IN BLOCKSCHRIFT!
P.17

⟶

HERRN. UND FRAU
WILHELM SCHORMANN
⑳ BODENFELDE /AN DER WESER
BAHNHOFSTRASSE, NR. 241

Gebühren-
frei

PRISONER OF WAR CAMP
191

IV. TEIL

Falls Addressant
unauffindbar,
Weitergabe an

⟶

HAUPTERMITTLUNGSSTELLE
HAMBURG

V. TEIL

Nur für den Dienst-
gebrauch durch die
Hauptermittlungsstelle
zweck Weiterbeförderung.

⟶

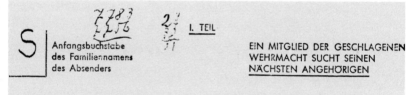

S | Anfangsbuchstabe
des Familiennamens
des Absenders

I. TEIL

EIN MITGLIED DER GESCHLAGENEN
WEHRMACHT SUCHT SEINEN
NÄCHSTEN ANGEHÖRIGEN

ich bin noch am Leben und befinde mich z. Z. in ~~amerikanischer~~ britischer ~~russischer~~ Hand

Ich bin gesund ~~im Lazarett~~ Meine Anschrift ist wie unten. Bitte die Karte sofort zurückzuschicken!

Datum **17. September** 1945   Unterschrift _Schormann, Egon_

Geburtsort und Geburtsdatum _BODENFELDE, 18.9.1924_

8a and b.   POW card from Egon Schormann to his parents, 17 September 1945

9a. Hill House Farm 1946/47, photograph provided by Siegfried Gabler

9b. The cast of a camp production, photograph provided by Siegfried Bandelow

10a and b.   Scenes from *Der falsche Kalif* at Crewe Camp, music by Fritz Heller.
Photographs provided by Kurt Bock

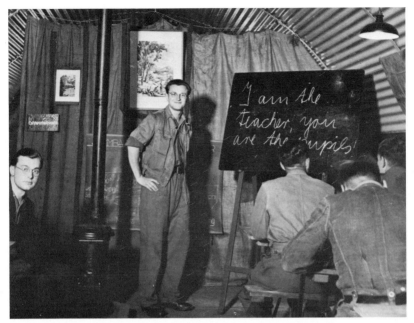

11a. Classes at Eynsham Park Camp, photograph by E. G. Waterman

11b. The Information Room at Eynsham Park Camp, photograph by
E. G. Waterman

12. Cartoon from *Der Postillon*, December 1946

13a and b.   Eynsham Park Camp, photographs by E. G. Waterman

14. Drawn by Robert Reuter and taken from the book presented to Sister Scott by German POWs

15a. POW football team, photograph provided by Siegfried Gabler

15b. Christmas 1946 at the Hostel Brandesbury, London. Photograph by
Dietrich Lotichius, Hamburg

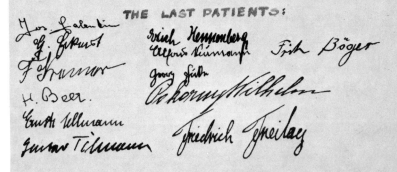

16.   From Sister Scott's book

17 Christmas Presents

Britain had little enough to give, that Christmas of 1946 – generous and conciliatory as she was feeling towards her POWs. With a devastated Europe to feed and keep warm, the country was fast moving towards one of the most serious fuel crises ever experienced. Food supplies were short, and rationing of most items persisted at home, in some cases on a more austere scale than during the war itself. There was no question this year, Mr Bellenger regretfully announced, of granting the German prisoners, or yet the British troops, extra rations for the Christmas festivities. Only very limited concessions had been possible even for the British people.

Lacking material gifts to bear as tokens of its growing goodwill, the Government instead granted relaxations in regulations restricting the prisoners' social activities. On 12 December, Bellenger announced that arrangements were afoot to allow well-conducted POWs to take unescorted walks within a 5-mile radius of their camp or billet until lighting-up time. But, even more significant, they were now permitted to converse with members of the general public and to accept invitations to private homes within the 5-mile radius. It must be added that all these privileges were already being tacitly sanctioned and uninterruptedly enjoyed by prisoners billeted on farms – and others.

Some prisoners would have preferred the food. Egon Schormann for one. On 21 December he wrote home disconsolately from Llanover Park, 'When the English gave us nothing for the festival (you only find that sort of thing in the newspapers) except the possibility of going outside the camp, then we gave up all hope of celebrating the festival as only a German Christmas can be celebrated. Don't worry about me on this count. We shall not let it get us down. We are young and it is the privilege of youth to be prepared for life by facing difficulties . . . . There will be a performance of a Christmas fairy story here over the holidays as well as a concert, and an operetta in the New Year.'

The British public, however, welcomed the innovations.

Agitation for these reforms had been vociferous. It was argued *inter alia* that familiarity with the British way of life, which could be obtained only by meeting the British people in their own homes, was the best possible form that re-education could take.

Now, with the Government's blessings, they were enabled to prove their point. They sprang into instantaneous activity. 'Go-as-you-please Christmas for good Germans', screamed the *Daily Mail's* headlines on 20 December 1946. 'Families Rush to Ask POWs Home.' With the Church setting the lead ('The Bishop of Rochester . . . will entertain a prisoner', the *Mail* reported. 'Three more prisoners will spend Christmas with the Archdeacon of Rochester'), families vied with one another to offer seasonable hospitality. 'Everyone was invited out', Siegfried Gabler told me. 'I went to my Freda for dinner.' 'It was amazing how many people made contact', said K. E. 'I didn't know anyone personally, but lots of my friends made contact with local families, with whom they spent Christmas, and were very well looked after.' The Revd A. S. Cooper, minister of St Columbia's Presbyterian Church at Cambridge, remembers that 'we made an effort to invite as many as possible to spend Christmas Day in homes of Church members'.

The reasons behind this afflux of hospitality varied considerably.

'It was my continued interest in the German language which ultimately led me to meet German POWs on the ending of the Second World War', writes C. V. W. Tarr. 'When I learned that POW camps had been established in the countryside around our ancient city of Exeter, I immediately conceived the idea that this might make it possible for me to take lessons in German from some POW able to teach. When the Government relaxed the restrictions on the movements of German POWs at Christmas-time 1946, the way was opened. My brother-in-law had been a POW in Germany for four years in the First World War and therefore had a certain sympathy for and understanding of the POW's situation. He invited Friedrich Riebenstahl to his home for Christmas and I invited Hans Kirchoff (a student) to my house . . . . Some neighbours of ours also invited German POWs to their house, so we got to know a number of the German boys . . . .'

A lady living in Middlesex, on the other hand, writes, 'Why did we issue invites to POWs? I think the word was compassion – Heinrich was about fifty-four years of age at the time. They were very happy to come. I think they mainly spoke about their families and homes (homesickness can be a terrible thing). They made a lot of fuss of my children, who were about two, four and ten years old at that time. There were quite a few people who invited them for Christmas. Of course, they had all been screened and vetted OK by the time they were allowed to work on contract. They were working in Church Lane for some months and local people were quite friendly to them and often gave them cigarettes. I remember one day I was standing at a bus stop and a well-dressed gentleman was gazing at the road-makers, and he turned to me and said, "That road will last for a hundred years." He has been right for twenty-nine of those years.'

Egon Schormann in Llanover Park stayed resolutely inside the camp. However, this did not mean that seasonal celebrations were completely ignored. In a letter to his mother on 9 January 1947, he describes how, in the face of all scarcities, they welcomed in the New Year.

My dear Mummy,
I received your parcel at midday on 28 December and after a short food-test it was put away for New Year's Eve. The atmosphere was sub-zero: there were no cigarettes. Who can describe the outcry as I laid the table on New Year's Eve (as always, we celebrated in fours)? Everyone got some of Mother's biscuits on his saucer and I distributed five cigarettes from Christmas bag 209. The oldest family men were allowed a sniff and then the cigarettes were wrapped up together in silver paper in the centre of the table. Children, we were rich! we had something to smoke on New Year's Day. A greyish-whitish hand towel was the tablecloth. On it, picturesquely distributed, lay fir twigs from the homeland. The coffee water bubbled in a tin pot. And then the New Year celebration began. The high point was mother's biscuits, and, although the comrades did not know you, they all said, 'My mother also baked like that.' Is that not praise indeed? At around eleven o'clock we lit the candle we had saved from Christmas and cigarette smoke drifted festively through the barracks. Say 'thank you' to the young lady in the dining room. As she happened to be there, she received a kiss from everyone. As a rattling alarm clock showed twelve, we all clasped hands, wishing each other nothing – for there is no one in our barracks who will still be there next New Year – yes, and then we went to sleep. You see, we did not forget the holiday (but without your parcel we would not have had anything), and, as we have a lot of

time at our disposal, any activity which is in any way out of the ordinary is the occasion for a certain amount of festivity. Yesterday a comrade received a small parcel with three biscuits for everybody. Those three biscuits were eaten in a half-hour feast. It is silly, but it still has a serious side to it. A year of unbroken monotony would be terrible for anyone who is depressed and sits around and quarrels with his fate. There are enough of such cases. Don't worry about me. We are small artists in life. We curse, but we also laugh. Often we have nothing, but we polish the window pane so that the sun can come in. We hate – and love – life.

The love is stronger.

18 The Worst Winter

The first months of 1947 will remain in the memories of those who lived through them as the time of one of the worst fuel shortages, in conjunction with one of the most severe winters, in British history. Coal stocks were run down to an unprecedently low level. Production could not be pushed up to its prewar figures. Gas and electricity supplies to the domestic consumer were mercilessly cut, so that the housewife would find herself without heat either to warm herself or to cook dinner for the family. Industry staggered to keep alive, with limited hours being worked in factories.

The cold and hardship were not peculiar to Britain. In Germany conditions were even worse. The waterways, which played so large a part in the German transport system, were frozen up. Road and rail connections had not been sufficiently restored, after wartime disruption, to carry the displaced traffic. There were no stocks of commodities to tide the country over the difficult period. As a result, rations could not be honoured, power stations ran out of coal, factories were forced to shut down.

The news from Germany added to the miseries of the cold endured by the POWs in Britain. Siegfried Bandelow writes, 'From the very beginning of winter, we were terribly cold. Fuel supplies were not functioning properly. The winter for England was very hard, with a great deal of snow. At this period, many of us were receiving news that elderly members of our families had not survived the hard times in Germany. I too heard that six elderly relatives as well as my mother had died. These unhappy news items depressed us all very much. Added to this was the uncertainty about our own fate. We did not know how much longer we were going to be kept in captivity.'

The relaxations granted to the prisoners in December were not retracted when the Christmas festivities had come to an end. They were still allowed outside their camps and permitted to mingle with the populace. Nor did the readiness of the British public to establish relationships with them diminish. Individual contacts made during the holiday period were followed up, while schemes to enable prisoners and public to meet socially were initiated by the Church and other institutions.

The Revd Cooper, with a POW camp a few miles away from his Cambridge parish, on the Trumpington Road, was involved in one such undertaking.

'It was decided', he writes, 'to open a social club for them on our Church premises every Sunday afternoon for a couple of hours. We had the co-operation of the camp commandant in this and transport was arranged to bring between thirty to fifty men each week. Members of the congregation and some other interested friends came along and refreshments were served free of charge. Most of the time was spent simply chatting individually or in small groups or in playing table games, and some music was provided, vocal or instrumental, as opportunity offered. Sometimes it was the prisoners who entertained us with songs or other musical items.

'Nothing was specially planned beyond this, though as a natural consequence individual contacts were made resulting in visits of individuals or small groups of two or three into people's homes.

'My recollection is that from the very beginning there was no sense of their being "enemies", but that they were just seen as people from abroad who like ourselves had been brought into a war situation. The personal contacts were quite natural and conversation was usually on personal and family matters. They were glad to talk about their folks, and not infrequently we sent letters of greeting to members of their family, especially perhaps to their children. Small gifts were occasionally exchanged, deliberately kept small because their resources were limited, and we did not want this to be a one-sided transaction.

'The whole affair lasted less than a year, as gradually they were drafted home. The impression that remains with me is that it was all so very natural, and very little different from what would have been the case with any other group of people with whom we felt that friendly contact might be beneficial. We like to think that it gave them pleasant memories of the last days of their enforced stay in England.'

Sonia Argyle was a post-graduate student at Newnham College, Cambridge, at that time, and participated in this scheme.

'It was the bad winter of 1947', she told me. 'It seemed so awful that these men were traipsing around when they were allowed out once a week. Although I was very anti-German indeed, I felt strongly that this was terrible and that something should be done. I heard that a meeting had been convened by a church council and I went along. The person I remember as being most involved was a friend of mine who'd been in the army and gone right through Europe hoiking out Nazis. He was going to be a Methodist minister. He was also on the committee.

'We had a big room where we gave the prisoners tea on Sunday afternoons. Thousands of them came. We gave them tea and then got people to sing or play to them. We were in charge of the recreation thing and we used to ask our friends to come and perform – for example, the music master at The Leys School. I remember a minister's German wife who sang. I remember it well because she sang *Wiegenlied*, and the words were very applicable. I remember one person refused to play the piano for us: his brother-in-law had been killed in the war. He himself didn't fight in the war.

'We used to go around talking to the POWs and we sent parcels for them. We used to ask little groups of them what they would like sent home, and every week we'd send one or two parcels to their families. Some people used to ask them to their homes.

'Although I was sympathetic to the whole thing, I was surprised to find that among these Germans there were gently born people who were men and not officers. One man, a very nice man, used to show us pictures of his wife and family. While I was talking to him one day, a young thug came up and spoke to him very roughly. He was obviously very shaken, but seemed to be used to it. The same thug, who was really foul, was convinced that we girls were only doing this for the men and he wanted to meet me. He couldn't understand that we were doing it for other reasons. There was one hilarious episode. Another man, a cultured, gentle person – I think he'd been a professor of art, in any case, he knew about art – wanted to take me and a friend to the Fitzwilliam Museum and show us round. We duly went and were conducted round. It was so absurd and pathetic, because he couldn't express himself properly in English.

'I remember starting a conversation with one young man by talking about Niemöller. He was about twenty or so. He said, "He says I am guilty. How can I be?" I merely wanted to know what they thought about it. The older men wouldn't talk about it at all. We had not seen this sort of thing (POWs in a camp) in our lives before. It was a very shaking experience. The first year that the prisoners were allowed out, seeing them made us conscious of their presence. We felt some trepidation as to what they'd be like. They turned out quite harmless and pathetic – such a contrast to what we'd expected, marching out, sieg-heiling! No one had any illusions about them: that they were wronged or unguilty but it was not appropriate for them to be treated in our country as they had treated others.'

Mrs Eva Glees, a dental surgeon living in Woodstock, Oxon, also offered hospitality to German POWs.

'In 1946 we lived off the Southern Bypass, near a POW camp [North Hinksey, Berks]. My mother had come over to England from the Continent at that time and was living with us. She had been in hiding in Holland during the war and therefore escaped being sent to a concentration camp. She was, of course, Jewish. She was quite pleased to have someone to speak German to, like the prisoners. One was asked to do a little bit to help the prisoners. Sometimes, when we went out for a walk, we saw them playing football. My husband felt kinder towards them than I did. I personally wouldn't have asked them to come to our house. We used to have an Italian POW to do the garden. He was very nice. There was a campaign in the papers to be helpful to the German POWs, so we asked some to come for Sunday afternoon tea. We had to write to the commandant of the camp and he sent us three men. One was called Friedrich. He was a schoolteacher at a gymnasium in Germany, and a very well educated man. He was interested in organising education at the camp. He was very soft spoken and he and my mother got on very well. My mother was a great admirer of Goethe and they found common ground talking about his work. The next one was a farmer from Bavaria called Herr G. It was a Jewish name but he certainly was not Jewish. I forget the name of the third man. He was an unhappy-looking man, well educated, which the farmer certainly was not.

'One day Herr G. appeared when we were out and my mother was at home alone. When we got back we found her in an agitated state. Herr G. had started talking politics: "We never wanted the war. We never wanted Hitler. The only good thing he did was to do away with the Jews. You have probably never met a Jew in your life", he told my mother. She was so overwhelmed she couldn't say anything. Two of my sisters had been killed in camps between 1941 and 1943. "I tell you what Jews are like", he said. "They only want to take. Otherwise, I am quite against Hitler." We dropped Herr G. He did not mind. When he was repatriated, there was not much food in Germany and we received a letter from him asking for food. The letter was not answered. Then we got another letter saying, "I know you have plenty to eat. Do send a parcel with sausage, coffee and sugar, and whenever you come to this part of Germany, you can stay with us." That was the end of Herr G.

'Friedrich was very grateful and wrote a letter of thanks when he left. Many of the people of North Hinksey village had befriended the prisoners, and, when they left, Oxford station was crowded with people crying, seeing them off. I also know that some of the German POWs went out working with English workmen, painting in Beaumont Street. The Germans worked so well that they were told not to work so hard.

'Once, at Christmas, we were invited to the camp by the commandant, and they acted *Charlie's Aunt*. It was terribly funny. Then there was a Christmas party. There were English soldiers running the camp and the atmosphere was really good. The prisoners sang some German Christmas carols. I felt absolutely ghastly sitting there with Germans. The play was silly but quite fun. We were treated as honoured guests by the commandant. The whole thing took place in a big hall with a stage. It was very amusing seeing the men playing women's parts, but they did it very well. I know that Friedrich felt apologetic. He felt that it was below our standard and his standard. I can still see his face.

'I have another memory. At that time we had a car but no garage. We kept it in the garden. My husband and I slept over the front door and he would often jump up in the night thinking someone was pinching our car. One night he let out a yell because he actually saw two men standing behind our car doing something to it. We rang the police and they found to their surprise that the car was filled with petrol (this was at the time of petrol rationing). They thought this might have been done by POWs hoping to escape.

'The people in North Hinksey village all entertained Germans. They were all kindly disposed towards them. There was far too little anti-German feeling. Some people, including my char, thought it was rather funny having people around who couldn't talk English. They used to talk a lot about food – for instance, that German sausage was quite different from English. No one was overfed at that time, but they were not particularly badly off.'

At this time Griselda Fyfe formed a lasting friendship.

'I myself had no contact with prisoners until 1947, when our friendship with Fritz started. My father bought a late Victorian villa and divided it into two houses. The house had previously been used as a school and had a Japanese garden. This had, with the occupation by the school and the builders' material being thrown on it, been neglected, and my father decided to employ a firm of landscape gardeners to redo the garden.

'Among the labourers was this German POW. He had been captured on D-Day and, owing to an injured hand, separated from his companions, and later sent to Gosford [POW Camp 16, Aberlady, Longniddry, East Lothian]. He worked on a farm belonging to a woman who owned a hotel in Edinburgh. She employed a few POWs and later the chef in her hotel was German. She is dead now.

'My father, who had a habit of befriending odd people, took an interest in Fritz and, on finding he liked to play the piano, asked him into the house to play ours and to feed him quantities of beer. He would come to spend the day with us, arriving off a lorry around breakfast time. My mother remembers cooking him bacon and eggs and giving him soap and oranges to take back to the camp. He would play the piano, chiefly, I remember, the *Moonlight Sonata*, the *Pathétique* and Brahms's *Lullaby* [*Wiegenlied*]. He was a very good pianist and could make our piano rise off the floor with some of the music he played. One Sunday, my father lent him a suit and took him up to the Conservative Club, a very exclusive place in those days, for a drink. I can also remember his family photographs being shown around, little thinking at the time they would all be like a second family to me.

'I don't really think I know why a forty-seven-year-old man should have made such an impression on an eleven-year-old girl. Our house, from 1939 on, was full of every nationality, especially Poles, but he was the only one whom I strived to keep in touch with. Perhaps it was because from an early age I was interested in everything German, owing to a book of German fairy tales given me early in the war.

'My lack of German makes it hard for me to understand some of his stories of those times. I know that one cold winter's day he and his friends walked from the camp at Frogston Road to the city centre, to see Edinburgh Castle. I don't think they were allowed on public transport. It's some walk! Somebody in town spoke to them and gave them either money or a meal. I think most people were sorry for them. The only person I can remember being unkind was a retired Church of Scotland minister. He, on being introduced, refused to shake hands with a German. I remember thinking "How un-Christian!" I never liked him much after that.'

But social life was not all-absorbing. Work continued, and more and more prisoners were being employed as drivers on the British roads. Not entirely to the satisfaction of some civilians. As early as May 1946 the Minister of Transport had been asked if his attention had been drawn to an incident in which a German POW had been driving a lorry on the wrong side of the road after only four days of driving in this country. In February 1947 John Freeman reported that eleven British civilians had been killed in accidents involving vehicles driven by POWs, but in ten cases the prisoner concerned had been exonerated. In fact, all potential POW drivers were carefully selected and subject to the same driving test as British soldier drivers. Officers in charge were also at great pains to explain the British Highway Code to them. Alf Eiserbeck was, I am sure, no better and no worse than any of the others.

'In January 1947 we were transferred to a camp in Tidworth, on Salisbury Plain [Aliwal Barracks, Camp No. 668]. The first night when we arrived we were all drunk. We had been taken there in three lorries. We sat in the back and, as it was cold, we drank our special brew. The same evening, we went into the canteen and had some more to drink – beer this time. There was no heating in the room where we were sleeping, so we broke the beds up. Outside the camp there was an old dump with anti-gas cream in tins and that burnt lovely. The tins expanded like foam.

'Two days later we were moved into a hut in Bulford itself. There were thirty drivers and two German interpreters, and we had to drive for an army company. There I got reported by a paratroop officer. I used to drive a 3-ton bread lorry, and one day a 15-hundredweight army truck in front of me was going at about 15 miles an hour, so I started overtaking him. He accelerated but I carried on, and he reported me to the POW camp. Six months later, I got seven days' detention for this as a punishment, for what could have happened. In the event, I only did one day of this detention before I was transferred.

'After one week in Bulford, we all got split up into army hospitals, driving ambulances. I was at Larkhill, near Amesbury, at the School of Artillery. I stayed there four or five months. There were two POW drivers and one army driver. I didn't know the area, the roads or the camps. I first had to go to Greenland Camp, taking a woman from married quarters to hospital in Salisbury, to have a baby. It was a hard winter and I couldn't see the roads because of the snow. When we transported service families, we had ATS girls with us. We drove open ambulances and had no winter clothes – no gloves, nothing. We complained to the doctor that it was too cold to drive. He wrote to the camp and we got special clothing from the camp: gloves, long pants, greatcoats, thick socks, gaiters. This doctor, Major Bennett, treated us like children. He was a very fair and very good chap.

'When there were cases from POW camps to take to hospital, they went to special POW hospitals. I met some Sheffield blokes in a hospital near Swindon; in Swindon cemetery there is quite a big patch of German POW graves. Some of them were genuinely ill, some had been ill treated by their guards.

'An incident I remember was when I took an ATS girl with suspected appendicitis to the military hospital at Tidworth. When I arrived, two medical orderlies took the stretcher along the corridor. As they were walking along carrying it, the bell went for 10 p.m. tea, so they dropped the stretcher and walked off. I got the first person I could find and we carried the stretcher ourselves to the surgery.

'At this point I was living in CMI rooms, which were heated, and I had my food in the regimental kitchens. I always got more than I should have. If one didn't get enough in one mess, one went in the truck to the next one. The POW camp was about two miles away and I could always go up there. There was a Polish camp just outside the army camp. One of their chaps cut his finger in the kitchen and rang for my ambulance. When I saw that it was just a cut finger, I made him walk – lazy sod. I went back empty and told the doctor. He just laughed.

'We were on duty twenty-four hours a day and we split it up as much as possible, but sometimes, when there were accidents or emergencies, we didn't have a couple of hours sleep a day.

'After five months we were pulled back into Tidworth and transferred to Westbury, Wilts [Camp 114, Eden Vale Camp]. Before we left, five POW drivers took their ambulances and went all the way to Didcot. They filled up with petrol and took 5 gallons of alcohol. They put up their Red Cross flags and flashed their lights and drove off as if with an emergency case.'

Meanwhile Egon Schormann, in Llanover Park Camp, continued to write his letters home:

22 January 1947

My dear father,

Your letter of 29 December came yesterday. I get the impression from it that the Christmas period was not too good for you. We were short of cigarettes. The day before yesterday, someone sat down on the stove and, looking innocent, smoked boiled-out tea-leaves (as they did in the East at one period). But he had to leave the room, or rather barracks, in a hurry.

So a description of the stove might be appropriate at this point. There it stands, an old frame which was already serving the same purpose 300 years ago. Sometimes it glows and sometimes it says *krrr*, thrusts out a few clouds of smoke and goes out. Unluckily for the wet socks and cardboard soles to which it lends a deserving edge. Around this model hearth sit all the POWs who are not reclining on their mattresses, for this also goes on in the daytime. I cannot reproduce the stove conversation, because it is composed of concentrated imbecility, fiction and fact, experiences with the fair sex and various curses. So some twenty men talk men's talk through the noise of the radio. . . . Over the double bunks hang damp socks (those which have not found a place on the stove), wet washing and, put there by prisoners who cannot come to terms with captivity, a naked woman (a characteristic of the Canadian POWs). Under the bunk, wire, wood (rotten), pieces of broken glass, nails (bent), straw, a lot of dirt and other things besides (which only a good chambermaid would find). Beside the bed, a box stands in state for the washing – 'Clean and dirty should please be separated!!!' – and a second with exercise books and books. On holidays, the covers are dusted. The next dusting: Easter Sunday evening. Everyone however, has his own standard of cleanliness. Those who are not sleeping and not sitting on the stove can be found washing. An insane arrangement for men to be doing this! All the same, I do not wash at all badly. You should see me. I don't soak it but use a lot of lather. Then a thorough rinse – and out to hang for a few hours in the rain. To Finish it off, I leave it to drip over the stove and to dry over the bed. Not bad, eh? . . . We are autarchs – and if children could be produced here mechanically . . . poor female sex – but until then it will hold its own.

1 February 1947

My loved ones,

According to the English newspapers, prisoners' parcels can now travel to the East. As for you, you have celebrated the pig-killing festival once again without me – and I barely know what a pig looks like any more. For this purpose, i.e. for supplementing ideas which have got mislaid, we have a dictionary here with pictures. For example: railways, chocolate (the latter will soon go back a decade now) and women. That is to say, we do have our women, but they have artificial breasts (which according to the civil code is a cause for divorce – once learned never forgotten – though the man would be a nit-wit if he did not notice until after the wedding, but that is going too far). As I said, women we have. Their legs are painted brown in place of silk stockings and their voices . . . . Only in the operettas do they need to play their parts fully, and I must say one gets used to it. After all, the Greeks also had all female parts played by men. It would hardly work in reverse . . . that would get a cat-call here – in addition, they are abominable in trousers.

The snow is lying very deep on the ground here. Deeper than for eighteen years; it is not cold. But what they call deep here and what cold . . . . They already have difficulties with the transport system at 10 degrees Centigrade, because that is equivalent to 25 degrees in our winter. Our winter sport is limited to snowballs, before the daily count, otherwise none of us moves from the stove. It is too dark to read there; now, you can imagine for yourselves what nine hours of conversation is like, until the light is switched on. Yesterday, the warm water was turned off just at the end of the big wash, and I had to rinse in cold. I shivered like a young poplar and cursed like ten pandours. A snowman has just been built in front of the hut. The work of a senior judge who acts as meteorologist and determines the weather (here in England it is always forecast wrongly) and is in addition our 'adviser on *Abitur* matters'. In reality, the schoolboy wants to trundle along, but the old man does not take him up. With luck spring will soon be here and then the atmosphere will improve again. Now we are too much on top of one another.

19 February 1947

Dear Mother,

In this letter I want to thank you for your parcel as a reminder of the pig-killing festival. I was so delighted with it. You know the way one sends a parcel is just as important, more important than its contents. And in that respect Mother's parcels are the finest. When I open any other, then it is somehow unexciting, for the contents are biscuits, for example. It is all over at the first glance. It would be ungrateful not to feel pleasure, but this glance shows immediately that it was not packed with love. And that is what matters. It is sterile somehow, if one sees and knows everything right away. You understand. You see, your parcel: first one comes to a lot of paper, then two small packets with butter, then one with *Wurst*, which needs to be unwrapped. After that a whole new box with a notebook on top. In the time this has taken, one has already smoked a third of a cigarette – for a year now, we have all only been smoking a third at a time, but on a wooden spike so there is no waste. When the box is open, another notebook. The enclosed reproduction of Urbino's Venus (which gave me special pleasure). Everything is immediately passed from hand to hand. For the comrades certainly receive the parcels with me. And they are delighted because the recipient is delighted. Now, the wooden case is taken out from among the biscuits, with a shout when we realise that it is not empty. Now we smoke a 'whole' cigarette! This is our finest hour, so fine that we forget the barbed wire, and even the swearing ceases. That is why Mother's parcels are the finest, because they are given with love, because they give us something to unpack. It is irrelevant what is in the parcel: as with all presents, when they arrive, the most important thing is how they were given. The biscuits were as good as in the best times. A short time ago, we were weighed: 113 pounds. Thank you for the parcel; but you ought only to send again when you can really spare it (otherwise my pleasure would be halved).

19 Thaw All Round

In March 1947, as the winter cold gradually receded, Mr Bellenger could announce that the results of the experimental relaxation of restrictions on the POWs had been favourable. He was therefore prepared to make further concessions. First and foremost, the patches and distinctive lettering on prisoners' clothing would gradually disappear as and when chocolate-coloured and blessedly undistinctive battledress became available for them. Next, provision was made in special cases for the extension of the 5-mile limit. Thirdly, prisoners were allowed to enter private houses on invitation, without first needing to obtain the camp commandant's permission – though the commandant still retained the right to place individual houses or areas out of bounds if he considered it advisable. In January this prerogative had actually been used in relation to the town of Gloucester, where, it was said, the privilege of walking unescorted in the town had been abused. In some cases, towns were put out of bounds because of the continuing hostility of the inhabitants towards the Germans. This could be the case with towns, such as Swansea, which had suffered heavily from enemy bombing.

Individual houses, on the other hand, were sometimes banned because the occupants were too friendly. In April 1947 a number of British fascists were sentenced to terms of imprisonment for helping escaped Nazi prisoners. Although the Imperial Fascist League had been disbanded in 1939, its sympathisers were still prepared to help POWs. Dramatic stories were told of the efficient ring which had operated for some months in 1946 and at the beginning of 1947, until it was finally broken by the British – while its members were harbouring two Dutch Nazis who had escaped from Kempton Park Camp.

None the less, despite attempts to prevent the German POWs from frequenting the homes of British fascists, no restriction was placed on their attendance at fascist political meetings. It was considered, said Mr Bellenger, that part of their education into the

British way of life was to allow free speech and to permit them to attend any type of public meeting during their off-duty hours. There was therefore no objection to their presence at weekly fascist meetings held at the gate of Victoria Park.

Another relaxation, also issued in March, allowed prisoners to attend football and other matches in organised parties at the invitation of the management or local authority, provided that they did not compete with the British public for the limited accommodation available. At least one precedent had already been established here when on 1 February twenty-five German POWs attended a football match between West Ham United and Bradford, gratefully using complimentary tickets sent by one of the clubs concerned. POW bands were also permitted to return the hospitality of their friends, where it was possible for a hut or hall outside the camp to be used, though they were not allowed to charge for admission. Finally, POWs were allowed to take part in educational activities outside their camps, provided that these were approved by the Control Office.

The way was now even more favourably paved for the gentle movement of the POWs into British society while they awaited repatriation. For repatriation, at the promised rate of some 15,000 a month, was systematically proceeding. In April 1947 came the turn of Harald Dreier: 'Hull', he writes, 'was the last stage on English soil before repatriation. I still remember with gratitude the English soldier at baggage control before embarkation, who deliberately overlooked my packet of coffee and cigarettes. On my arrival at Easter 1947, I was thus able to give some small pleasure to my parents, who had been brutally driven from the homeland by the Polish militia and were now living in a tiny attic room in Schleswig-Holstein.'

The 290,300 prisoners who remained were engaged in deepening their relationships with their British hosts. Kurt Bock and Egon Schormann at this juncture both found themselves at Llanmartin, Monmouthshire, Camp 184.

Bock recalls his first such relationship.

'Freedom covered a radius of 5 miles. The town of Newport was 6 miles away. We had volunteered to be together in an English-speaking hut. We had been learning English for our two years in Britain, but whom could we talk to? We talked to each other in English and had quite a good vocabulary. But we only talked to each other because there was nobody else. It was impossible to have any contact with people outside the camp. At last, in 1947, after two years, we were allowed to. We could not go into a shop to buy anything with our token money (issued in the camp). Was there in fact a shop in the vicinity of the camp? The weather stayed cold for a long time in the spring of 1947 and the food was barely adequate. Applications for transfer to a hostel for farmwork were rarely granted.

'Beyond the road to Newport there were field paths running up the hill. The slope was steeper if you walked along beside the fence, but, on the other hand, you got to the top more quickly. The spring sunshine tempted me higher and higher. Once up there, it was very lonely, but the view was beautiful. Unfortunately we had to be back in camp for meals – and we needed them. What could we do with our permission to leave the camp in the morning and stay out till 10 p.m. if we had no friends to meet. We – from Hamburg – were anxious to make contact. Did the British families feel the same? The spring and our greater freedom rapidly brought us together. Anyone looking for friends will find them.

'In the morning at eight o'clock I marched up the hill. The walk was through low undergrowth which had once been a forest. Even before the war there must have been extensive forests on the slopes of these hills. The smaller paths, away from the main roads, were covered with tarmac, but I preferred to walk along a footpath through fields and woods for miles until I reached the very lonely spot where Wentwood Cottage stood.

'I went there to meet Mrs Pugsley. The large tea-kettle hummed continuously on the hob in the wide chimney. I felt at home there; she was like my mother. To start with, I always had a very good breakfast and especially a nice cup of tea. She had never had children of her own. I, Kurt, was now her son. A second son, "Martin", who hailed from southern Germany, was also adopted for a while. She talked to us as she did to her neighbours, who lived miles away. There was such a lot to talk about: of the old days in England, about the Queen (Victoria) – yes, over and over again about the Royal Family. I talked about Germany. There were no end of subjects.

'There was no electric light and no main water supply but the large garden was wonderful. To the south-west, one could see far across the Bristol Channel. The Atlantic Ocean must have been somewhere out there. To the north, the River Usk wound its way through the hills. I was becoming familiar with the local names:

Caerlon, Chepstow, Tintern Abbey, but in actual fact I had never been there – or, at least, not yet.

'John Pugsley would come in. I think he must have been in his mid sixties. There was always a pipe in his toothless mouth. He was saving up for and dreaming of a Petersen Pipe. "What shall we do today?", he would ask. We would harness his pony to the cart and drive for a few hundred metres into the wilderness, into the erstwhile forest. Only a few trees were still standing, but there were one or two immense trunks lying in the undergrowth: beech, oak and ash. We would think about which to start with first and how much of it we would be able to manage. Then we would start work with the long tree-saw. John would light his pipe time and time again. It was impossible to talk while sawing, but we stopped every so often. The pipe was always going out; a Petersen would probably not need to be lit as often. John did not speak Oxford English; many of his words would not be found in *The Times*; but nevertheless this was the language we used. John talked about the First World War. He had never been a soldier but had been a "conchie". It took me half an hour to understand his definition. Nor was he too sure why the word meant what it did. Only later, with the help of Mrs Pugsley, did we find out that it meant conscientious objector. He talked very impressively about thirty years ago and the Great Strike of the 1920s.

'In between talking, we would have sawn through a large tree trunk with a diameter of perhaps 80 centimetres. Then came the problem of how to get it onto the cart. If we could not do it, then we would have to have another go the next day. Martin might be there to help then. Slowly we would drive back. Lunchtime: how long was it since we had eaten meals as good as Mrs Pugsley's? She cooked nearly everything over the wood fire in the chimney and only used a small paraffin stove for baking. By the time we returned she would have used up all the water. I would go down the hill from the cottage with two buckets to the well: at such a well as this Siegfried must once have refreshed himself. I would carry the two buckets 150 metres uphill, and repeat the process a second time. How on earth did the old people do it, especially in winter?

'The chickens were always cackling furiously. The fox was the great enemy. There were lots of stories of how "she" (the fox) often stole hens or chickens. I also kept watch for her. I looked for the eggs which the hens sometimes laid under the bushes or in the thick undergrowth. The goat had to be milked. I tried once or twice but was never skilful enough to do it properly. The distant neighbours were always told about this and they would laugh with me about my inability to milk a goat.

'In the afternoon we would continue chopping up the tree trunk. First, a thick slice was sawn off; then, with the help of wedges, this was reduced to smaller and smaller pieces until we had the right size logs to suit the fireplaces in the town. One trunk yielded a tremendous amount of firewood, which was then loaded into sacks. It was great fun sawing and chopping up wood.

'Sometimes I missed tea-time, because I liked visiting the neighbours as well. Perhaps I would meet Flossie Richards. She was a pretty and hard-working girl. It was a pity I did not get to know her better. Mrs X (I forget her name) lived with her daughter in a cottage a mile away. There was also a baby; the husband was in the army. I found out that he was Polish; I never met him.

'It was strawberry time. They were picked and sold in the market. At that particular time, one could still get a good price for them, but a few days later there would be a glut, so that the profit would be halved. I helped pick them and was given 2s. I gave the money to Mrs X to put on a horse for me. The St Leger? I was absorbing new ideas: I got to know the names of horses. I must have won because the 2s. were given back to me. Small odds: only the stake. At Mrs X's house the things we discussed were quite different. Do you like the Americans? Do you like the Italians? Do you like the Poles (the son-in-law?)? There were no stories about the Royal Family. There, stories and articles from the *Daily Mirror* formed the topic of conversation. Neighbours who did not know me hardly noticed that I was German. "Are you Canadian?" "Are you Scottish?" Great surprise when they found out that I was a German with whom they could talk about anything.

'In the evening I would be back with Mrs Pugsley. There it was really cosy. The fire was poked up and the flames rose in the enormous fireplace. We did not have to economise on wood. There were plenty of off-cuts which could not be sold. The sacks were loaded onto the small cart for John to take to town early in the morning. It was suggested that I could meet him somewhere on the way; I was not allowed to enter the town itself. At 8.30 p.m. I had to leave and return to camp. Sometimes I stayed later and then had to run down the hill. I had to be inside the camp gate by 10 p.m. In fact we should really have been in our barracks by then, but in any case I would go there again the next day.

'During the winter I had asked to be transferred to work in a hostel, with heated Nissen huts and more and better food. This was postponed again. There in Llanmartin, I was very happy as long as I could visit Wentworth Cottage as often as I liked. Mrs Pugsley hoped that I would still be there at Christmas, although this was about nine months away. Of course, she also wanted me to return to my parents as soon as possible, but if Martin and I were still in Britain at Christmas then we ought to see how Christmas was celebrated there with plum pudding and turkey.

'It took me an hour and a half to get back to camp over the isolated fields in darkness, because it was very early spring. When I reached the Newport Road things livened up. At about 10 p.m. people were flocking back to the camp. POWs were returning from "their" families. Cars were passing by, bringing prisoners back to camp. Some had made contact with POSH PEOPLE, as Mrs Pugsley called them. For her the class system was still a reality. Do any young people still know about it today? In the end, there was a veritable column of cars bringing POWs home. Fantastic stories circulated. There were a lot of talented people who could use their knowledge in some way. One of them tuned the neighbourhood pianos, day in day out, for 10s. a time. For my part, I was quite satisfied with my simple surroundings. I was doing quite well, even if I had to carry water-buckets about 200 metres up a hill. It gave me a great deal of pleasure and I had no intention of spoiling it merely to find somebody who would take me back to camp by car.'

Egon Schormann's letters home continued:

Llanmartin Camp, 3 March 1947

. . . Everybody knows what moving house does to the nerves, and we were no exception when we marched across England with our trunks, cardboard boxes, jam tins, cans, potato sacks (sewn up into pockets); the traditional kitbags (hallmark of the POW), little carts, and other means of transport which defy description. The screening involved in a move like this meant 'packing' four times and unpacking three. As you see from the address, we have stayed in the same country. An improvement as far as comfort is concerned: stone barracks instead of Nissen huts. But there are thirty-six men in each. It is a good thing that summer is coming. Food and canteen provisions have stayed as before.

The scenery here is beautiful. Only there are no trees or bushes in the camp. Camps 191 and 200 were better in that respect. I have met up with some old acquaintances here, but we have been separated from the friends we had been with for two years. However, the main thing in captivity is a good bed and room to work, for all one's life revolves around one's bed.

Two days after my arrival, Mother's package arrived, with sausage, dripping, butter, biscuits and cigarettes. I was absolutely delighted. The sweet tin is standing on the table in front of me, and the salt cellar looked very sophisticated yesterday evening. We immediately spread out our grey-white festive hand-towel – tablecloth, to give it the right environment. I had a very bad conscience when I unpacked this lovely parcel. You are taking the food out of your own mouth and having to work, and I sit here on my bed all day and receive parcels.

Writing during the day has now come to a halt; we cannot light a fire until 16.00. But the sun is already very warm and in four weeks' time it will be Easter. . . .

23 March 1947

. . . All England is under water at the moment and food supplies are completely disrupted. There has not been a winter like this since 1794. They are never at a loss for a superlative here. Fortunately, we are situated on a ridge. In good weather we can see the sea, and beyond the sea, we know, lies Germany. After talking and writing about it for months, we have now received a considerable relaxation: freedom to go out walking from nine in the morning till twilight. . . . I am almost afraid you worry too much about me. There is no need. You can see from the photos that things are all right with us. I also have enough work to fill up the day. You must not brood so much about the time aspect of repatriation. It cannot be changed. And, when you think how fast the time has gone by since my twentieth birthday (my last leave), it is some consolation for the time left until Group 26's turn comes round. The all-day walks mean we can now go out for hours into the woods; then we don't see the barbed wire or anything associated with it. And, in bed in the evenings with the searchlights shining in through the windows, we have the reassuring sense of someone watching over us and preventing any evil entering.

Easter Sunday, 1947

. . . The ice has now melted on the streams and brooks – and we have never longed so much for spring as after this winter. Yesterday we heard Goethe's *Osterspaziergang* read, and in the evening we listened to an Easter cantata for soloist, choir and orchestra. It is now Easter Sunday, and, although the rain is still drumming on the windows (when doesn't it rain here?), winter is over. According to the last announcement by the British Minister of War, Group 19 (that is to say, prisoners taken in July 1944) will be repatriated by 31 October this year. This information is official. In our experience, such time limits have been punctually observed in the past. Whatever one has had against promises in the course of the last two years, you will have seen for yourself the accuracy of the dictum: the Englishman's word is his bond.

Now a request: please look after my watch. I should be cross if it didn't work when I came home, after I have not had a clock for years on end (since imprisonment). It would be lovely if you could hunt out an old 3-mark clock for me. It would help us considerably during the remaining seventeen months of captivity. The Easter parcel has still not arrived, but that is a good thing, because food here is always plentiful at holiday times.

13 April 1947

. . . Your Easter parcel with the sandcake arrived the day before yesterday. The cake was only slightly broken. Special thanks, dear Mother, for the sugar. We put the first spring flowers on the cake and everyone asked if it was someone's birthday. I have put the sausage aside for a rainy day. We now have sufficient food and there should be no transport difficulties until next winter. The sun is so warm that we hardly remember the winter any more.

Now may I ask you, please don't send me any more sausage. You need it urgently and I have enough to eat. If you can bake me a cake now and then, that will give me a great deal of pleasure. You more than anyone know how much I like sweet things. But you must not take the food out of your own mouth. This must not be allowed! The cigarettes were as good as the 'Nameless' which we buy here (twenty-five a week, often only twenty). . . .

We have just heard of a new relaxation: only concerning the length of the day. We can now be out of the camp from nine in the morning till 9 p.m. The countryside here is beautiful. From the mountains, you can see the Bristol Channel like a silver band on the horizon, and on a clear day, the sun glints on the sea. Not far from the camp, the Usk (a small river) winds through green meadows: mirror image of the Mosel valley. Only the *Weinberge* are missing and those lovely weeks I once spent in Trier. We often sit on a mountain in the shade of a ruined castle wall for hours on end, without saying a word, and the Eichendorff verse runs through our hearts: 'The morning is our joy! Then in the silent hours I climb on to the highest mountain into space, greet Germany from the bottom of my heart.' Do not be sad, dear Mother. We certainly are not.

19 April 1947

. . . It is raining. I could begin every letter with the sentence: It is raining. This must be why the Englishman begins every conversation with a sentence about the weather, for it changes daily, often hourly, and weather forecasts are very hazardous. If we ask an Englishman the time on our walks, the dialogue goes as follows: 'Good day!' 'Day', he says. I: 'Beautiful weather today.' 'Lovely weather today – marvellous sunshine – fine sunshine – a fine day. A really beautiful day.' Then one can ask, 'What is the time?' There is no other way of greeting; perhaps between loved ones, but I do not know about that.

Today we were given a plot of land: our allotment. We had our own gardens when we were at Crewe as well, and shortly before the harvest, we were moved. Let's hope this won't happen again. The English supply us with seeds. That is something they really do supply us with.

24 April 1947

My dear Mother,

I am writing this letter to you for Mother's Day, and so many memories float into my mind. If I were not writing to you, I should have to start every sentence with 'Do you still remember . . . ?' But mothers certainly do not forget. How often have you and I sat together in the evenings until long after midnight? I will never forget those hours. The steamer trip to Hann. Munden, a week before I became a soldier. To me, it is as if these five years have never been. But sometimes I feel very old –

I suppose mainly because (especially in England but already in Russia as well) I have always been the youngest in a community of older men, and have lived with them through all their family fortunes (which is probably the reason too why the soldiers so often come to me for advice and to pour out their hearts and completely forget that, at first at least, I was just nineteen years old). Here my age is particularly noticeable, because of course there are no young men coming into the camp and therefore I am often afraid that I have completely lost contact. What twenty-two year old, in normal life, is continually in the company of forty to fifty year olds? (I already think of the thirty year olds as contemporaries.) I often wonder if I will ever be able to celebrate a carefree party again, dancing and laughing for hours on end, forgetting everything – and there is so much to forget.

I have a little English friend. One day, when I was out for a walk by myself, she spoke to me. Now I go and see her every few days to play with her. She is, to be precise, $3\frac{1}{2}$ years old. We play ball, or pick flowers for Mutti, as she tells me. I always come home happy from these walks. You know how much I love children.

Otherwise, we do not come into contact with the population. They regard us more or less as the evil Germans or are indifferent to us. How long will it last, especially as the children think the same way? A day or so ago, I met a man with a young boy. He raised his hat and greeted me. Scarcely had I gone a step when I heard, 'Father, was that a Hun?' 'Yes, that was a Hun.' Thirty seconds before, he had greeted me. Practical understanding between peoples, with education of the children thrown in. . . .

1 May 1947

. . . All credit to what you at home call 'growing it yourself'. The tobacco (rolled into cigarettes) is as good as the stuff they now sell us as 'Mixture'. Thank you for the large quantity, which will – together with our weekly ration (thirty at the moment) – last us over the summer. In the first month of captivity (especially during the war), we got fifty to 100 cigarettes a week. When the KZ propaganda set in, in summer '45, it suddenly fell to ten. In the course of the year we have now gone back to twenty-five to thirty, and, as we now smoke a third at a time, one ends up with ninety thirds a week. Such are our problems.

Yesterday, our radishes hazarded a step above the surface and our pride as allotment holders soared, for there are beds where nothing is showing. There is hardly any occasion to use a watering-can in this region, as it rains every day. Today, when little girls in Germany are wearing white dresses and singing 'May has come', water is rattling down from the sky as if the weather god had gone mad.

In a year's time I hope you will put up Dr Stephan for a night before he goes on to the Russian zone, because he needs the British zone as a repatriation point. Today he was moved into the Nazi Camp 165 for the first time as a newly-fledged C+ man, but he will emerge again before he is repatriated (Group 23). Dr Wenzel will also sleep the night in my future bed (again in about a year) on his way to Thuringia. Please write if this is not possible. Neither of them knows where to stay and I am in the fortunate position of having my parents' house. Wenzel is a refugee (a lawyer) from the Sudetenland. who has lost everything, and his wife is sitting in Thuringia with a dress and a three-year-old child whom he has not yet seen.

Yesterday, a marvellous comedy was enacted: our oldest POW here, who had waited $7\frac{1}{2}$ years to return home, was suddenly given three hours to get ready for repatriation: 63,388 hours against three! That's life!

Whitsunday Evening, 25 May 1947.

. . . Time has never passed so quickly as these fifty days between Easter and Whitsun. A correspondingly heavy programme will carry us through the day. In the morning: Whitsun cantata (choir and orchestra); evening: symphony concert, Mozart. The day after tomorrow: *Schatzkästlein*; evening: *Lumpacivagabundes, Spiel von Nestroy*. And all accompanied by good food and light music. The three Whitsuntides in captivity offer no grounds for complaint.

And in Germany· the food position is becoming increasingly subhuman. With the annihilation of the Third Reich and the Nuremberg trials, the so-called world conscience has again been laid to rest, in order to awake if Germany should become strong again. There is only a malicious sneer, in any event, indifference, towards the hungering German women and children and the 2 million prisoners whom Russia has stolen from the world and who will never see their homeland again. And, if you think I have turned into a pessimist as a result of the length of my captivity, then ask yourself, how could you know more than what you read in the newspapers and what the wireless reports? There are men here, such as Stokes, who intervene on our behalf daily (less from love of us than from recognition that hatred only breeds hatred), but their warning voices do not break through; their importance is likewise nil. Many men of the external and internal emigration movements, the resistance movement and both churches, who worked with the enemy so honestly, today realise with alarm that the victors were concerned with more than solely the annihilation of National Socialism. They had not imagined this. But how could they have known? And the Viennese, who celebrated the first day of liberation with joy, flags and music, have gone quite quiet this year.

If this letter falls into the wrong hands, it will be called a typical D Nazi case, of misled youth. Naturally anyone who does not unconditionally lie at the feet of the victors and say 'yes' and 'amen' to everything is a Nazi. How I hate this slimy fawning! If I had already gone into a KZ because of my convictions, then I would not have let myself roll like a slave in the dirt today and renounce everything with the words 'I knew it and you Germans have deserved no better' – although I am one myself. As I insist, I am a slave. If it is difficult to be a German today, we must certainly be Germans, for our parents are German and today (as at all times) we have sufficient reason to be proud of it.

In April 1947, George Weiser was also on the move.
'We were told to pack our stuff together as we were going to be transferred up north, but no one said where. They put us on a train and we went up north. We ended up in Carlisle, the draughtiest station in the country. We went on to Kelso, Roxburghshire, and were put in a camp just outside Kelso [Sunlaws Camp No. 120]. We were there for four to five months doing nothing and then we were transferred to a small annexe, two miles away, "Windywalls". Even on the hottest day, the wind was howling through it. It was just a small camp, two huts with twenty people all told and with no barbed-wire fence. It had a Northern Irish corporal as the guard. A good chap, he was: he didn't bother us, but he got sozzled every weekend and we had to go to Kelso to collect him. Medical orderlies didn't have to work so I didn't do much. I went for walks around the countryside. I went into pubs, even in uniform. Though we weren't supposed to, no one minded.'

20 'The Inevitable Course of Nature'

In June 1947 there were still some 275,342 German POWs in the United Kingdom. Over the months, relaxations of the restrictions governing their activity had followed thick and fast. An important milestone was passed when on 24 June Mr Bellenger announced in the House of Commons that, as from the middle of July, POWs – except those classified as ardent Nazis – would be allowed to draw part of their pay in sterling and to use shops, cinemas, restaurants, and public transport within a 5-mile radius of their camps. Pubs, however, were still theoretically out of bounds. So was fraternisation.

With so many personable young men roaming the countryside, and with young British womanhood suffering from the aftermath of the war, which had robbed them of a regrettably large number of British youth, the consequences were predictable.

On 10 June, Mr Freeman reported that he had received fifty-four written applications from British women who wished to marry German prisoners. In the same month, the Minister of War was asked in the House of Commons whether it was not unreasonable to allow social intercourse and rule out the probable effects. Would it not be reasonable to allow both? 'I have never', Bellenger retorted, 'attempted to resist the inevitable course of nature.'

And resistance indeed was impracticable. The inevitable had already occurred before his words were spoken. A secret marriage had taken place between an ATS girl, Monica Cann, and a German soldier, Leo Gunter. Their story was carried by the press: the *Sunday Express* proclaimed, 'ATS Girl Who Wed German Says "I'd Do It Again"' and *Pflugschar*, the magazine of Camp 250 (Old Malton, Yorks), told the story in verse:

A real-life love story

There was a girl called Monica,
In the ATS, no less,
Young, happy, beautiful . . . and one day,
Wearing a pretty dress.

She met a 'sergeant' prisoner,
Who by a ditch was sitting,
Eating bread and 'Churchillwurst',
And drinking tea as fitting.

And that is how it all began:
She loved him then and there,
What a particularly handsome man,
Slim, and with yellow hair!

And he saw her . . . saw all her charm,
Her laughing invitation.
His heart grew warm, though well he knew
The prisoner's resignation.

Before he could remember this,
Her question met his ear –
In German too – his mother tongue –
Was he quite happy here?

'O thank-you lady, very well.
O you are very kind',
He spoke good English and quite soon
She came to know his mind.

They met again, at first by chance,
Then, in the gentle twilight,
They often met on silent paths
And walked into the night.

And came one evening, grey and still,
A milestone in his life,
He asked her softly, 'Monica,
When will you be my wife?'

His heart was full of joy and tears,
'My Monica, I love you',
'Beloved Leo, give me time,
Before I say "I do." '

And then they really reached their goal,
She in a velvet gown,
He radiant in civilian dress:
The registry in town.

As lovingly, she said, 'I will',
Her happy gaze he saw,
He, the POW,
Was married by the law.

Outside, she said, 'Come, Leo, quick!'
To a hotel they hurried,
They went inside (she knew enough)
And they were truly married.

But O! the unkind element,
Reality said 'No'.
When nations hate each other,
Then true love has to go.

He was transferred quite secretly,
To where, she did not know,
And there is only this small rhyme,
To hope they meet somehow.

She found him – and they met again.
'Twas full of joy and sorrow,
For they could only sadly hope
That he'd come back one morrow.

Then pulled the mighty father-State
A very angry face,
And took the pair before a judge
For such a grave disgrace.

Because they had not told the truth
And said he was a German,
Monica was now accused
And preached a solemn sermon.

Her punishment was not too grave:
One pound was cheap to pay
For such a lovely union
With Leo on that day.

For Monica, I understand,
Your fame has spread to all ears,
And every prisoner raves of you,
For you love – without frontiers!

Whatever the fame of Monica and Leo, the real test-case came in July and concerned one Werner Vetter. This POW, aged twenty-two, was sentenced to twelve months' imprisonment by a court martial at Droitwich, Worcs for associating with a British girl. 'Would not the British Minister of War take steps to enable Vetter to marry the mother of his child?' a member of Parliament asked. A woman MP, Leah Manning, asked why the War Office exercised sex discrimination against British women wishing to marry German prisoners when no such embargo was placed on British servicemen wanting to marry German girls.

On 8 July, Bellenger agreed that no obstacle would henceforth be placed in the way of such marriages – provided that the parties concerned fully understood the implications thereof. Not that the implications were negligible. The British woman who married a German would forfeit her British nationality. Furthermore, no undertaking could be given that her husband would be allowed to stay in Britain when his turn for repatriation came round. But, most daunting of all, no provision could be made for her to live with her husband after the wedding. He would be required to return to his camp at night, and be subject to all the restrictions still governing POW life.

British womanhood was not daunted and such marriages did take place: 796 in all. In August, Bellenger announced that he had examined the proceedings of twenty-seven military courts which had awarded sentences of imprisonment or detention to POWs for establishing relations of an amorous nature with members of the public. As this was no longer an offence, the sentences were remitted where prisoners of good character were concerned. In September, Werner Vetter married Olive Reynolds in Hampton Lovett church, Worcs 100 yards from his camp, in front of 150 German prisoners.

The *Daily Express* staff reporter wrote on 18 September 1947,

To the singing of a German prisoners' choir, Schubert's *Sanctus*, anthems and hymns – they were married by the Rector, the Reverend Eric Bartlam.

As the couple signed the register, there was an *Ave Maria* duet. Outside there was more singing – a German song, 'Hoch, Hoch, Hoch', and Vetter found some pennies to scatter in the crowd.

Then they went off to spend the rest of the day at their reception, held in a Girl Guides' hut . . . .

There were about sixty altogether. They ate three meals, cooked by prisoners with food saved from their rations, including a wedding breakfast of soup, roast beef, potatoes and carrots, and fruit dessert.

They saw two wedding cakes cut. They heard speeches in German and English. Then came German folk songs, dancing and games, to the music of a prison camp orchestra.

It all ended at ten tonight and everyone went home: Vetter to his camp in Hampton Lovett, and Olive to Droitwich, one and a half miles away . . . .

Not all German POWs were thinking of marriage at this period. Alf Eiserbeck was one of them.

'Camp 114, Westbury, Wilts: The "democratic camp of England". In the parade-ground they had planted a tree called "Konrad Adenauer Tree". We were all rebels then; we pinned a notice up saying "Joseph Stalin Tree". We didn't work there. We were under direct order from HQ Southern Command. That's when my seven days' detention notice arrived. We lazed around all day playing snooker in the canteen. We only stayed there one week and then were transferred to Camp 124, Bedminster Camp, Ashton Gate, Bristol.

'From there we were sent to Hambrook hostel, just outside Bristol. It was a large camp, an old army camp. They only put us in there so that squatters wouldn't take it over (at that time, squatters were taking over camps). There were forty of us plus two guards. It was the only camp I knew where civilians from the village came in to take baths and showers. The camp was in the middle of the village. Most of the POWs worked on farms in the area. We didn't work. After three to four weeks, we were moved to the Failand Hostel, on the Bristol-Clevedon Road. There we had to start work driving lorries. At that time we were given new clothes with all the patches off, though they were the same chocolate-brown clothes. Already quite a lot of us had civilian clothes, but the authorities didn't like that much. At that time we could go anywhere – Bristol and so on – as long as we were back by 10 p. m. When we had our patches, civilians gave us lifts. After the patches were off, there were no lifts and we had to walk all the way.

'Behind the hostel there was a golf course. One of the holes must have been at our end of the camp, and when people used to play golf, we watched where the balls landed and picked them up. When civilians came over looking for them, we sold the balls to them for 6*d*.

'When we were there, we used to do a lot of part-time evening work for farmers. Farmers who were well liked by the POWs had no trouble and used to get their harvest done before anyone else. We were picked up after tea and worked till nine. Then the farmer gave us supper, took us back and paid us into the bargain. We only worked for farmers who were recommended by POWs. For example, there used to be one farmer and every morning when we stopped with the lorry dropping off prisoners (he had five working there), he asked every one what service they had been in. No one liked to work on that farm, so a couple of times when he asked they said, "SS" – so he didn't keep them after that, and I had to take them back to the hostel. After a few weeks, he found that everyone who came to his farm had been in the SS, so he kept them. He told them to go and hoe the mangels. He didn't send anyone with them, so the five men hoed the mangels and left the weeds. At about 10 a.m. he 'phoned the camp and I had to go out and pick them up. He didn't have anyone after that. Everyone refused to work for him.

'In Bristol itself, in the evenings or at weekends, we used to go to cinemas or pubs now and again, and we went for walks. In Bristol, the meeting place where POWs met local girls was Ashton Park – girls came from miles around. One of our POWs married a local girl. On his wedding day, he had to go back and sleep in the camp and the girl slept at her home. He was still living in the camp when we left there.'

K. E. also writes about this period.

'Then came a change: we were allowed to have half our pay in cash and allowed out within a 5-mile radius of the camp. The money we got on the quiet supplemented this (if we were caught, the money was taken away from us and probably kept by the guards. This danger was eliminated when we were allowed to have cash). We were also allowed to go to shops and cinemas, which gave us a better chance of getting into touch with ordinary people. That spring I got to know Uncle Jack and Aunt Lizzie, who were caretakers at a school in Woodstock Road, Oxford. I met them through a friend of mine who spoke English. I went out with him and he took me to see Uncle Jack (Hughes). I got very fond of them. I went up on Sundays for tea. When we were first allowed to go out, we were invited home to university professors, generally for tea and chats. The YMCA also entertained us and there were church dos. Uncle Jack and Aunt Lizzie were very trusting. When I went there on Sundays, if they were out, they allowed me to go in and make the tea – such a good relationship we had. I was always welcome there.'

Egon Schormann reminisces about that period.

'Early summer, 1947: picture-book weather. We recovered from the cold winter, forgot our anger that we could only heat the Nissen huts after six o'clock in the evening, and were also managing better with our food. I found out years later that the general situation in England at that time had not improved. We had regarded the coal rationing in the winter of 1946–7 and the miserable low-calorie food in the officers' camp at Llanmartin as unnecessary aggravation.

'We could walk 5 miles in the vicinity of the camp from morning to evening, and, if we acquired British money, we could travel on buses. There were no controls. Generally the camp staff and the bus drivers were nice chaps. The population scarcely seemed to notice us in public conveyances. In our unmistakable POW uniforms we were part of the general scene.

'What we needed was money. We were driven around the countryside in twos and threes, knocking on farmers' or artisans' doors asking for work. Without any technical skills – since we had become soldiers or officers straight from classroom or university – we did each task set with varying degrees of success.

'I remember a farm where we papered a bedroom and, while doing it, were fed on ham and eggs and white bread, with real English marmalade, cups of tea and cigarettes. We were in high spirits. We were given 10s. in cash for the work. We never declared this payment. In the later afternoon, the first sheets of wallpaper started peeling off the wall, and soon the room looked dreadful. We threw in the sponge and only offered to do painting in future. Next time round, we avoided that farm.

'Over the Easter holidays we obtained a four-day job hoeing weeds in a market-gardener's greenhouses. We agreed on a payment of breakfast and lunch, cigarettes and £2. It was suffocatingly hot in the greenhouses and the work was hard on the bones. The weeds had to be pulled up by hand. We lay on the ground for three and a half days. From time to time we showered ourselves with a garden hose to wash off the sweat and filth. When we asked for our money on the last afternoon, the proprietor decided that we had eaten well, had received cigarettes – and that our camp might be somewhat further than 5 miles away. That we knew. What the good man had not considered however, was the situation of a POW. We certainly had no rights; but we also had little to lose. We reached a decision amongst ourselves by a series of quick jerks of the head, and began to pull out the plants as carefully as we had previously pulled out the weeds. In a few minutes we were paid. The boss disappeared into his house and we worked (it was Easter Monday) for another three-quarters of an hour until the agreed time was up. When we wanted to leave the nursery, the boss came up to us and invited us for a drink in the pub. We never referred to the former matter and even worked in the greenhouses on other occasions. However, we never went to the pub with the gardener again.

'Money gave us a certain sense of freedom. We could climb on a bus and search out places in the neighbourhood. We could go shopping in the typical little village store. In those days, one still got change from a shilling.

'One POW on one of these round trips discovered a public swimming baths, and five of us to a man determined to have a swim. For that purpose, we needed swimming trunks. Jupp, a young officer from Eifel, had acquired certain skills in the costume department of the theatre workshop at Crewe Hall Camp, and he offered to cut out the trunks. We had long since learned how to sew and darn and also how to knit. Some POWs knitted scarves 3–4 metres long, in the hope of taking them home with them one day.

'We needed material for the trunks. I acquired two bed-sheets in exchange for some cakes, various natural-history curiosities and a month's guaranteed delivery of hot water for the morning shave. The bed belonging to the sheets I allowed to vanish into a heating installation, though I was still able to sell a good part of the wooden frame as carving wood.

'Jupp cut out the trunks and we sewed the pieces together. The trunks creased a bit between the legs: we had forgotten the gusset. We disregarded such trifles. We were equipped for the baths.

'On a Saturday evening, we set off. The new trunks rolled up in a hand towel seemed to us very professional. We went by bus to the neighbouring town where the public baths were said to be. This information was correct: there were public baths there but we could not find them. No one knew the English designation. We asked passers-by, held out our towels and the home-made trunks, and one of us made swimming motions. Amidst friendly laughter, we were put on the right road.

'As we stood in front of the little cash desk, we were very tense in case we would be forbidden to enter. But the girl there barely raised her head and let us go in. The swimming instructor came up to us in a friendly way and asked if we needed swimming trunks. We shook our heads and showed him our home-made trunks. He took us into a large communal changing room and told us we should leave our clothes there. He then disappeared. We changed and went out somewhat hesitantly onto the lawn of the swimming pool. Were we free now? A peaceful scene lay before us: children were fooling around as they fool around at any bathing place, young girls and boys lay on the grass or played ball or made love. We squatted on the grass. Popular music came over the loudspeaker. We looked at each other. "I wonder if they know we are prisoners?" asked one of us. "Nonsense!" I said. "We are young men who are going for a swim after a week's work and who will shortly ask the blonde on the steps to come dancing with us – and to bring all her friends with her." "The sun is not shining for you", said another. "You ought to look for the shade." But all of us looked the blonde up and down and we all thought the same thing: "Damn it! Why was it so impossible simply to speak to the girl?" She could obviously sense that we were looking at her. She stood up and slowly sauntered off. "If she turns round now," said one, "I'm going to speak to her." She did not look round. She strolled away on the other side of the pool.

'Did we want to swim? Naturally we wanted to; that was why we were there. But no one made a move. "OK. Come on. I'll count up to three!" Then we hurled ourselves bodily into the pool. With headers and belly-flops, we were in the water. Nobody bothered about us. We were free. Five young men moving about in the water on a Saturday afternoon, like any others. We forgot everything: the camp; the uncertainty about repatriation. In summer 1947, we still did not know when we would be released. Interrogations were still going on, screening into "A", "B" and "C", and re-grading from "B" to "C" – which meant some relapse into fascism and little prospect of release.

'We laughed, splashed each other with water, dived, arranged little swimming races and felt good. We then swam back to the edge of the pool and scrambled out. Then I saw the shocked face of Hans, who was in front of me and had turned round to face us others. "All lie down!" he shouted. Immediately, accustomed to obeying orders, we threw ourselves down on our stomachs on to the grass. "Man – oh, Man", he groaned, and almost choked in a burst of hysterical laughter. "We shall have to stay lying here until the baths close. The trunks made out of bed-sheets are transparent!" We looked cautiously all round. No one was taking any notice of us. "The trunks were all right before we bathed", one of us interjected. The trunks at that point had been dry. We stood up. That was really it. In this hot summer weather the material had dried quickly. We fetched our money from the changing room and bought ourselves ice-creams. We had not eaten ice-cream for years. What a wonderful world!

'An hour later we were reminded that it was not our world. The swimming instructor came over and said we had to disappear: it was not allowed and he was very sorry, but a complaint had been made. We got dressed. The swimming instructor stayed with us. He did not say a word as we went to the ice-cream stand yet again, this time in our POW clothing, and bought a farewell ice. At the door he said something like, "Sorry", and we could perhaps come one weekday morning when it would be empty, and so on. We never went there again.

'On the way to the bus, a police car came towards us. It was driving to the baths. We still had a bit of trouble about the bed, but that passed over. For me, the visit to the public baths was to have a dramatic sequel: the operation.'

THE OPERATION

'On the evening after the visit to the public baths, I got a pain in my stomach. The pain was bad; I felt ill. Apart from my wounds, I had never been ill during the war nor during captivity. I lay down on the

bed and tried to sleep. It was impossible. The pain became
unbearable towards morning and I was absent from the yard at the
morning count. Someone informed the German camp doctor. He
examined me and diagnosed bad stomach pains as a result of the
unaccustomed quantity of ice-cream I had consumed the previous
day at the public baths. In the evening I was feverish and shivering,
but managed to get some sleep in the ensuing night. The next day
the fever increased considerably and the pain spread to my whole
body.

'Towards the evening of the second day, the camp doctor, who
had returned to visit me, became nervous. This could not be just a
stomach-ache. He examined me again: was the pain worse on the
right side? He diagnosed appendicitis. Towards nine o'clock in the
evening, the camp doctor came in with a stretcher. He had ordered
and obtained an ambulance. An English soldier – the driver – and a
German prisoner – the co-driver – carried me to the car. My friends
had thrown my possessions into my kitbag and laid it at my feet.

'I was aware of a great deal of what was happening but only
through a mist of fever. However, I still heard the doctor say to the
co-driver in German, "Drive slowly, no bumping." Then we drove
off. I dozed on and off, shivering and feverish. From time to time,
waves of pain ran through my body alternating with periods when I
felt nothing at all.

'I thought about the camp, about the public baths. I thought
about home and about who would take over the heating installations at the camp for me. After all, the job carried a second
ration of food with it. The car stopped. I heard voices. Doors
banged. The car drove on. This was repeated a few times. When we
stopped again, the German POW came behind and said, "We can
not get rid of you. Either they do not want POWs or they have no
beds. I have spoken to the tommy. He knows a military hospital in
the vicinity but our instructions were to take you to an infirmary
and this has taken us further afield. We shall drive up to the
entrance, lay you down on the road and take off." I am sorry I did
not succeed in contacting the tommy or the POW afterwards –
perhaps they saved my life that night.

'We stopped in front of the military hospital – also left behind by
the Americans. Both drivers said goodbye to me. In the darkness I
saw a nursing sister approach my stretcher. The Lanka drove off.
The sister looked me over quickly, took an envelope from my breast,
then ran back into the house. Immediately afterwards a doctor

came out. His skin was dark. "A negro", I thought. A black as a doctor was exotic for me. As he bent over me, I recognised my error. He was an Indian. He opened my coat, pulled a pin out of the revers and stroked the pin over my stomach. At the same time, he seemed to be watching me. When he stood up again, he seemed to be in a hurry. He called the sister over with a few words which I did not understand, and hurried into the house. Shortly afterwards, I was already in an operating theatre and washed. A man in a dinner jacket came into the room and was helped into a smock. I was conscious of a certain agitation in the room and suddenly saw immense lamps over my head and a mask was placed over my face. "Was the sister also coloured?", I thought. Then I had the feeling of falling – deeply and endlessly.

'The sister was white and laughing. The sun shone on my bed. I was thirsty. "What is the time?", I asked. "It is eleven o'clock in the morning. You have slept for a long time." "I am thirsty", I said. She nodded. I tried to sit up a bit, but she pushed me back on to the pillows with both hands. And what a pleasant sensation: female hands on my shoulders! And how tender they felt! I tried the same thing again. She immediately understood the ploy. I was energetically pushed back. "Please", she said. At least I had produced another laugh.

'I lay in a large room with some thirty beds. Around me lay soldiers. I was the only POW.'

21 'That Distracted Country'

At the end of July 1947, a major debate on the future of German POWs took place in the British Parliament. Should those who wished to stay in Britain permanently be permitted to do so? There were many points both in favour and against.

When the idea had first been mooted, as early as 17 October 1946, Martin Lindsay, Tory MP for Solihull, had suggested several advantages to be reaped from the scheme. First and foremost, it would augment Britain's then-deficient labour force by thousands of industrious, skilled workers. Next, it would introduce the ethnological benefits of an admixture of foreign blood. Lastly, it would help absorb the surplus of British women of marriageable age, i.e. between twenty and forty – placed by Mr Lindsay at 200,000. 'I would make it a qualification for those who wish to remain', he said, 'that they should be bachelors.'

Already in November 1946, prisoners were given the opportunity of volunteering to stay in Britain for a further six months when their turn for repatriation came up. By February 1947 those men who had taken advantage of this offer were permitted to ask for a further deferment in the fifth month, and so on each time. The following month, when it was reported that 819 German POWs had volunteered to remain, Ness Edwards, Parliamentary Secretary to the Minister of Labour, said that his Department was prepared to consider an arrangement whereby a farmer who could provide accommodation might retain POWs on a civilian basis provided that this was not to the detriment of British workers.

However, it was not only the interests of the British workers as represented by the trade-union movement that were causing the Government to take a somewhat ambivalent attitude to the scheme. In making good Britain's labour shortage, there was also a strong feeling that the country owed greater allegiance to the victims of fascism and to former allies – in other words, to the hundreds of thousands of displaced persons whom the war had strewn over Europe. Should they not have first chance of working in Britain?

There were 100,000 Poles in the country; a million displaced persons in Germany and Austria. . . .

There was also the well-being of Germany itself to be considered. No one wanted to place any impediment in the way of German economic recovery in this difficult postwar period. However, as Mr Rankin, a Glasgow MP, explained to the House on 31 July 1947, in addition to a coal shortage in 'that distracted country' there was unemployment in many of the ancillary industries. It was therefore better to employ prisoners who were willing to remain in Britain on useful work 'than to have them rotting in Germany'. In view of the British economic situation, in view of the fact that several British industries were undermanned, we needed them. Moreover, there was a great housing shortage in Germany, making absorption of repatriated prisoners difficult.

Rankin's advice was supported in November 1947 by a broadcast made by an ex-prisoner currently working in the mines in the Ruhr. He appealed to all POWs in Great Britain to stay there as long as they were able.

Meanwhile, while the prisoners remained as prisoners and awaited repatriation, relaxations of restrictions continued. In July they were allowed to remain outside camp till ten o'clock in the evening throughout the year. In August it was announced that the rate of repatriation on compassionate grounds would be raised from 500 a month to 1500.

At the end of September 1947 some 110,000 German POWs were expected to be working in British agriculture. One such was Kurt Bock, somewhat regretting the success of his earlier application for a transfer from Llanmartin Camp to work on the land at Warren Hostel, Castlemartin, Pembrokeshire.

'I did not really want anything else. I was quite content at Wentwood Cottage in Llanmartin, Monmouthshire. You were not allowed to withdraw. You had to work in the fields for three months at this hostel once you had applied and been accepted. There was no barbed wire round the few small barracks. During the war a small contingent was stationed here protecting the coast. We had electric light; the farmer on the other side of the road did not. Most farmers in the area had no electricity supply and any machinery there was was driven by a small generator. Unfortunately, the summer of 1947 was *the* summer; I do not remember a rainy day. It was relatively warm or even hot and, of course, very sunny. I did not manage to make contact with the farmers. Sometimes we worked in different places. For the first few days we made hay; later we gathered in the potatoes and dug up turnips. There were also days when there was no work, because not enough hands had been rounded up, especially at the end of June and July at haymaking time. The fact that we were on "double summertime" often meant that it was damp and wet for too long in the mornings. Six o'clock DBST coincided with four o'clock Greenwich Mean Time – and sunrise by GMT was 6 a.m.! So, when the sun had dried the hay at about 7 or 8 a.m. GMT, it was already 10 o'clock by DBST, and that was too late for the farmers, especially if they could not correctly forecast when the early morning mist would rise. They would have to pay us for the whole day if they decided that we should work, and for that reason they preferred to do without us. It was all the same to us. We were not paid anyway. We just received a certain number of tokens as our basic pay as soldiers. I think I was given £5 8s. every month. The pay for a lieutenant was 2.70 marks a day, which multiplied by thirty equals 81 marks a month. The pound was worth 15 Reichsmark at that time. The farmer for his part had to pay the Government the normal wage for our work, and was not supposed to give us extra – not even lunch or supper and certainly not alcohol. However, all the farmers knew that they could not hope to get much work out of us without giving us at least breakfast, lunch and tea. The cleverest farmers managed things so that we worked at least one extra hour in the evening. For the sake of simplicity they paid us half the standard rate, although it was not allowed: 1s. per hour, perhaps 1s. 6d. It might have been more.

'In any case, in these conditions the work in the summer of 1947 was pleasant enough. We worked in the burning heat in the potato fields, dressed only in shorts. The man in charge of the potatoes rode on his round along the rows between the potatoes, which were overgrown with weeds the height of a man. The fields were not far from the sea. If we looked out, and we certainly had time so to do, we could see far out over the Atlantic. In my home-made shorts (not made by me), I had the previous day's *Daily Express* folded up very small. When the man in charge of the potatoes rode by, I quickly collected potatoes in my particular section and folded the paper up. The bucket emptied, I sat down and read until he came round again. By that time I had read at least half a column and I read everything from the front to the back page, even the soccer results and horse racing. I read the longer articles by Sefton Delmer with special interest.

'The farm where we worked not only arranged overtime working in groups of two to five men, but, in addition, groups of about twenty men were organised to plant cauliflowers in the evenings. It was light for several hours after 7 p.m. and we planted several acres in the evenings. We put up fences sunk 20–30 centimetres into the ground round these fields as protection from the dozens if not hundreds of rabbits. Rabbits were absolutely everywhere: they overran the fields and burrowed in every sandhill. Doing overtime was the only way we could earn money to spend in the shops – and that was only from 1947 onwards. I think the maximum amount of money we were allowed was £2. For most of us, it had been three years since we had been able to buy anything we wanted: a cigar; an ice-cream; everything we could not buy by saving our tokens.

'I did not care about overtime or the work. I wanted to make contact with the people. Since we were changing work all the time, we could not make friends. This was neither helped nor hindered by the fact that the hostel was isolated: there were only a few cottages nearby and one farmer – but there was no work on his farm. Children find it easy to make friends and one bright evening I played with a brother and sister about eight or nine years old. Their mother lived alone in a house with a garden. I do not remember their name, but I got so friendly with them that I had constant use of a bicycle belonging to the family. This must have been in my capacity as a friend of the children, for I cannot remember any great service I rendered them, though I would gladly have done so, but no opportunity arose. I wondered, could I paint a window? The window in the loft could not be opened from the inside and a number of appendages also had to be painted apart from the frame. I was happy that I could do something to please the woman or at least offer to do something. In my mind's eye I can still see myself high on a ladder with pallet and paintbrush. My work was bad. And I knew it, but could do no better (I could not do any better now). And I knew that the friendly woman had also noticed that I was no good with my hands.

'I still had the use of the bicycle and it was a stimulating experience to cycle down to the coast on my evenings off. To East or West Freshwater Beach. There were hundreds of metres of sandy beach between projecting rocks where one was almost alone. I did not worry about the tide. I swam out and then wanted to get back to the shore, but I could not make it. I could not see anyone on the shore; nobody to come to my assistance. My strength was ebbing, but I could not swim against the tide. Suddenly I felt the rocky bottom; a second wave pulled me away. Another wave pushed me on to a rock. At last I got on to firm ground but the waves made it difficult to stay there. I struggled slowly for maybe about half an hour to get onto the beach, and I succeeded. Exhausted, I stretched out on the sand until I could retrieve the clothes I had taken off and find the bicycle to go back to the hostel.

'Walter, who was from the "English-speaking hut" in Llanmartin had the same problem as I: we needed other people we could speak to, a family we could visit. No longer solely for a cup of tea. To mix with ordinary people was important. We moved about freely and betook ourselves on Sunday evenings to Pembroke. The church bells were ringing. We went inside. "Abide with me . . ." A beautiful soprano immediately behind us, so close that it became torture not to turn round and see where this bell-like sound was coming from. Carefully and pretending that I had lost something on the floor, I turned round and glanced behind me. I took a deep breath: an extraordinary beautiful girl. It was not difficult to express my appreciation. She really sang enchantingly. Walter and I stood talking to her for a long time outside the church. Evidently we had attracted other people's attention, and we were accosted by old ladies who asked about our families and invited us to tea. We would willingly have accepted, but unfortunately we could not let our prima donna get away. We still did not know her name.

'Gwynneth ("child of the white wave", as she translated for me from the Welsh) was really beautiful. We met again in church on the following Sunday and all three of us went for a long walk. Topics of conversation were inexhaustible. This is not the tale of an eternal triangle, but we did not remain unnoticed. The evenings were so light. We, like a three-leafed clover, were noticed strolling around for hours, lying in the grass high above the Atlantic looking out over the sea, Gwynneth between Walter and myself. It became an integral part of our life. She came on her bicycle. I gave up the advantage of my bicycle. Both men walked, one pushed her bicycle when we went over the dunes. Someone saw me pushing it and produced the *bon mot* "Whoever pushes, will be given the cold shoulder." He was right, but at that time the decision had not been made.

'Walter and I never talked about the tension between us. We both liked her very much, but neither of us expected the other to hold back for his sake. Unconsciously we waited for a chance to sort out the problem undramatically. We observed our own and her reactions. Did she show whom she liked best? It was a neck-and-neck race. I am certain that often enough I was a nose-length ahead. We never went into her house; her parents never got to know us. In Pembroke we passed back and forth in front of the home of an aunt who watched us from her window, and Gwynneth, relieved, told us this aunt spoke favourably of us, because we gave the impression of being "very nice boys". But her parents wanted to have nothing to do with us Germans and even Gwynneth could not understand how she herself had changed her own mind. "If I had met you in the war I would have shot you!"

I had bad news from Hamburg. My father was in hospital. He had cancer. My brother wrote that the doctor said that he would not live for more than six months. I continued to hope, but in August news came that he was dead. Disoriented, I withdrew into myself. For the next few weeks I roamed the countryside. Officially we had an outing to Tenby organised. We wandered through the wild romantic coastal strip. There were a lot of people on East Freshwater beach on Sundays. Walter and Gwynneth were a couple. There were still outings together. I still have a programme for 25 September 1947, with Gwynneth's signature above it and my translation of her names, Gwynneth and Vanora.

'Another occasion: in the upper part of the Pembroke cinema. I was sitting at the edge of the hall when suddenly a muffled explosion shook the room. There was great excitement but not exactly panic. The floorboards in the centre of the hall had sunk 30–40 centimetres. There could really have been a catastrophe if the people and seats on the higher level had tumbled onto the lower level when the cinema was full.

'Ten o'clock was lights-out for everyone. It was unbearable, because of the brightness as a result of double summertime and the heat and because I was alone. The farmers held a fete. In the afternoon there were sack-races, relay races and singing. People poured in from all around. Everyone was very friendly. We took part in the competitions, making up a team of our own. We felt accepted as part of them. For the evening a large tent was erected. The farmer's ball. Should we take part? We had to be back by ten. How could we get back to the hostel quickly? The first chap paid his shilling and was given a ticket. Then the second and the third. It had not yet begun. But we were not to take part. The organiser got cold feet about letting us in to the tent. We argued with him but in vain. The people responsible for the ball did not want to take any risks, but, although they were uncertain about their decision, they never went back on what they had first said. It was a pity, but they still said no. We protested and repeated our protests to the officials the next day. What regulations, what rules allowed us POWs in the late summer of 1947 to take part in a country-club party in the afternoon but not in an evening dance? A few days later the apology came. We must appreciate their position. We were so surprised. We had never expected that at all. But, on top of it all, they were going to organise a ball especially for us as a compensation. It was held on Friday 19 September 1947, and was a great success. We did not have to be in by ten o'clock. It seemed like heaven to us. The guests paid 1*s*. 3*d*., "including light refreshments".

'I liked dancing but I was no good at it, for I had never been taught. I had to ask the girls to excuse my dancing and give me a quick lesson. We spent several evenings in Pembroke. But the enjoyment was limited. Even if we started at 8 p.m. it was soon 8.30 and at ten we had to be back in the hostel. A taxi was ordered in advance for 9.45 and we had to start saying goodbye to our friends at 9.30. Then at 9.45 we left the girls standing, jumped into the taxi and were back in the hostel just on ten.

'Castlemartin with its romantic church! The minister gave an address on the history of the area. We visited a castle. I forget the name of it, but it was in any case very impressive. The pastor invited us to tea and we had a lively discussion. His special interest was the seventeenth century. Allusions in the newspaper could only be understood if you knew the background. *Gone with the Wind* and now *Amber* as well. I only knew that this was a book – a bestseller. He explained it to us. Now I have read *Forever Amber* for myself.'

22 Autumn 1947

As the year 1947 drew to its close, the German POWs were imperceptibly taking a place of their own in British life. Their numbers had, of course, diminished considerably, as a result of repatriation. The conditions of captivity of those who remained were constantly eased. In October all restrictions on the number of letters they might send home were removed, while the scheme which had enabled those who wished to remain in Britain after repatriation, as civilian agricultural workers in farm billets, was extended to 1948. They were even granted clothing coupons, so that they could purchase civilian garments under the British clothes-rationing system. Certain Germans were allowed to volunteer for employment as civilian workers with the War Agricultural Executive Committees. And, for those who wished to return, the announcement came in October that the monthly rate of repatriation was to be raised to 20,000 starting in December.

Meanwhile, Kurt Bock, his stint of agricultural work completed and his repatriation date still some months away, returned to his beloved Llanmartin.

'The wonderful summer of 1947 was over. For me, too, my time in Castlemartin Hostel, Pembrokeshire. I would not have missed it for the world but now I wanted to see Mrs Pugsley again. I had volunteered to work on a farm for three months. I had volunteered at a time when it was very cold and the barracks were unheated and the food was not enough really to satisfy us. Nearly everybody stayed on at Castlemartin. I was the only one who went back to Llanmartin Camp at the beginning of November.

'A soldier acting as a guard accompanied me on the long railway journey. He was glad of the opportunity of the break in the routine of guarding the hostel. In any case there was not much to guard. No barbed wire. Just administration, deciding where everybody had to work. He was also responsible for taking the men to work and bringing them back. On the whole, we were now quite free and were allowed to go anywhere we liked, the only condition being that we should be back at the hostel at 10 p.m.

'In my pocket I had £1 10s. In reality, I also had a few more pounds. For a few months now we had been allowed to have real money. Even so, only small amounts. Everything was well hidden. The coins were squeezed into shoe-polish and Vaseline tins. Part of it was also hidden in the side of a cardboard box which my friend Wilhelm had covered with sacking material for me.

'I do not remember anything else about the return to the camp. How did we get from the train to the camp? They did not usually take us to and from the station by car. How much luggage did I have at the time? Was I able to carry it myself for several kilometres? A few months later, when I was repatriated, it would have been impossible.

'In the camp I had the usual routine examination. The luggage was thoroughly looked over, the books especially were properly checked. The soldier asked where my money was. I showed him the £1 10s. but he did not believe that I had so little. Some careless people had obviously fallen into the trap and had to hand over their hard-earned money to the screener. They did not discover anything on me. They tried to intimidate me but did not succeed. I took a chance that they would not find my money. They would have sent me to prison if they had found something. OK. I had nothing as long as they could not prove it. In the end they gave up.

'The camp was no longer full. A large group had already been transferred to the Scottish border (Featherstone Park Camp near Haltwhistle). For me too, it was not worthwhile settling down again. I was only waiting for the next morning. I wanted to go to Wentwood Cottage as soon as possible. We should have such a lot to talk about. As it was, we had corresponded, but they did not know exactly when I would be back.

'It was a grey foggy autumn day. One could not see the top of the hill and, when I came to the crest, I could not see the valley either; visibility was only 100–200 metres. Then I saw the cottage. Everything was quiet. No smoke was coming from the chimney and the door was locked. I looked through the window. Nothing was stirring. Disappointment. I began to get very worried. Were they ill? Perhaps they had only gone to Newport. The chickens were still there. John must have been taking logs to his customers and Mrs Pugsley had gone with him. I walked round. I could not see Flossie either. I did not meet a single human being up there. There was nobody whom I could ask. If John had gone to Newport he would probably be back between twelve and one. In any case, I would wait till then. I walked along the familiar footpaths. Complete stillness. Scarcely a bird calling.

'There – in the west, a slight grinding noise. I turned in that direction, stopped and listened; slowly it came nearer. One could hear every noise for miles in that stillness. The noise continued to approach. Clear enough – that could be a cart grinding through the sand. Time went by. Nothing was visible yet, but the sound was growing louder. At last a dark outline gradually emerged. I quickly went towards it. There they were. I was lucky. "Kurt, Kurt!" The old people were tremendously happy to see me.

'I fetched a few buckets of water. The fire was blazing high in the fireplace. I was enjoying it, especially in that weather. We talked about our experiences in the last few months and made plans for the future. It would soon be Christmas. But I knew that my time in the camp was coming to an end. Now I only had a short time left to spend there. Who knew whether we should ever see each other again? We all felt it was farewell forever, because in 1947 nobody dared think that it would ever again be possible to travel wherever one wanted without any restrictions. We did not think of twenty years ahead, when Mr and Mrs Pugsley would be too old to live on their own any more at Wentwood Cottage.'

The relationship between Kurt Bock and the Pugsleys, between the German POW and his British hosts, was not one-sided. The affection the Pugsleys felt for Bock is amply demonstrated in the letters they sent him:

29 July 1947

Dear Kort,

   We thank you for your kind letter and are glad to know you are well and happy also to hear you can get about a bit more you must find it much better Dear Kort we are all well at Wentwood and Christine is here for 2 weeks Mrs. Tomkins when back home on Sunday she could not get a film for the camra so we could not have a Photo taken to send you will see what she can do next time she comes down do you think you will be able to come back here after you finish there I hope you will as we miss you and would like you to come up to us if you can do come . . . I am sending you a little smoak.

   I dont think I can tell you any more this time so wishing you all the best and love from all at Wentwood.

6 November 1947

Dear Connie [*sic*],

I expect you will think we have forgotten you well I am sorry
not to have wrote to you before but we were expecting to see you
but I don't think so now as your Men are all going away from
Llan Martin. Well how are you getting on this long time. If you
will answer this letter I will send you some sigs but I am not sure if
you are in the same place . . . . This is all for now with. Best
wishes from R and J Pugsley.

27 November 1947

Dear Kurt,

I received your ever welcome letter and was glad to hear all is
well but was so sorry to hear that Theo was not well and hope he is
well by the time this letter reaches you I hope you got off
alright . . . Jack is shouting . . . tell Kurt the Fox came the
Night the Snow was down and killed all the Ducks so now we are
worried every Night for fear she will come for the chickens before
Xmas . . . .

2 December 1947

Dear Kurt,

I received your kind letter also Parcel and will you please
thank Theo from me and will you let me know where he is going
and how long he will be in Hospital and will you be able to go and
see him. I hope he is much better. I wish he was near us so as we
could go and see him. I am just going to Gloucester only for a day.
Dear Kurt Hilda and her Friend was here last week it was
Moonlight and very nice at Wentwood but very cold I was
surprised to know it was Raining with you we have not had Rain
for a long time everything is frose up. Dear Kurt did you and
Theo get my letters as they must have crossed in Post. I dont think
I have any more to say this time only hope Theo is getting better
so Cheerio for now . . . .

1 January 1948

Dear Kurt,

Just a few lines and hope to find you well and happy I received
the Parcel you so kindly sent me and did you paint the Card it is
very nice and Jack was very pleased with sig papers it was very
kind of you. Did you get the little Parcel we sent you I would like

to know because there was so much getting lost at Xmas will you send me a line and let me know dear Kurt the weather is very bad here now lots of Rain but not very cold yet no snow up to now only one night I can hear you have had snow up there have you got Fire in Camp I don't think I have any more to say to you this time so hope to hear from you soon with best wishes from your Friends Ruby and John Pugsley.

18 January 1948

Dear Kurt,

I received your most kind letter also sig papers for which we thank you I am sending you a little smoak and hope you will enjoy it Dear Kurt is Theo gone home yet could you please tell me because I do not get a letter from him since before Xmas I have sent him a Parcel and a few letters but no answer to any I also sent him stamps thinking he had no English money will you please try and let me know some thing about him. I hope your little Dutch girl have been to see you again hope you are well with all our Best wishes to you we remain your Friends Ruby and John Pugsley.

12 February 1948

Dear Kurt,

I received your kind letter and Parcel and thank you very much for it also Jack thank you for papers. I am sending you a few sigs and I will send you a smoak next week I hope you enjoyed the pictures and hope you will have a nice time in Newcastle on Tyne and do hope you will be able to go to the Camp near London I would like you to see it before you go home Dear Kurt we would like to see you before you go home we were talking about you to day Jack was chopping stick in the Barn and he said he wished you was here to help him. I am glad you heard from Theo I expect he is home by now. I may get a letter from him soon.

So with all our best wishes we Remain your Friends Ruby and John Pugsley.

27 February 1948

Dear Kurt,

I just received your Parcel all safe all in order I was very surprised to get such a Big Parcel from you I do think it most very kind of you to think of us as you do well I send you my very Best thanks for them we do hope you will be able to go to London before you go home the Weather is dreadful here but one thing we can get a good fire I am sending you a smoke and a few shillings I hope you get them. Can you go in to a shop and get a meal for yourself I hope you can Dear Kurt when you go home you must try to come back to Wentwood for a holiday you know you will always be wellcome I have not had a letter from Theo yet have you had one I think this is all I can say for now with all our Best wishes to you your Friends R & J Pugsley.

19 March 1948

Dear Kurt,

I was very pleased to get your kind letter and also very glad to hear of you going home so soon it must be grate for you and we hope you may be able to come to England some time and come to Wentwood and see us I was sorry to know that you have not heard from Theo you may be able to see him when you go home and please will you tell him we would like to get a letter from him.

I don't think I have any more to say this time wishing you all the Best. I remain your Friends R & J Pugsley.

Undated

Dear Kurt,

I now write these few lines to answer to your kind letter also little Parcel for which I thank you very much and I was very pleased to know that you had been to London and that you had a good time and what do you think of our fine sity well Kurt I expect you are getting ready to go home and you will be glad when you go home do you think you will see Theo we have not heard from him I am sending you a little smoke

so will finish now with all our Best Wishes to you from all I remain your Friends R & J Pugsley.

'We kept up the correspondence for several years', Bock explains; 'then it stopped. I travelled to England with my family in 1973. I had told them about Mrs Pugsley and John. Coming from Abergavenny we were near Newport. In the evening I wanted to be in Bristol. I had an appointment there with a business friend.

'How would I find Wentwood Cottage? The rain was pouring down. There was heavy traffic towards the bridge. I was trying to find my bearings. Where was the path going up the hill? Where was Llanmartin Camp? A great deal had changed and I had too little time. Twenty-six years had passed. Another twenty-four hours and better weather might have helped me find the spot again. A friend from Bristol tried to find out after I told him my story. He even heard about Wentwood Cottage, but there are no traces any more of John and his wife.'

23 The Featherstone Spirit

By November 1947, when Kurt Bock was transferred to Camp 18, Featherstone Park, near Haltwhistle, Northumberland, it had in the opinion of many of those who passed through it become something of a model of its type. One of the largest officers' camps in Britain, with around 3000 prisoners at most times, skilled leadership had made it, in the words of Swiss journalist Peter Durenmatt, 'a cell of reconstruction'.

Under the guidance of its enlightened commandant, Colonel Vickers, the indomitable, gentle interpreter officer, Captain Herbert Sulzbach, and an exceptional German camp leader, selected by Sulzbach, the camp had grown into a hive of democracy, education and re-education, based to a large extent on mutual trust. Lectures were held on every subject under the sun, with, obviously, a marked slant towards democratic institutions. Speakers included the famous Pastor Niemöller on 'The Question of Guilt', and 'our MP', Richard Stokes, on 'The Situation of Europe as I See It', as well as Professor Hugh Trevor-Roper ('Beginning and End of an Ideology'). From autumn 1946 the prisoners themselves had run a regular civics course in the camp, supplemented by visits to Northumberland County Council, county courts and other institutions. The camp contained an information room, well stocked with newspapers, periodicals, and pamphlets from Britain, America, France and Germany. There was also a camp library, with a relatively good selection of books. A 'POW Cultural Division' organised a complex educational programme, which covered not only academic subjects but also training in practical skills. This camp, like so many others, produced its own newspaper, *The Tyne Times* (which, to the surprise of the prisoners, was entirely uncensored) – and the editorial board was also responsible for news broadcasts, transmitted over the camp radio and translations of extracts from the English press, pinned on the camp noticeboard. The camp had four theatres: two for serious productions, one for lighter entertainment, and one puppet theatre.

Coach excursions about the surrounding countryside were regularly organised for the prisoners; as early as November 1946, over thirty large buses had carried nearly a thousand POWs to a combined English–German Armistice Day service in Hexham Abbey.

Not only cultural activities, but also sport, flourished in the camp. Games on the sports ground were first permitted in summer 1945, and in the autumn of the same year the POWs themselves had set about building a proper sports pitch. Football, punchball and handball matches were arranged, at first between teams chosen from individual huts; then camp championships were organised. After relaxations in October 1946, games were played against teams from other POW camps, and, by autumn 1947, against English army, university and amateur teams.

This camp was, as we have seen, one of the first to send out its officer POWs on voluntary agricultural work. In summer 1946 it set up its first hostel outside the camp, in Catton. This was rapidly followed by two others: Coswell, housing sixty men, and Rayless, with 100. When, in summer 1947, POW labour was to some extent replaced by that of displaced persons, these hostels closed, but Camp 18 opened others.

Meanwhile, within the camp, every type of do-it-yourself workshop flourished, from shoe-repairing, hair-dressing and tailoring to the camp bakery, which also provided bread for all British military units in the surrounding area, and the camp post office, where the prisoners themselves dealt with the vast mail received and transmitted.

It was to Featherstone Park that Kurt Bock, then in the final stages of his life as a POW, came in November 1947.

'It was a great disappointment for Mrs Pugsley that I could not join them for Christmas 1947, as I was transferred north, to near Haltwhistle, some time around 15 November 1947. Repatriation according to schedule was already in full swing. It was therefore quite normal to dissolve camps and concentrate those still waiting in even fewer camps.

'Life for a POW had become more and more comfortable. There was no roll-call in the morning or at night. But we had to stay in camp between 10 p.m. and 8 a.m. It was from Featherstone that I escaped to London for one week. [More of that in Chapter 25.]

'I think the huts were the Nissen type, but I am not sure. In Abergavenny they were Nissen, in Crewe not. As they were less crowded, I was pretty comfortable. We even had a radio, so that we could listen to the news and music, though this was an exception; most huts were only equipped with loudspeakers for camp broadcasts. There were no double bunks and our beds therefore served during the day as easy chairs to relax in. Our personal property was increasing and we needed room to store it.

'There was an iron stove in the middle of the hut. Unlike the winter of '46–7 there was much more fuel to burn and I do not remember the winter I spent there with any horror.

'With no friends like the Pugsleys outside the camp, I had to make do with the standard food rations, but, as I do not remember much about it, they must at least have been sufficient, with the extras we were now able to buy ourselves if we had the money, and fortunately I had. I am sure we were much better off than our relatives in Germany at that time. Of course, all this was on a very modest scale; no rolls in the morning, no fruit, no fish, no alcoholic drinks etc. But at that time I think I was happy with what I had.

'At this advanced stage of our captivity, the overwhelming topic was repatriation and the corresponding preparations for the day. When I came to Featherstone Park, I was already able to reckon that I would return to Germany at the latest in six months' time, and many of us earlier, according to the date we were taken prisoner.

'Courses were still continuing and those who participated with a fixed target, such as the *Abitur*, were very serious about it. Teachers had already been partially repatriated or were perhaps going in a few weeks. I did not participate in a target course but nevertheless attended a lot of lectures. All this was, however, much less than at Crewe Hall at its high point. Günther, in my hut, was already far advanced in the Chinese language, though he had known nothing about it before, and after my repatriation I read articles by him in papers. The Chinese language became his profession, I think, though I do not know what he is doing now. Probably a professor of oriental, or, rather, Chinese, language and art.

'I went for long walks with Joachim in the Tyne Valley and to Hadrian's Wall and I remember it as a beautiful and remarkable landscape, though I saw it only in the winter months. Now, thinking about it again, I should like to go there again as soon as I can find the time.

'Joachim, a straightforward and honest man, I think about ten years older than myself and married, with children, a qualified engineer employed by the State, naturally had other views on many problems. I think the time he had to spend as a POW was more bitter to him as he was missing his family more and his children were growing up without him. On the other hand, he was absolutely sure about his profession as an engineer and he knew he would be needed. I do not think he was afraid of the future. Nor was I, though with me it was more my generally optimistic view.

'POWs could receive female visitors at Featherstone Park, and they also met them in Haltwhistle. Gwynneth came to see Walter – and it was quite a journey from Pembroke. We had a nice tea-party together. A Dutch girl came to see Wilhelm. He knew her from his time in Holland and had already persuaded me to learn Dutch with him in camp from a Berlitz book I bought. I still have this book, but do not really understand Dutch, though we northern Germans can understand a little of the written language. I found this out recently when corresponding with a boat-builder, who got my letters in German and replied in his own language. This Dutch girl managed to come to England with a friend as a kind of au-pair girl, and as soon as they had got enough money they came north from London to Haltwhistle to spend a fortnight with her old friends. I had to entertain the friend in the intervals when we were not all four together. This girlfriend from Holland was older than I. She was just a nice girl but not one to arouse any dazzling memories when I think about that period.

'Featherstone Camp was the only place where we had the opportunity to attend cinema performances in the camp fairly regularly. Maybe once a week or every fortnight – just ordinary cinema films but I do not know the titles. I just remember one or two with Deanna Durbin, another with Gregory Peck. We had to pay for it – first 3*d*., then 6*d*. – and not everybody could afford to go. I treated my friends now and again, though I was not even rich in camp token money and had to work out my finances carefully so that they were not used up before I went back and also so that I could buy as much as possible to take to Germany. It is interesting, though, that some people still had more money than their monthly allowance and others just had to live on it.

'It was quite useful to have enough money in Featherstone Park. We were still only allowed to have one or two pounds in "real" money, but opportunities to get things for token money were quite good. Books could be ordered from lists held by a POW who organised it. We bought books from Swiss publishers in the German language, and a number of English editions. I took home quite a lot, and these titles serve as the basis for my present library. Newspapers could already be ordered privately in summer 1947. I took the

Sphere, an illustrated periodical, and the *Manchester Guardian* as well as the *Daily Express*. I read everything intensely and my knowledge of English life and my command of the language were therefore far above average. I did not smoke but bought cigarettes and tobacco for the post-POW time in Germany. I permitted myself the luxury of having my laundry washed, which was not possible before, but this is also proof that I thought I had enough money.

'I bought a gramophone, an ugly, clumsy grey box worked by a crank handle. The cost: £3 – or a little more. I was glad to sell it again before I got home. I bought leather soles, bicycle tyres and tubes. As I knew my mother now had to get water from a pump at least 150 metres away (and the garden also had to be watered by it!), I seriously discussed the possibility of getting all necessary material for our own pump. The difficulties exceeded my capacity and I therefore had to rely on cigarettes and coffee in Germany to achieve this.

'Apart from films, there were still theatres and concerts. The established groups co-operated as long as possible after one by one their members were sent home. At Christmas I saw *Kapitän Brassbound's Bekehrung* [Shaw's *Captain Brassbound's Conversion*]. Maybe it was the last performance? There were also invitations to outside events, such as Haltwhistle Youth Club performing *Blithe Spirit*, which I enjoyed and still remember vividly. On one occasion I was in Carlisle attending a concert. Most probably some POWs did not return to the camp the same night; opportunities for these nights off were to be had, but with the exception of the week in London I did not use them.

'Featherstone was my last residential camp before we were sent home. Of course, there were others, but I do not know the names. Sheffield was only a transit camp. Letters from friends who had already returned arrived, telling of their experiences and adventures. Most of us were comparatively rich in material completely unavailable in Germany at that time. We knew about the fantastic prices for cigarettes, coffee, etc., on the black market. It was therefore vital to take these home and the topic of endless discussions. Friends, collecting and saving cigarettes for this purpose, found them months later covered with mildew: the tobacco was taken out, after slitting the paper, and put into tins, which were supposed to keep the flavour better. As there was nothing to be had in Germany, anything taken home would be useful, but coffee and cigarettes could also serve as a kind of money.'

24 Hard Times All Round

Prosperity had not returned to Europe in the winter months of 1947–8. Germany, in particular, urgently needed to reform her currency. Nazi policy during the war had put large quantities of money into circulation, and now the country was feeling the effects. Although the occupying powers continually employed wage and price controls, they were unable to reduce the circulation, and the people were utilising legal channels of trade less and less as money assumed a decreasing degree of importance. Transactions tended to take the form of barter, either between goods and goods or else between goods and money substitutes, such as cigarettes and coffee – which retained their value to a greater extent than mere money.

Letters such as a grateful former patient wrote to Sister Scott from Grossgarnstadt on 28 January 1948 could not have been rare:

I arrived here safe and sound on Christmas, 1946, and I am still living with my mother. We cannot speak of a real home because we have lost all our property by this war. Mother had to leave our little house in which our ancestors had lived, with all our family and inventory [*sic*] to the Poles. Today we are living at a small village near the town of Coburg with its beautiful surroundings. Our conditions are rather primitive, one can say. This is very hard for my mother who is so attached to her beloved native country. I don't believe that she will overcome all this. But the worst is that one cannot buy anything. One earns quite a lot of money, but one cannot purchase anything for it, because there is nothing to be had. Many people are suffering from malnutrition. I am again working as a clerk at the post-office as before, and besides I am trying to continue my study. One must make the best of it, you know, and I hope that I shall have a good job again soon. By the way, I intend marrying towards the end of February. I think it will not be easy at the beginning, but I hope that we are a little lucky and that we shall succeed in building up a new home for us. . . .

Britain too had by no means completely emerged from her economic problems, and the line taken by the new Labour Secretary of State for War, Emanuel Shinwell, towards the remaining German POWs (195,000 in November 1947) was often dictated by economic necessity. In November, for example, Christopher Mayhew announced in Parliament that it was not possible to bring to Britain the families of German prisoners who had volunteered to remain in the country beyond their repatriation date in order to undertake essential employment. Accommodation was very short and priority had to be given to the families of European voluntary workers. Likewise, in December, the ban on POW bands playing at concerts – even charity concerts – where an entrance charge was made was reiterated, following protests by the Musicians' Union. 'It would not be fair for POWs to entertain as artistes in direct competition with British civilians', said Shinwell, despite the somewhat caustic question, 'Does the Minister realise that a charity concert at which there is no charge for admission is of very little use?' The problem partly arose because a very successful concert had been held in October when POW artistes had performed to raise funds for the East Grinstead children's home. When, however, a second such concert was planned at Ashurstwood, the Musicians' Union became disturbed.

Another symptom of governmental stringency appeared in December, when an order was published forbidding prisoners to wear civilian ties, collars and shirts, and, especially, civilian suits. 'Until these men are released to civilian status or are discharged in Germany on repatriation,' said Shinwell, 'they are military prisoners of war and must wear uniforms for reasons of discipline and control.' Asked if he would see that more suits without 'beastly patches' were made available to them, he replied, 'I am afraid that patches are not peculiar to German POWs.'

The parcels that POWs could send home post-free every three months were limited to essential relief items such as rationed soap, toilet articles (other than shaving soap), clothing, medicines and the like, and non-perishable rationed food. But these restrictions also applied to parcels sent to Germany by British civilians, and arose solely from the limited stocks of many commodities in Britain.

The prisoners, in any case, found a multitude of ways of circumventing these regulations, as Kurt Bock writes.

'In 1947 we were allowed to send parcels to Germany. The contents had to be checked by the guards; we could not go to the post office to dispatch them. We were permitted to send personal property (the great majority had none!), books, flour, Ovaltine, Oxo, etc. No coffee, tea, cigarettes or cocoa. But these things were valuable in Germany and in 1947 we had the opportunity to buy them for our own use.

'The POWs now developed ingenious packing methods. I remember that cocoa felt just the same as flour, so the paper bag containing cocoa was put inside a bigger bag containing flour in such a way that even a careful check could not disclose the illegal contents.

'Ground coffee was put into empty tins which had formerly held baked beans (we were allowed to send these). The lid was carefully soldered on and the Heinz label securely wrapped round. Some guards seem to have been clever enough to find out false declarations – in which case the coffee was lost. After this had happened, the method was refined. Before closing and soldering on the lid, a carefully prepared small shoe-polish tin was put in on top of the coffee. When the guards shook the tin, they were now convinced that it contained Heinz baked beans, as the shoe-polish tin was filled with water and gave the impression that the contents of the whole tin conformed to the label.

'Leather soles were also much in demand in Germany, but forbidden to be sent. Useless old books, regardless of the contents but large enough for soles, were prepared by carefully cutting out the pages to insert the soles.

'Some prisoners made a profession – even a hobby – of this sort of thing, which was quite understandable. I never did it, but I saw others doing it. There were certainly many other methods which these POWs, who spent all their time inventing and practising them, devised. I did not have the time, and my mastery of handicrafts is also limited. I therefore used more simple methods. A big Ovaltine tin contained a small tin of coffee – and, quite naturally, I was detected committing this fraud, as the guard simply poked his finger into the opened tin and easily discovered the coffee tin. The result was not too serious. I was put on a list of people who were not allowed to send any more parcels for the next nine months.

'However, I tried my luck again when my official turn next came round and found I had judged the situation correctly. They did not check the list of "criminals". I handed in my parcel and it was actually received in Hamburg with a great deal of pleasure. The preparation had not involved too much work either. I just wrapped my old uniform round several small, hard items: a brush, some books – five tins each containing one pound of Lyons coffee! This was a fortune in Germany. My optimistic view of the situation had turned out correct, though usually I am not a very successful gambler.'

Opportunities to employ these subterfuges and skills were increased when, as a special concession for Christmas, prisoners were allowed to send an additional post-free parcel during November 1947. If they had sufficient sterling to buy postage stamps, they were also permitted to send one gift food parcel and one gift parcel per month at normal postage rates.

Christmas 1947 also saw the easing of other restrictions, to allow prisoners to enjoy the festive season. Those who were eligible were permitted to be absent from their camps or hostels between 2 p.m. on Christmas Eve and 6 p.m. on Boxing Day. They were thus able to accept invitations to stay with members of the public, the only conditions being that their hosts should accept full responsibility for their guests, and that the addresses to which they went were within a 100-mile radius of their camps. The latter provision was intended to reduce the strain on public transport, but, nevertheless, people in Oldham anxious to entertain POW friends who had been moved to Ashton-in-Makerfield (Lancs) were allowed to do so.

It was not until after Christmas, in the first months of 1948, that Egon Schormann made his most interesting contacts with the British civilian population. He was then at Malvern Hostel, Worcs.

'One evening Hans, who slept in the bed next to mine, told me about a school concert that we could go to free. We always had enough money for the bus. We cleaned up our POW uniforms and got ready to go to a small-town cultural event. I have forgotten the name of the private school, but I still have a mental image of the stairs going up to the hall and hear us tentatively asking whether we could go to the concert. We could.

'The hall was like the one at Kaiser Wilhelm School: musty, spartan, with a platform and hard seats. When we came in and sat down, the hall was not full. We saw parents with their older children sitting between them, and we felt like schoolchildren again ourselves.

' "Don't draw attention to yourselves", an old soldier's dictum, was also valid for a POW. With this in mind we sat by the gangway in the second row from the back. This row and the one behind it were empty. No one took any notice of us, although we were recognisable as POWs by our awful chocolate-brown uniforms with patches at the back and on the knee. "Can you imagine an occasion like this at a German school?", Hans whispered to me. "No", and I had absolutely no doubt about it. Local Germans mixing with prisoners at a concert? How was such a thing possible in England?

'The concert began like all school concerts begin, with the school head, an old lady straight from the picture books, welcoming the audience. She welcomed the mayor, teachers from other schools, parents, pupils and then us; she must have glanced at us at the back for a brief moment. But we were not self-conscious after three years in prison. We expected a musical evening and not a red carpet for two unknown POWs.

'As she was bidding us welcome, the door opened and in walked several young ladies. I had never seen anything like this before, except in films, where it was not taken as seriously as this. In pairs they entered the hall and marched in military style down the gangway to the back. What a sight! England's female youth was coming towards us. Our hands shook. But there was no way out of the situation. It was lucky that we had combed our hair. The girls, who were sixth-formers from a neighbouring school in Malvern, spread out in our row and the one behind us. They had not all taken their seats when a teacher very much like the head suddenly noticed our presence and asked the girls to clear our row again. There was a commotion, the audience turned round; the girls stood along the back wall. The concert began.

'What was the matter with us? Why had they left us amicably alone at first and were now making such a performance? Does anyone understand the English? After our anger had subsided, we agreed not to move from our seats, and, as it turned out, this pedagogical measure was quite a friendly thing for both us POWs. They were strung out in front of us like a chain enclosing the outsiders, and had nothing against a little flirtation. Perhaps from the mere fact that we were enclosed we were not so strange after all.

'The concert – in parts good, in others boring, as school concerts are – took its course. People spoke to us during the interval and at the end, but the girls, even after the interval, stood in the gangway against the wall.

'When we left the school, nine o'clock was striking. We had to be in the hostel by ten but at the beginning of 1948 we did not have to be so punctual. The last roll-call was at six, in the evening; the next would be at seven in the morning of the next day. If it was discovered that we had in fact overstayed our pass it meant twenty-eight days' solitary confinement. It was cold, damp and dark as we walked to the bus stop, or, more exactly, to the square from which our bus and other cross-country buses left. As we hurried through the empty streets we heard steady footsteps behind us. A man in a dark overcoat seemed to be following us. The street lights twinkled on the asphalt. It was like a scene from an Edgar Wallace novel.

'Just before the bus stop, we came to an underground urinal. We had been looking for a urinal. We had not found one in the school and had not liked to ask. The man came down the steps after us. Did he represent the military police in civvies, checking that we would be back in camp on time? Was he someone affected by the particular brand of hysteria that saw Russians everywhere, checking if we had a rendezvous with a contact?

'Nothing like that. He was from Malvern and wanted to apologise, even in this ghastly place, for the goings-on in the hall. He said that he was an architect and that he and his wife had been hurt by the way the people had found it amusing: "Ridiculous", he said. "My wife and I would very much like you to come in for a cup of tea." We forgot the time. The architect's wife, when she was introduced to us, was an enchanting, charming lady, with refined manners. She had studied music at Dresden for two terms but had not completed her studies. She spoke only a little German but it helped, since our knowledge of English was deficient. We went hot and cold as our beautiful hostess passed us tea and urged us to eat her cakes. Here was a person who was concerned about us, friendly towards us, interested in us and could laugh heartily with us at our attempts to speak English. Never again would this charming English lady meet two young men who on the first evening were so prepared to lay their glowing grateful hearts at her feet.

'Many similar happy evenings followed this first occasion. After conversing for three years with dull-witted guards, the architect gave us an insight into the world of the English middle and upper-middle class. Conservative, obsessed by the British Empire, with little idea about the Continent but a passionate defender of democracy. There was nothing we did not discuss: the dictator, Hitler's annihilation policy, the loyal devotion to Hitler of most of the youth who had grown up under him (and that included us), the murder of the Jews and the Polish intelligentsia. They were tough weeks for us. We defended a belief which had been ruptured for a long time. It was re-education such as the British Government had pursued since the end of the war but had imposed so ineptly in the camps.

'We shall never forget this couple from Malvern. They made us feel after so many years in prison in England that we must question everything that we had accepted as maxims: that our culture, history, politics, economics were supreme, and that those of other countries were as nothing.

'On one of these beautiful, exciting, happy evenings, my friend Hans could not come. I went alone. The lady of the house had bought some coffee, although she herself only drank tea. She asked me into the kitchen and I made some of the strong black coffee which we Germans love. We played Monopoly, a game that we had learnt over this period. For the first time, some of the architect's friends were there. The first few evenings we had spent alone with them. All of a sudden I realised I had to run to catch my bus. There it was, as usual, under the clock-tower. I got on but did not have time to pay, because the driver beckoned me to hurry up and find a seat. The bus was full – it was usually empty at this time of day. I sat down at the back. It seemed to me that there were a good many soldiers on the bus that day. The bus moved off. A sergeant with a moustache turned round and eyed me up and down conspicuously. "Now what?" I thought. I looked round the bus again and realised I was on a military bus going to a military camp (left behind by the Americans before the invasion). "Good night", I thought. "Fare-was on a military bus going to a military camp (left behind by the Americans before the invasion). "Good night", I thought. "Fare-well Malvern." This would mean a transfer, but, before that, the dentist). That meant twenty-eight days hard labour, and deferment of repatriation for a few months more, and I wanted to go home, I did so want to go home at last! Soon!

'The bus drove for half an hour, much longer than it took to go to the hostel, its headlights lighting up the night. A large wooden gate, Nissen huts – not much better than our camp, barbed wire. We were there. The bus stopped in the middle of the camp and the soldiers got out. The sergeant hesitated at the door and looked at me in a penetrating way again. I followed the other soldiers as I had learnt to do as a POW. I did not know what he was thinking. Perhaps nothing. But he must have been thinking a great deal. Whatever the case, he got out. I looked at the driver, he looked at me. I shrugged my shoulders. He came round to the back of the bus and beckoned me to lie on the floor under the seats. The bus drove to the gates. A guard opened the driver's door. I could not understand what was going on. Ten seconds later the door slammed shut and the bus drove off. As the lights of the camp disappeared into the distance, the driver stopped. I pulled myself together and went and sat with him in front.

'It was February 1948, the month I was to be repatriated. I could have hugged the man. "Where are you going?" I asked. "To Malvern? I could find my way to my hostel at village X from there." "OK", he said, and we drove off. We both smoked. He was an older civilian, forty-five to fifty perhaps. I wondered whether we had ever fought against each other during the invasion, or at Arnhem or Reichswald. After three-quarters of an hour, my little village came into view. He stopped by the church and smiled at me. I offered him my cigarettes and said thank you. "Scram!" he said. "That's quite all right." I climbed through the fence, glanced at the barracks, where the soldiers were playing cards, and strolled over to my Nissen hut. It was after midnight. As I opened the door to my barracks, I was met with "What's her name?", "Was it good?" "Leave me alone", I said. I was dog tired.'

25 Last Act

On 31 December 1947 there were some 59,000 German POWs employed in Britain. No one at this stage would question the fact that they were good workers. As C. V. W. Tarr writes, 'the POWs at first were only allowed to do agricultural work. When the restrictions on their movements were relaxed, however, the German boys who had trades and professions were able to earn a lot of money by working in their off-duty time, for English people. Of course, a good many English people employed them out of self-interest rather than sympathy with the Germans, because they got first-class workmanship at low cost to themselves. I can assure you these German POWs were great ambassadors for German efficiency and industriousness, which English people speak of to this day and, considering our present disastrous decline in standards, devoutly wish that English productivity and efficiency could match. I remember a surveyor to a large local authority telling me that two German POWs constructed an inspection chamber in a road. The brickwork, he said, was so perfect that it "was a shame it had to be covered in".'

More to the point, were the British good employers? In February 1948, cases were cited of exploitation by the officials in charge of the POW workforce. One such public servant had used prisoners to repair and redecorate his own home. Another had been used to dig an official's garden. In neither instance was the prisoner paid for his services. Moreover, the methods of payment by farmers generally were wide open to abuse. 'The prisoners are virtually slaves', thundered Mr Dye, MP for Norfolk, South West, in the House of Commons. 'They are sent hither and thither by the officials, according to the demands of the farmers, and they cannot complain. They have no interest in what they do and no organisation to speak for them . . . .'

But there were, after all, only 109,800 German prisoners left in Britain by the end of February 1948. Camps were being closed down. Those left open were being reorganised. Emanuel Shinwell,

Minister of War, at this point doubted whether he could give the
POWs permission to travel around Britain to see their friends over
the Easter and Whitsun holidays that year. It would, he said,
increase the administrative problems involved and might even
interfere with the repatriation programme. It should be added that
by March Shinwell had relented and leave was granted.

Kurt Bock did not wait for leave.

'I bought myself a pair of shoes in London.

'At the beginning of March the time had really come to put an old
idea into practice, otherwise I might have the ill fortune to be
repatriated to Germany before I had seen London. There, near the
Scottish border, it was lovely in the spring. Although spring had not
yet come it felt as though it was not far off. We went for walks in the
countryside, but this did not cure my impatience. How far was it to
London? I did not know, but it was certainly not as far from there as
from Germany, and, once I was back on the Continent, who was
going to give me the chance to see London?

'I had tried it once before, when I was still in Monmouthshire, in
November 1947, when Mrs Pugsley was filling me up with royal-
wedding gossip. At the time, Llanmartin Camp was in the process of
being closed down and I had thought that it would be very easy. We
would be marched to the station early in the morning for our
transfer to the new camp in the north. I would simply disappear and
get onto another train in the direction of London. There must be a
lot of trains to London and I was not completely without experience
in escaping from ticket collectors and the like. I had enough
confidence in my ability to find my way: I would get to London
somehow and, once there, find some form of board and lodging. In a
town that size you can always find somebody who will help you. It
was the getting there which was difficult and I did not have a ticket.

'My little suitcase – 18 × 12 × 4 inches – was packed: toothbrush
and shaving kit, spare underwear and socks. The departure from
Llanmartin had been fixed for three days prior to the wedding. It
really could not have been better.

'The royal wedding took place as arranged, but unfortunately I
was not present. The hour-long march started at 6 a.m. –
snowstorm, no coat; the little suitcase and I were completely
soaked. That time I had to give up. For me the royal wedding took
place only on the radio, and I listened to it near the Scottish border.
My turn had not yet come; nevertheless, I was determined to take a
little trip to London before I went back to Hamburg.

'Friday 12 March 1948: the suitcase was packed again. I went to stand amongst a group of men about to be repatriated. Fifty men with their hand luggage. We knew each other by sight: "You here too?" – "Sure." We agreed to watch each other's luggage on the journey. Despite my small suitcase I did not look suspicious, although the others had much heavier luggage. We were counted and moved about while the count took place; we were counted again. Nobody said anything about the result of the count, but since we were then marched off, I assumed that nobody was missing or superfluous. But I was certainly not on the sergeant's list. Just as well that I was only 5 foot 7 inches tall. I would not have been able to get away with it if I had been 6 foot. We marched through the gate to the station and the first recount was taken inside the train. There, it was even more difficult, as nobody was supposed to leave their place. It was imperative that the sergeant should not see me, nor my companions notice that I was trying to get away without the sergeant seeing me. It was a kind of war on two fronts. So I tried to behave like the others who would be home in Germany in four or five days, after three or 3½ years as POWs, which meant that they had often been away from their loved ones for four years.

'So far, so good. The train was going to Sheffield, where we were going to spend a night in a camp before going on board ship. Sheffield might not be London but at least it was a few kilometres further south than Haltwhistle. If, at Sheffield station, I could move a few steps "sideways", I might be able to miss the connection to the camp. After all, there was always a lot of movement at a station and it would not be noticed. Wrong again. In Sheffield I was noticed at the station. I did not even know which station it was. There were no crowds there. I mumbled, "I must just nip around the corner." But it was not easy to get out of sight. However, if there was another count when they got onto the bus, at least it would be right without me. Then, when the bus had gone, I could show myself again. So I moved slowly in the opposite direction. There were far too few people walking around there. I would obviously be noticed. I looked around carefully: the bus was still there, but the POWs were now ready to get into it. What I had to do was try to get around the corner of one of the buildings. It was a long way to the corner, but at last I made it and the bus left. I made my way to the main exit of the station, trying to look as normal as possible. I needed a tram to get me to the south of the city; after all, I could not very well try to hitch a lift in front of the station. What I really needed was a map of the area. I imagined that Nottingham was the next major town. I was wrong: Chesterfield and Derby came first. Hitch-hiking was easy. Everybody gave me lifts, although mostly only for short distances. 30 kilometres was very good, because nobody was going straight through to London. Nobody asked questions, and I did not have to give explanations; people just took me along. How far was Derby from London?

'Leicester – what did I know about Leicester? Nothing. By then it was evening. Would I get any further? Certainly not as far as London. Where could I stay the night? It would not be a hotel. Somewhere at the station? No. But there were POW camps all over the place. Surely I should be able to find room there. Where was the nearest camp?

' "Excuse me, madam, I've lost my way – could you kindly tell me where I can find my camp?." '

' "Yes, of course, you just take that bus." '

'It was getting late but there were other POWs sitting in the bus and some more got on on the way. Nobody took any notice of me after all; I would simply follow them. Although everybody knew everybody else, this did not mean that a new face does not appear in a large camp from time to time. This was a large camp, probably with between 1500 and 2000 POWs in it. The guards at the gate looked bored. I passed through with a slight wave of the hand. Some of the others also waved. I walked around inside the Nissen huts. If I had known where I could find an empty bed, I could simply have lain down in it. Hardly anybody would take any notice of me; I knew the drill. But the trouble was I did not know which of the beds was not in use. I wondered who was in charge of this hut. I saw a man in a small office and went up to him. He was the camp elder. He probably had been a sergeant major or a warrant officer originally. I wondered if it still mattered to him. I needed his help but I did not know him. Had he got a sense of humour or a sense of adventure, or was he so full of his own self-importance that he had become a bureaucrat? Camp elders were often very full of themselves, very convinced of the importance of their rank. This made it difficult and you could not be certain of success. I ought to call him by his first name. This was not the practice in our officers' camp, but I did not want to give myself away. I wanted him to take me for a sergeant major. But there was no time to give this much thought, as he was on his own at that particular moment and I preferred to speak to him by himself.

'As I should have expected, the attempt failed. I said to him:
"Listen, I am from a camp near the Scottish border and I want to
visit my brother in London. Can you put me up for one night?" He
was almost speechless. "What . . . what . . . who are you? Have
you been sent here by the English?"

' "No, I want to visit my brother, it's a private visit and, of course,
nobody must know about it. I just want to stay here for one night on
my way."

' "I'll have nothing to do with it. I really ought to report you. For
goodness sake, get out of this camp as soon as you can. I don't know
anything and haven't seen anything, but if you stay I'll report you."

' "I'm only asking you to give me a hint in which of the huts
there's a free place."

' "Get out, get out quickly, I am not doing anything for you. Do
you think I am going to get myself into trouble for your sake?
SCRAM! I've seen nothing and I want to see nothing."

'There was nothing to be done; a good civil servant knows his
limitations and he knows the rules and he keeps to them.

'The next question for me was: how was I to get out of the camp
without being seen, and, once out, where would I spend the night?

'It was already about 9.30, the gate was open and well lit. The
guards were a little more alert, because they had to close the gate at
10 p.m. and were then relieved. Many POWs were only just coming
back, all walking quickly in; nobody was going out of the camp.
What should I say if I were asked why I was leaving so late. I could
say, "I must have lost my purse on my way from the bus, but I will
be back before ten."

'However, the guards were not particularly watchful and nobody
asked any questions as I left the camp. It was certainly the trickiest
situation on the trip so far. Where did I go then? Where in fact was I
then? A long night still lay ahead of me, but the sky was clear and I
could see in which direction I had to go. If I went from west to east I
should meet one of the roads leading southwards, perhaps even one
of the main roads to London. The road meandered, there were a
number of small side roads. I met hardly anybody and no cars. In
any case, how could I hitch a lift there at that time of night? So I
continued, but I was slowly getting exhausted. I wondered what the
time was, but had no idea and was gradually growing very very
thirsty.

'At last I seemed to have reached the highway, although there
was hardly any traffic at all. Everything was quiet; there were very

few houses, and no lights. Where in Heaven's name could I hide myself for a few hours? I could not go on walking all night, and I certainly would not get a lift then. I saw a petrol station, but it was in darkness. In front of it was a lorry. I saw that the cab was open and so I crept inside and tried to sleep. But it got very cold and I heard voices and I certainly could not sleep, as I was still very thirsty. Carefully I looked around me. There was nothing to be seen. However, a hundred yards down the road there was a light, actually quite a bright one, and the sound of a lot of voices. Perhaps I would be able to find a water tap. I crawled out of the lorry. Except for the pub, everything was dead quiet. I did not want to look suspicious. There was no tap to be seen. Should I take the risk of going into the pub to try and get something to drink? Being thirsty was worse than being homesick: I decided to risk it. I went in with a poker face. No doubt I would think of something if I was asked any questions. Nobody asked anything; they just stared at me. But then, of course, they stared at any stranger. I wondered if they could see that I was a POW. I drank my glass of beer, and I did not seem to be particularly conspicuous. "Last orders please, gentlemen." I disappeared before "time" was called and crawled back into the cab of the lorry. I hoped that the night would soon come to an end. I decided that it would be best if I were out by 5 a.m., because I certainly must not be caught there asleep. Although the road was quiet and hardly a car passed, I did not sleep too well. In the pub too, everything was quiet. I dozed a little, woke a little, dozed again. Suddenly I woke up! Was somebody coming towards the lorry? No, all was quiet; I dozed again.

'A car passed, then another. It was still quite dark but it must be early morning already. I had to get out. I was very cold and it was better to move about rather than stay there. I wondered if I would be able to get a lift then. What was the next large town and how far was it from Leicester to London? I had no road map, no idea of the towns between there and London, so I could only ask for a lift to London. A car stopped and the driver threw out a parcel of newspapers. "Will you give me a lift?" "Where to?" "To London." "I'm not going very far, I've only got a few more customers, but if you want to come, okay", and I joined him. At least I was making some progress. The newspaper man finished his rounds at an all-night cafe. That suited me fine, because, not only was it warm inside and crowded, but I might even hear of somebody going to London who would be willing to give me a lift. I sat down, ordered my baked beans, fried egg and cup of tea. At last some solid food, after all that time. There was a constant coming and going, but nobody talked to me and I did not see anybody whom I felt I could approach. On the wall facing me there was a mirror in which I could see the door. It opened and shut suddenly and I saw a policeman come into the cafe. I must not turn round. The copper stood at the bar two yards away from me, ordered tea and talked to the girl behind the counter. Nobody looked at me, but while he was standing there I certainly could not get up.

'Although it was Saturday morning I still thought it should be possible to get a lift to London. But it was not so easy and I was very happy when I at last got a lift with somebody going as far as St Albans. He seemed a nice chap, though quiet. St Albans . . . that should be very near London; I tried to find out from him how I could get from St Albans to London, specifically to Shepherds Bush. "Hmm, you had better go to . . ." – quite incomprehensible cockney slang. He talked about greyhound racing at the White City, soccer, and so on. I was a very attentive listener – when he had anything to say – but that was not very often. "Thank you, thank you very much for giving me a lift, it's very kind of you."

'Where could I find a bus to take me into London? Could one in fact ask the way to London from St Albans or was it already part of the metropolis and must one name a more specific destination? The signs on the buses meant nothing to me. How did other people manage? I did not even understand them, and yet surely I was able to speak English. I just said, "I want to go to the White City Stadium." "EIOIO . . . ." Not a syllable could I understand. I gave him the money and said, "Will that do?" It seemed to be okay and the bus moved off. I had no doubt that I would land somewhere where there was more to be seen, perhaps even White City. A lot of people went there, and I would not look suspicious, and in any case it was not far from Shepherds Bush.

'Whether I would succeed in getting into the camp was another matter. My experience so far was not very encouraging, but if I met one of the four officers whom I had known in Crewe Hall Camp I might be able to pull it off. The best thing I could think of to do was to ask the camp doctor: doctors were officers and they knew everybody, even in a camp containing 2000 POWs.

'White City: thousands upon thousands of people streaming into the stadium. I asked my way to Shepherds Bush. There was supposed to be a camp there, in the centre of London. It was really quite incredible: it was now 2 p.m. and there was the camp gate in front of me. The situation then was the exact opposite of the night before in Leicester. POWs were coming out for their afternoon walk with their friends. I wondered where they were all going. Tired and unshaven as I was, I simply marched through the gate and neither of the guards looked at me or talked to me. And why should they? Surely if somebody went into a camp, of his own free will, he must be okay?

'It was a huge camp, and I felt a little lost as I entered it. It was full of clean, well-shaven and well-dressed POWs. Nobody knew me and nobody took any notice of me. And yet I must be conspicuous with my little suitcase and unkempt appearance. I looked for and found the washroom; inside a number of men were cleaning up and preparing for going out. As soon as I had washed and freshened up and had a good shave, I could start looking for the doctor. But I did not even have to ask. During a tour of the camp, I soon noticed the hospital and the doctor – well, at least his little room. He really was well off, with a room to himself, even if it was small. Hoping he would be in, I knocked on the door. I saw a civilian in a brown suit. "Doctor?" "No, my name is Klein, Lieutenant Klein." "I am Lieutenant Bock, I have come from Featherstone Park Camp, Haltwhistle. I want to ask the doctor whether he can put me up for a few days. I so much wanted to visit London before being repatriated to Germany."

'My luck was in, the doctor was not in the camp, but Lieutenant Klein was a friend. We had a quick cup of tea and then Klein took me to see the real London: Piccadilly Circus, Westminster, Houses of Parliament, Buckingham Palace, Whitehall, Downing Street, Trafalgar Square, Strand; even Leicester Square, with its huge cinemas and the long queues of people waiting for tickets. Klein knew everything, because he had had this dream job for several months. He was able to walk about in civilian clothes, but, like all the others, he had to be back in camp by 10 p.m.

'How did one get around with very little money and travel on the tube as much as possible? Klein knew how. How did one get back into camp, even if it were after ten o'clock and the gates were closed? Klein knew that too. He showed me a free bunk, obtained breakfast and an evening meal for me. Everything was very simple. I could have stayed there for weeks, as long as the doctor in the hospital did not see me, because he lived in fear of losing his job. This was understandable, of course, because he too had a dream job: camp doctor in Shepherds Bush Camp. But the doctor never saw me, although I spent the nights in his hospital and had breakfast there in the mornings.

'During the next few days I had to make my visits to London by myself. Klein was my mentor although we only saw each other rarely. He constantly gave me new tips and I was even able to save a few shillings to buy a guide to London.

'I had made it at last. If I got caught now, and even got twenty-eight days solitary in Haltwhistle, nobody could take this away from me: I had been to London.

'How much money would I need for my stay? How much would it cost me to return? Obviously I would not have enough money for a dinner at the Savoy, but I wanted to see as much as I possibly could. For a few pennies I travelled from one side of London to the other and back again, and after two days I did not even have to look at the Underground map in the stations, because I then knew all the important places I wanted to see. I wanted to include at least one visit to a theatre; obviously I could not afford more. The possibilities were enormous. I decided on a popular production such as *Annie Get your Gun* or *Oklahoma!*: everybody at that time was singing the tunes from these shows. I chose the matinée performance of *Oklahoma!*, which was cheaper and also less difficult to get tickets for. 'Oh What a Beautiful Morning'; porridge and tea in the camp, and off I went. By 9.30 I was at the theatre and had hired a little stool. The stool was only for the queue for the ticket. It was a very practical arrangement. You hired a stool and put it down in the queue, and in the meantime you could go off and discover London. Do such excellent arrangements exist anywhere else? I have never heard of any and yet it was a marvellous system.

'Once again I was on the move: Trafalgar Square, Haymarket, Hyde Park Corner, the Serpentine, crossing and re-crossing London. I walked for miles in my heavy boots and ate lunch at Lyons. Once more into the huge Underground network with its enormous escalators. What a life!

'The Changing of the Guard at Buckingham Palace, that was my aim for Wednesday 17 March 1948, after I had hired my little stool in front of Drury Lane. The diary for that date records the following: "Shamrock People [Irish Guards], colours marching to and fro, no goose step, but . . . ." Afterwards it would appear that I was looking for a telephone and found it at Victoria Station, but I did not make a note of whom I wanted to talk to. Further notes:

Vauxhall Bridge, Tate Gallery, Paul Nash, spiv in a car. The last item means nothing to me now, although I vaguely remember a speech by Attlee in which he mentioned "spivs and drones".

'I finally returned to the theatre, a bus ride to Aldwych for 1½d. As I rejoined the queue I ate a buttered roll and some cake. By then there was a large crowd in front of the theatre, but thanks to my stool I was in a very advantageous position. "Queueing with sailor and charming wife", says my little diary, but again this means little to me today. However, I do remember that I did not find queueing in front of the theatre boring, and that I had an interesting conversation with the sailor and his wife. "Oklahoma – Overture, people smoking and eating." This entry in my diary reminds me how surprised I was that smoking and eating were allowed in the theatre. Tea was served on a tray, brought to your seat. The sailor gave me some chocolate; I had told him that I was a POW. He noticed how enthusiastic I was about the performance and told me that in the past he used to hate the Germans.

'The words and music were of course familiar, because the papers had been full of them for a long time. In fact, talking of papers, never since have I read as many papers as I did in camp. For months I even subscribed to *The Times* and the *Daily Express*, and apart from these I also bought the *Sphere*. In fact I read everything, every word, including the Stock Exchange report, and the racing results. So much reading sometimes led me astray in conversations with Englishmen. Not everyone was as well up on what was "in" in the London theatre, or in the book world. Not everyone read all the reviews and cricket reports. For me, even the soccer tables and cinema programmes were of interest, and therefore I knew everything that was going on – but only from the papers. And now I found myself in London, and could actually see and experience what so far I had only read about.

'Houses of Parliament: There was no entry fee, and of course it was something I had to see, and would have seen even if I had had to pay. In fact I went twice, although even there queueing was the rule. POWs were not a normal feature of the queue, which consisted mostly of visitors to London from the provinces and abroad: Americans, New Zealanders, South Africans. The impression was one of practical re-education and you felt as if you were living through history. You saw Mr Speaker in action. Would somebody speak to me there? They must have known that I was a POW, as I was wearing a dark battledress. But nobody made any objection and a lot of the people probably did not even know who I was. And why should they worry about me there in London?

'A girl walked past dressed in the "new look". You did not see it very often yet at that time, and I exclaimed in pleasure, "Actually the new look!" The man next to me heard me and said, ". . . and good-looking into the bargain!"

'In the lobby there was constant coming and going. I knew the names of the ministers and the more important MPs by their speeches, and from newspaper and radio reports; there I actually saw them in the flesh. A typist passed, and dropped a few letters; I picked them up and handed them to her, and she thanked me with a most beautiful smile. I was sure she did not know that I was a POW. If she gave me a thought at all it could only be that I was peculiarly dressed.

'I visited the British Museum, the Tate Gallery, the National Gallery and, of course, St Paul's. I had no system, except that I was determined to visit all the important and well-known places, including, of course, Regent's Park, the Tower and Madame Tussaud's. Ah no, Madame Tussaud's was out, because the ticket was too expensive. I would just have to admire it from the outside. I also visited the big stores, but only for a short time, because I had not got enough money to buy things – except for a pair of shoes with crepe soles. These I had to have because I could not continue to run around in my heavy boots.

'Wednesday 17 March: a symphony concert at the Royal Albert Hall. I would simply have to fork out the necessary shillings to hear this. A seat in the fourth row cost 2s. and the programme was 6d. They were playing the Sinfonia from the *Easter Oratorio* by J. S. Bach, the Violin Concerto in D by Beethoven, with the solo violin played by Ginette Neveu. After the interval they played a symphony by William Walton. The conductor was Sir Adrian Boult. The gallery under the dome was crowded, mostly with young people. I moved around freely without fear of being discovered. On the contrary, I was looking for people to talk to, have a conversation with, but without having to tell them the circumstances in which I was there. I had bought a packet of cigarettes, not because I wanted to smoke, but so that I could offer them to other people. I walked right round the enormous hall looking for a suitable seat and finally found one in the first row. I studied the faces in the stalls and in the rows and rows of seats around me.

' "Will you have a cigarette?" The question, addressed to me in

German, startled me. The man immediately behind me was about forty years old, wore a dark suit and had a puffy face. Was he from the CID? Almost automatically I replied in English, and, without taking his, offered him one of my cigarettes. He spoke to me again in German. Although he spoke it very well, he was certainly not German, nor English. He spoke very good German, but somehow his intonation was not right.

'The concert began and I turned into an enthusiastic listener, because this was a great event for me. It was not the music, which I knew and had often heard, but the fact that I was listening to it in the world-famous Albert Hall. In the camp they might well be listening to it on the radio, but I was hearing it live. After the Bach symphony, again a few words of German from the stranger behind me; I replied at first in English, but then also in German. By now he knew that I was a POW. No, he must have known that from the start and only wanted me to confirm it, otherwise why would he have addressed me in German? Needless to say, I did not tell him I had come down from the Scottish border.

'The violin concerto was finished. Some of the audience rushed out and we applauded furiously. I turned and looked behind me; the stranger had vanished. This was the interval and so I got up, went out and walked around the hall with the rest of the audience. It was odd that the dark stranger had vanished. Was he a policeman after all and just waiting to pounce on me? There he was again, leaning against a pillar. He saw me coming. "How did you like it?" "Marvellous, excellent, a really great event for me." We started discussing Beethoven and Mozart, and then he suddenly said, "I have to go home now and boil a couple of eggs for myself." "Don't you want to stay?" I asked him in English. "The William Walton symphony is long and boring", he answered in German. "You won't enjoy it; come with me, and we can talk at home and cook a few eggs and, if you really want, you can listen to the symphony on the radio." An invitation! I could save the cost of an evening meal, have a bit of personal contact and maybe there would be help and advantages in it which would be useful to me while I was in London. I accepted his invitation, although I did find the circumstances unusual. Not that I was afraid; it just did not seem quite right. On the other hand, it was not "right" for me to be in London at all, was it?

'We got into his small car which was parked in front of the Albert Hall. As we drove I tried to see the names of the streets. My host obviously noticed. "It's not far, we will soon be there." We finally reached a block of flats in Kensington: not bad, but nothing special and the furniture was ordinary; small square entrance hall, large living-room. He looked out of the window, and offered me cigarettes behind his back, not noticing that there were no cigarettes in the box. It did not matter as I did not want to smoke anyway. "Whisky with or without lemon?" I had never had either before. He poured me a whisky and soda, told me that he was living alone at the moment, because his housekeeper – his Jewish housekeeper – was away on holiday. Then he drew the curtains. "I have to be careful; the English are always very suspicious about foreigners. I am a foreigner myself." He repeated this a couple of times. "People are inquisitive. I don't know what they will think or do if they notice that I am entertaining a POW." For my part, I told him about my friends in Monmouthshire and Pembroke.

'He was obviously a cultured man. We talked about concerts we had heard. He put on a record of a Vaughan Williams symphony and we continued discussing music. There was no mention of food until he remembered his offer. Whereupon we went into the kitchen together. He made a cup of Nescafé, and two fried eggs. The gas cooker had an eye-level grill and I had never seen one like it before. The eggs were soon done. He gave them both to me. He ate nothing – and yet it was he who had wanted to leave the concert before the end, to "boil some eggs". I had not told him my name yet, so I introduced myself. He asked me which part of Germany I came from, but he did not seem to want to tell me his name. He mentioned that Englishmen were always reticent about this with strangers and tried to avoid difficulties. I did not really know what he meant by this, but of course pretended to understand: "Where do you come from then, perhaps from Holland?" My guess was correct and nothing further was said about that either. He had stopped talking about music, and now discussed painting. This was something I knew less about, but I could answer the question "What do you think of Picasso" easily enough. My host got up from his chair, looked for a book of reproductions and sat down on the sofa. He flicked through the book, commenting on the pictures. I had to sit next to him and we looked at the pictures together. I listened carefully as he instructed me; he praised my diligence and took my hand. Was he going to read the lines of my hand? He looked puzzled when he put my right hand into his left. His index finger traced the lines and he explained that I was very sensual. I was beginning to feel uncomfortable in this unknown and unusual situation. I thought he also sensed that I was somewhat tense, and was wondering what to make of it all. I just stared straight in front of me and said nothing. Then suddenly he tried to put his arm round me. Without a second thought, my fist landed in his belly and I got up. I had to get out. He followed, looking completely helpless. "At least let me kiss you" – he held a pound note and a box of cigarettes in his hand. I grabbed both and dashed out of the door like lightning. He followed moaning, helpless, with his arms outstretched. Outside, I looked at the name of the block of flats and then made for Knightsbridge station and on to Shepherds Bush as fast as I could.

'Thursday 18 March 1948. I enjoyed my day in London. As usual I got home late, because I had to make the most of the twenty-four hours. My return to the camp between 11 p.m. and midnight had become routine. About 200 yards before the gate I left the road at an angle of 45 degrees and crossed a field which brought me to the barbed-wire fence, well away from the gate. I walked a further 300 yards along the fence, turned, and then continued for another 100 or 150 yards until I reached the "gap". You could only see it if you bent down and even then you had to keep a sharp look out for it. However, the gap was large enough to get through.

'I had already crossed the field and was happily walking along beside the fence. It was particularly dark that night and I had to walk slowly so as not to trip. Otherwise, there was no need to be too careful because there were no guards and nobody was going to take a shot at you. "Stop!" A torch flashed and a policeman was standing in front of me. He did not ask many questions: he knew whom to expect there. Unfortunately, Lieutenant Klein had not warned me about that, so that the policeman had expected me, but I had not expected him. I wondered what would happen to me – how long would I be locked up for getting back late? "Your identity card please." That was all I needed; of course I could not show it to him: I did not belong to that camp. I fumbled in my pockets: nothing. "Sorry, sir, I must have left it in the camp." "Your name?" I told him my name, but he did not write it down. "Stand over there", he said, pointing to the fence and shone his torch on a man standing ten yards away. I noted that I was already his second victim that night. I did not know the man and he did not know me, but then, of course, I hardly knew anybody there. "What's this going to cost me?" I whispered. "Don't know either." I wondered what to do, how to get out of this jam. The policeman was standing next to us, saying not a word. Nothing happened. The minutes ticked by, but time seemed endless. I wondered what he was waiting for. Did he hope to catch still more victims? How could I escape? I simply had to wait.

'There . . . far away from us, there was a movement, a shadow. It became more visible, but made no noise at all. The copper waited for the shadow to approach, like a spider waiting for its victim. A few more steps, a few more seconds, then he moved forward shining his torch upon the approaching figure. That was the second I needed. Without looking round, and as fast as my legs would carry me I ran along beside the barbed wire to the corner, and then a little more slowly, bent double, towards the gap in the fence. There it was – at last – and I squeezed through it quickly and then took cover behind a hut, to get my breath back. I listened for sounds of movement, but everything was quiet, nothing at all. I moved forward carefully, in case there were guards patrolling the camp. I finally reached the hospital block and my bunk. Fortunately nobody had seen me. I wondered how many POWs the policeman had caught that night; I did not really know how much "time" it would have meant for them or me if we had been reported. It was a calculated risk, but it was rumoured that nobody ever got more than twenty-eight days solitary for this sort of thing. As I say, this was only rumour, because I never knew anyone actually to be caught.

The return

My financial reserves did not permit a permanent stay in London. It had been an overwhelming experience, but I had to return to Featherstone Park Camp. I was not going to be able to get a train to get me northwards fast, free and for nothing. I was beginning to regret not having drawn a map of the route northwards, with as many towns marked on it as possible. I knew my way around, but not sufficiently for the journey ahead. The first question was how to get out of London and how to hitch a lift northwards. Bayswater Underground Station, Euston, High Barnet? I still have these names jotted down on a small piece of paper, but cannot remember who gave me these tips. I should have to get to St Albans somehow, because I wanted to leave London by the same way I came in. I trusted my intuition. It was not easy in this vast city to find the right place to hitch a lift. I looked around, walked a little way, asked a few questions, and was finally picked up by two CID men in civilian clothes. "What are you looking for? Where do you come from?"

Experts that they were, they knew that I was a POW and obviously such people had no business there. In such a situation it is best to tell the truth. Perhaps it is not essential to tell the whole truth. Sometimes half is enough. Anyway, once I was in the hands of the police, they would soon find out all about me. The Metropolitan Police!

'I showed my identity card. For such occasions, I always had a picture of my mother on top of it, so that the police then saw not only my identity card, but also the old lady. She looked pathetic on this photo and I had no other picture of her on me. "Your mother?" "Yes, sir." "She will be waiting for you, will she?" "Yes, sir." "When are you going home?" "I don't know, maybe in May or June." "What are you doing round here?" "I've got a brother in Shepherd's Bush Camp, whom I have not seen for years, and the British camp commander in my camp in the north was kind enough to give me permission to go and see him for a week. Actually he doesn't have the authority to grant this, so I am not supposed to tell anybody about it, or he will be reprimanded. I ask you, gentlemen, not to make a fuss, but just tell me how I can get a good lift north."

'This little story was highly successful. I went on to tell them about my London week, including the visit to the concert at the Royal Albert Hall. They asked me for the address of the Dutchman, but I did not give it to them. Finally, they wished me good luck. It was Friday, midday.

'My chances appeared less than average. However, I got to St Albans and hitched another lift to Leicester – in fact, even a few miles beyond the town. I wondered whether I could not find a lorry which would take me a couple of hundred miles further north. It was already getting dark, so I took a bus to Derby. I did not really want to spend money on fares. Another short lift, but now I realised that I would have to spend the night somewhere. I was lucky that it was not raining. As it was dark I could not get another lift. I began walking and was even wondering if I was actually on the right road. I walked for hours and found that it was already about 11 p.m. I met a group of happy young people coming out of a dance. We started talking, but they could not help or advise me. I would not be able to go on much longer. On the other hand, I could not see anywhere to spend the night.

'Suddenly I saw a car coming towards me at high speed; it braked sharply and stopped beside me. Two men got out – a police car! They asked brusquely for my identity card and looked at my little suitcase, which I had to open for them. They did not give me a chance to say much, but I could easily prove my harmlessness. However, I had to explain my presence there: a POW on a lonely road at midnight. I repeated my little story about my brother in London, and once again it was believed. They would let me go on. However, I would like a little more from them. I hoped that the two policemen, having heard my story, would be able to help me find somewhere to spend the night. Unfortunately, they had a job to do, looking for a burglar, so they could do nothing then. But perhaps the police station in Chesterfield, only seven miles away, would be able to help. I was to tell their colleagues there that they should put me up for the night. Maybe it was lucky that Chesterfield was still so far away. A little further on I saw a haystack and nothing could hold me back. I made myself a "nest" for protection from the cold, crawled into it, and was asleep within minutes.

'At sunrise, I heard a milk lorry passing. There was still very little traffic, but I had to use every minute of the day. It was still a long way to Haltwhistle and I had to get back to camp by evening. I was lucky: a delivery van stopped and took me to Chesterfield. However, once there, I was again in trouble. A short ride on the bus, and then a lift to Sheffield. From there, by tram to Rotherham. It was 9 a.m. and I was still unwashed and unshaved, and had not had breakfast either.

'A policeman beckoned me over. "You look a bit rough." Too true – anybody could see I had slept in a haystack.

'"Well, sir . . .", and then once again I trotted out the story about my visit to my brother, showed the photo of my mother, and appealed to the policeman to tell me where I could wash and shave before going on. He directed me to a public lavatory and from there to a lorry drivers' cafe which was not far away. There I had a cup of tea and some baked beans. Then, whom could I talk to there, who would be able to help me on my way? The drivers in the cafe were all very nice, but nobody was going anywhere approaching my direction. The outlook was poor and I had already lost a good deal of time. It would soon be midday and I had not covered many miles since morning. However, a little later on I found myself on a main road to Doncaster. There there was heavy traffic with a constant stream of private cars and buses, but still very little chance of stopping anybody and asking for a lift. Everything was rushing past, even the buses were packed and did not stop at bus stops. There was a big football match at Doncaster! I no longer had much hope of getting a lift and was just trotting blindly along. When I heard a car I put my thumb up without even looking back, since nobody was going to stop anyway. And yet I kept on trying. Suddenly a large limousine stopped, with a squeal of brakes. The driver started off immediately I got in and asked where I wanted to go. He was dressed in a dark suit and did not look as if he was going to a football match. I asked politely whether he could take me to York, perhaps even further. He could not: he was only going as far as Doncaster. We chatted for a while, then I asked him, "Are you going to a wedding?" "No, I am an undertaker." So there I was, riding in a hearse, and I had not even noticed it!

'This lift was less than 20 kilometres but he gave me a 10s. note when he said goodbye. To get out of Doncaster in the afternoon was impossible: there was not a car in sight. I walked along in the direction of York, and nothing whatsoever passed me. If only I were in York! I had no option; I would have to take a bus. Thus, I reached York early in the afternoon, had a cup of tea and a piece of cake. But how did I get from there to Haltwhistle? I had very little money left, but I had no chance at all of hitch-hiking on a Saturday afternoon. If the experiences of the morning were anything to go by, it would take me another forty-eight hours. A thought crossed my mind: I might as well spend the money that I would need for food and drink during this time on the fare from York to Haltwhistle via Newcastle. How much could this be? Probably more than I had got. However, there was a train which stopped at nearly every station on the way. I bought a ticket to the next station, which cost 6s. 1d. – a fortune.

'I found that I still had time to walk around York. I wanted to see as much as possible, including the beautiful cathedral. But I only enjoyed it in a half-hearted way. Subconsciously the same question kept worrying me: how did I get to Newcastle, and from there to Haltwhistle, on my ticket? Once I reached Newcastle, it would not be too bad. I simply crossed from one platform to the other, and caught the train to Haltwhistle. It would, I imagined, be the same procedure as if I had arrived in Hamburg from Hanover and had to change to another platform to catch the train to Elmshorn or Lüneburg. My plan had to succeed.

'Nobody worried about me as I got on to the train with my ticket. It was somewhere between 4 and 5 p.m. and the train was not very crowded. The guard looked at my ticket and I looked round the carriages. Most of them were half empty. After twenty minutes we reached the first station and this was my time to disappear. I went into the toilet and made myself comfortable. Later, at another station, I used another toilet, and then, for the third stop, I returned to the first. I did not know any of the stations except Durham, and I had never actually been there either. It could not be much further now, maybe half an hour, and in the meantime it had got quite dark. I opened the lavatory door carefully. I put on a very sad face. I would simply say that I felt ill if another guard or ticket collector should by any unfortunate chance appear. But nothing happened; the train rumbled on towards Newcastle. The thought of changing trains there was worrying me all the time. One of the problems was that I did not know the station at all. In addition, I had no ticket, I did not know at which platform the train arrived and at which I could get a train to Haltwhistle – if indeed there was another one that night. I should have to think of a way of finding out, without making myself conspicuous. The train slowed down and we arrived at Newcastle.

'I did not hurry, but moved slowly and kept a very careful watch. I looked for the platform for the Haltwhistle train, but the situation was difficult. Only very few passengers left our train and they walked purposefully to the exit. Surely it was possible to get to the other platforms without passing through the ticket barrier? By then I was by myself; all the other travellers had disappeared. The train had also gone. Thirty yards ahead of me the ticket collector was sitting inside his office. He was waiting for me to pass him, but I stayed where I was. We looked at each other. I put my little suitcase on the ground. I simply could not go through the barrier because I had not got a valid ticket. The one I did have was useless, since it was not even valid to Newcastle and I needed one to take me as far as Haltwhistle. I decided that if there was any trouble I should have to say that I came from Durham, the station before Newcastle, and that I had lost my ticket. I had to pretend I was very worried and started rummaging in my pockets, slowly one by one. I opened the suitcase, and looked through it very carefully, pretending to look for the ticket. The expression on my face was of complete incredulity, as if I had just seen my ticket a few minutes before. I glanced over to the barrier; the ticket collector was still waiting for me, and watching me. I repeated the performance of looking through my pockets, very slowly this time. The man waited. I wished he would come over to me, I could not stand there for ever. I decided to walk slowly towards the barrier, again with a miserable face. I tried to find the right words. "Sir, I have just arrived from Durham and I have to get to Haltwhistle to Featherstone Park Camp." "Well?" He looks at me. "Hmm, the problem is that I have lost my ticket. I definitely had it in this pocket, and I still had it when the guard came round. Then I pulled a newspaper out of my pocket, and I suppose that is when it must have fallen out. I didn't notice, but now I am really in trouble. I have to get to Haltwhistle tonight. I should be there at 10 p.m. What can I do? By the way, when does the Haltwhistle train leave?"

'The ticket collector could not give me any advice, except to suggest that I look through my pockets yet again. I fumbled in my pockets once more, being careful not to pull out the ticket from York. By then I wished I had got rid of it earlier on. The collector watched me opening my little suitcase, looking through that as well, and was finally convinced that the ticket really was lost. He thought for a moment, and then went to consult his colleagues. I was left alone for ten minutes before he reappeared and waved me to follow him. He took me to the correct platform for my train – he had found the only suitable solution! The train for Haltwhistle left in approximately thirty minutes and we looked for the guard. The ticket collector explained the situation fully and put me in the guard's care. He immediately appreciated the fact that a POW such as I had no money and that it was a calamity if he lost his ticket. There was no longer a problem; he would not only get me to Haltwhistle, he would do so quite officially. The hide-and-seek in the lavatories was thus a thing of the past and I then travelled as a proper passenger. Although it was late, the tension had gone and I enjoyed the journey and looked forward to my bed in camp. It was a full hour's walk from the station to the camp, but what was that after the hundreds of miles I had covered between London and Scotland?

'I wondered who would have noticed my absence. Very few, I thought. All I wanted to do was sleep – and as soon as possible. But before that I had to have a quick shower and speak to a friend.

' "Where have you been?"

' "I bought myself a pair of shoes in London." '

26 The End of the Affair

The end was now truly in sight. As 1948 advanced, more and more prisoners were going home to their families. Their English friends were genuinely sorry to see them depart – though, in many cases, the parting was only temporary. Farewell suppers were held and goodbyes said.

Griselda Fyfe writes, 'New Year's day 1948, he [Fritz] joined our family party. I think this was probably his last visit to us before his return home. He brought me all the music he had bought with his earnings, five morocco-bound volumes of Brahms's songs he had got second-hand. I kept these for years and then sent them back to him. How many people were in our house that day I can't remember; I can only remember the roast beef and horseradish sauce – a thing I always connect with Fritz, as it was the first and last time I tasted it.

'After he returned home, he wrote and gave us his address. I still have the tail-end of his letter and a letter he wrote in 1949 saying he had all his family with him again . . . .'

C. V. W. Tarr also recalls the departure: 'There is no doubt that there were many, many friendships formed as a result of meeting German POWs, acting as a permanent lubricant to Anglo-German friendly relations. When the boys went back to Germany, we gave them suits – old suits – shoes, and so on, and we helped defray the expenses of sending huge parcels back to Germany before they were repatriated. We knew that they returned to a country devastated, without many of the essentials of daily life, and they were deeply grateful for the kindness shown to them.'

In April 1948 it was the turn of Kurt Bock. When he had been taken prisoner, in February 1945, his personal property had been officially listed as one shirt, one belt, one wallet, one cigar case and two handkerchiefs. And he himself questions the accuracy of the inventory. 'I definitely had no handkerchief then, but got one small red-coloured one from another POW a few days later. I also did not have a shirt, but of course I had trousers and a uniform jacket, even a uniform coat.'

On Christmas Eve 1945, apart from the clothes he stood up in, he still owned only one bag, containing nothing but a spare set of underwear and a pair of socks. The bag, in his own words, hung limp next to the bunk beds in C5 barracks in Crewe Hall Camp.

By the date of his repatriation, the single bag had been doubled by sewing another one on to it and his possessions had increased beyond recognition. The original jacket and trousers 'did not exist any more after three years of wearing them and I remember that they were already quite worn in 1945'. The list of what he did have in April 1948 is too long to reproduce and includes items varying from Oxo to writing pads, from fish-paste to shoe brushes, from baked beans to coloured pencils.

Prisoners on repatriation were allowed to take back with them the same amount of baggage as British troops: that is to say, all personal property which they had acquired legitimately, except articles of which Board of Trade regulations prohibited the export. They could also take up to 15 pounds weight of foodstuffs and 300 cigarettes or the equivalent in tobacco. In addition, every prisoner was permitted to carry a parcel of books, and his small kit, and could send his surplus baggage in advance by parcel post.

Generous enough it would seem. But none the less it seemed to pose certain problems, as Kurt Bock writes.

'We knew that we could take one big bag or box with a gross weight of 112 pounds and in addition one piece of hand luggage. They were not as particular about the latter as the air companies are today. Anyhow, you had to carry it. An extra piece of luggage marked "books only" was permitted, without any limitations on its weight. With a lot of books in my possession, I could not smuggle many cigarettes or much coffee in this extra box – a very strong one, which I also had to buy, and it was not even cheap.

'The vague definition of hand luggage (that you should be able to carry it) I interpreted as doubling the otherwise limited weight of 112 pounds. I had a huge bag which a friend sewed together for me out of two standard bags. As we had no scales to experiment with, we could only guess the weight and hope for the best. This bag was far in excess of the 112 pounds. The hand luggage was an aluminium suitcase – 10s. I still have it but do not use it. There is also a brown canvas holdall, on which you can still read my POW number. It later accompanied us to beaches in several parts of Europe. Altogether four pieces of extremely valuable luggage –

comparatively much more valuable than the suitcase which disappeared at Algiers airport last year!

'We were not allowed to take more than one tin of coffee, tea and sugar, and a few cigarettes to Germany. I had over 50 pounds of Lyons coffee hidden in my bags. Although a non-smoker, I had thousands of cigarettes, tobacco (Three Nuns), cigarette paper, sugar, a NAAFI cake, four oranges . . . .

'It was a gamble to pass through the several controls, frontiers, checks, and so on, and once in Germany we were also afraid of robbers, as it might well be that everyone knew that POWs arriving from England were not exactly beggars. The check in the camp was not too meticulous and the big bag and the books box were transported in a special van. We would only see them again when we arrived in Germany. We organised guards ourselves and did everything to watch the van by night and day for the five days or so it took to go from Featherstone to the Sheffield transit camp, Harwich, the Hook of Holland and finally Munsterlager. I have hardly any memory of the Sheffield camp. I think I went to the cinema to see *Gone with the Wind*.

'At Harwich we were crowded into the ship, only hoping that our main luggage was safe. It was impossible to keep watch, as it went in a separate van. I was already below deck on the crowded ship when the loudspeaker announced a final check of the luggage. Names were taken at random of POWs who had to leave the ship to be present when their bags were opened for the check. I can still feel the tension, the absolute quietness as everyone waited for their names to be called and I can also feel the shiver when I heard my own name and number clearly, without possibility of mistake.

'I climbed the ladder very slowly, watchful, thinking, "How can I save my property?" If they opened it, they would confiscate the coffee and cigarettes and many other things, maybe the whole bag with all its contents.

'Nobody took any notice of me. I saw officers searching bags, like the customs officials looking for weapons at the airport today, with the POWs standing in front of them. I did not see my own bag and nobody talked to me. Then I found my bag, lying all by itself. I made no move however, I just waited – fifteen, twenty, thirty minutes. Then suddenly there was a new announcement: everybody had to go on board. I told the officers that my bag had to be taken on board. Nobody noticed that it had not been checked and, much relieved at seeing it hoisted aboard, I went too. No search: no one had detected my coffee and the other extremely valuable goods.

'There was a personal check at the Hook of Holland. We boarded a train and could only hope that our luggage was in the same train. No control was possible. It was found when we unloaded the luggage van ourselves at the final destination, Munster, about 80 kilometres south of Hamburg.

'I had to spend about forty-eight hours in the most primitive barracks there while we were waiting to go on to our home towns. Our group of friends stayed together the whole time and we never let our luggage out of our sight. I sent a cable to my family from there. Hardly anyone had a private telephone after the bombing. I announced my exact arrival at Hamburg *Hauptbahnhof* and asked that several able-bodied men and, if possible, a wheelbarrow should meet me at Poppenbüttel (my suburban station) to help me carry and to protect the luggage. I could not expect to get a taxi at the station.

'While we were in Munsterlager, another train arrived. It also carried German soldiers, but they did not come from England. They had extremely worn-out uniforms. Many of them had no boots but just rags around their feet. If they carried anything, it was a minute bundle like a knotted handkerchief, with a piece of dry bread. We were ashamed, but what could we do except distribute cigarettes?

'All went well with me. I got home safely and presented each of my nephews with an orange. They were ten and seven years old and had never tasted one before. They liked them. I had bought them in Sheffield only five days before with my last English money. How long was it since I had myself last eaten an orange?

'I think I had half thought of selling the oranges on the black market, but I did not do so. My family had practically no connections with those circles. Of course, I gave a lot of presents and received civilian clothes from my relatives in exchange. It helped a lot. A cigarette at that time could be sold for 5 Reichsmark, or more. When I returned to Hamburg, I had my hair cut in the city, paid 2 Reichsmark and gave a tip of five cigarettes.

'I think I was in repatriation group 26 and we benefited from the experience of those who had come home earlier.'

On 13 July 1948, Emanuel Shinwell announced in the House of Commons that the repatriation of German POWs from Britain had been completed the previous day – except for 'a small number of invalids and others'. The 'others' presumably included the sizable group of prisoners who had elected to remain in Britain as agricultural workers. And the numbers who volunteered to do so rapidly exceeded the quota set by the Government. Adjustments to this quota were frequently requested and sometimes made. In April 1948 Tom Williams, Minister of Agriculture, categorically stated, 'We are only able to go beyond the 16,000 referred to, first, where Germans are married to British wives and, secondly, where Germans wish to stay with the farmer who has been employing them regularly as a POW. We got permission first to retain 10,000 willing volunteers. We found that more than 10,000 volunteers were available and the number was increased to 20,000, including Scotland.'

With a limited number of places and too large a number of candidates, factors taken into consideration were the character of the POW concerned, the quality of his work while he was a prisoner and his physical suitability for agricultural labour. The decision was made by a committee consisting of the commandant of the camp, a representative of the County Agricultural Committee and an official of the German sector of the Foreign Office, but the medical officer and the camp leader were also available to give evidence.

George Weiser writes, 'At the beginning of 1949 we were given the chance either of going back or staying here. The condition of staying was of doing at least twelve months' agricultural work here, as there was a shortage of agricultural labour in Britain. As my home was in East Germany, I volunteered to stay. Home Office officials came to screen you and find out if you were a Nazi. Were you a member of the Hitler Youth? I wasn't, but I had been a member of the youth movement from twelve to fourteen. But it was a case of having to. Even your schoolteacher told you to.

'Were you a member of the Nazi Party? I was too young.

'Had I been working? What did I intend to do if I stayed? Settle down.

'So I was released. I worked on a farm near the camp and lived in a hut for two or three weeks, like a shepherd's hut. This was not good enough for me, so I got lodgings in Sprowston, a nearby village. I worked on a farm for five years or so and then went into a foundry for eighteen months. While I was in the foundry, I met my first wife. I was married in 1958 and moved to Hawick.'

Alf Eiserbeck was another volunteer who was accepted. 'In

Faringdon, I had civilian status as an alien. After that I applied for a second year of agricultural work; got married. I didn't go back home till 1965.'

An interesting slant was added to the experience of staying in Britain when on 12 April 1948 Christopher Mayhew, for the Government, announced that 'should any German ex-prisoner of war be offered employment in Great Britain after the end of 1948 and accept such an offer, they will be given the opportunity of a visit to Germany before the end of the year'. Siegfried Gabler was one of the lucky ones.

'Those captured first went home first. I had to make up my mind whether to go home or stay on and go on holiday. I decided to stay on, as things were fairly bad in East Germany.

'On 30 December 1948 some 800 blokes met at Reading station. We were not allowed to have any money. We went to Germany for five weeks' holiday and there we got paid out quite a sum of money and told that we had to spend it, as we were not allowed to take it back to England. We had to pick up the money at Munsterlager, and while we were there a transport of prisoners was arriving from the East at the same time – not Russia, I think, but Romania or Hungary. Well, compared with us . . . ! We were dressed in our best: suits, camel coats, polished shoes. Kids were waiting on the platform, on the lines. We threw them sweets and things. We saw this transport from the East. They were in rags. We had suitcases, they had nothing. We thought then how relatively lucky we were. We were not allowed to go home to East Germany, but I managed to slip over for ten days. Otherwise, I stayed with a friend in West Germany and we lived it up for four weeks. When we came back, I actually got properly demobbed. The only condition was that I had to work on a farm for £4 a week, as they did. I heard about one or two prisoners in every village doing the same.'

George Weiser was also in the party.

'I was released as a POW in late 1948, and the Government said, you can have a month's holiday on us. They paid our fare to Germany – wherever we wanted to go. They took us under British escort and put us into a collective camp. They paid us any money we had accumulated as POWs and also back money from the German army from the moment we were taken prisoner, plus our discharge money. It came to DM 3000 or 4000. When we had it, we could either spend it or leave it there. We couldn't bring it back. I went down to Bad Homburg, where my sister lived, and spent the month there with her. After the month was up, I went back to the collection camp (I left the rest of the money with my sister) and back to Scotland. I then got my official release papers as a POW.'

Postscript

For the prisoners who went back to Germany with the intention of staying there, the repatriation they had dreamed of over the years of captivity was at last a reality. But the long-awaited reunion with loved ones, families and friends, the return to the homeland, the reacquisition of freedom, were coloured by the physical conditions in defeated Germany.

Not that Germany's political and economic state was not improving. In spring 1948 the way lay wide open to the much needed reform of her currency. At a conference held in London in April, France joined with America and Britain to merge her zone of West Germany with their two, and also agreed to permit this area to embark upon the work of drafting a democratic constitution. It was at this juncture that the break with Russia effectively took place, marking an end to the epoch of four-power control – though it was not formally wound up for a further fourteen months. On 20 March, Marshall Sokolovsky walked out of the Control Commission in Berlin. From 1 April, restrictions on personal travel between East Germany and the West tightened considerably.

On 20 June 1948 the currency reform was finally introduced. The old Reichsmark became valueless in the three Western zones. It was replaced by the new Deutschmark. Everyone was immediately allowed to exchange forty of the old for forty new. For any currency over and above this, they could obtain DM 6.5 for 100 Reichsmark.

To the political economist, the reform was an overwhelming success. Goods began to appear in the shops, partly because factory production was increasing in volume (and had the capacity to increase still more), partly because the issue of the new currency had been small enough to leave everyone short of money and therefore the demand for cash exceeded demand for stocks. In other words, goods that had been hoarded were unloaded. The black market virtually disappeared.

None of this happened overnight. For the returning ex-prisoner the path back to normality was a hard, slow haul.

In any case, when Siegfried Bandelow went home in October 1947, these events lay in the future.

'We were transported back to Germany via Harwich and the Hook of Holland. We left Holland by night and travelled through the Rhine–Ruhr district. It was a memorable journey through the heavily destroyed industrial area. For hours we travelled through ruins. Most of us, myself included, had last been in Germany on leave in 1943. At that time there had only been a few ruins. I still remember very distinctly that journey in 1947 through our destroyed country, in the cold, under a full moon to home.

'We arrived at Munsterlager, where at that time, as far as I remember, all prisoners from the British zone were released. Our demobilisation was then further delayed for some three or four days because a British general wanted to inspect the camp. After that, we were driven on lorries to Hanover station and were suddenly "free" men. Together with some comrades, I found a train to Göttingen and was home by evening.

'At that time a great deal was still destroyed. Reconstruction had only slowly begun; large numbers of men were still in captivity; others were ill, hungry, wounded and so on. Destruction in Hanover had been extensive and life was only just beginning amidst the ruins. Black-marketeers were thriving. This was our first impression at Hanover station. We had to guard our luggage so that it was not stolen. The black-marketeers could see at a glance that we had come from England and naturally wanted to cheat us. Göttingen had not suffered so much. There were several hospitals there. All that had been damaged was a couple of churches and a few university buildings.

'My wife had lost all her possessions. Her parents' home in Stuttgart in Württemberg had been destroyed. With a great deal of difficulty, she had made her way to my mother in Göttingen and was waiting for me there. One of my sisters had stayed in Berlin as a nurse and had looked after Russian soldiers, amongst others. She had contracted tuberculosis there and died from it. My brother had also been an officer and had been taken prisoner by the US army at Nuremberg. He had then been handed over to the Russians for their work camp. He was in Russian captivity for five years and came home ill in 1950. The husband of my third sister, equally an officer, was still in an American POW camp in 1947. My eldest sister's husband was half Jewish. He had been a lawyer in Berlin and was imprisoned by the Russians while he was walking from Berlin to

Göttingen on foot. He was able to escape and, when I came home, was working as a judge in the courts. My wife's father was still in American captivity. Every German family had the same or similar situations to face. Before the war I had had a circle of some twenty-five friends in Göttingen. After the war we established that only three of them had survived.

'Food distribution was very bad at the time when I arrived home and we never really had enough to eat. I had brought 300 cigarettes back with me and this was of great help in enabling my family to buy food on the black market. Various families of relatives, fleeing from the Russians, had come to Göttingen since 1945 and had stayed there until they found further accommodation.

'I would have had great difficulty in finding a job in my own profession as a bookseller. I therefore decided to study. In either case, I would have had to starve and work. As neither my wife nor I had any money (my savings were in the Russian-occupied zone), I looked for a steady job to support us while I studied. From autumn 1948 until summer 1949 I worked in an aluminium works – from six o'clock in the evening until 3.40 in the morning; in the daytime, I attended lectures. This job folded up and I found a new one in a sawmill where I could work the same hours. I did this until early in 1953. This was the only way I could achieve my goal. My story was not exceptional. It was the same or similar for all of us.

'In 1952–3 I took the examinations and have taught at the gymnasium ever since.

'For us, so much had been destroyed that only two possibilities remained: either to die of hunger or to set to work and put everything to rights again.'

By April 1948, when Kurt Bock returned, the position was not appreciably easier.

'I knew what the home I was going back to when I was repatriated looked like. After our flat had been completely destroyed, like tens of thousands of other houses in 1943, my father had converted a small garden cottage about 16 kilometres from the centre of Hamburg and twenty-five minutes on foot from the nearest station, into a permanent home of about 50 square metres, divided into five very tiny rooms. It took him several years gradually to increase the space. It was mainly built of wood or bricks, which were taken from the debris of destroyed homes. In the end, it was quite comfortable, as he was lucky enough to get wood panels and doors from dismantled ships. However, the roof was not leak-proof; for years it was impossible to get tarred paper; but this aggravation was quite common to most of our neighbours. The kitchen was also the entrance from the garden. The small cellar, only about 1·50 metres underground and not under the cottage but on one side of it, had been used as an air-raid shelter in the last years until May 1945. The few potatoes, fruit and vegetables left over from summer were stored there for the winter, and my mother took a very old-fashioned iron (I do not know where she found this), filled it with glowing coal, or rather charcoal, to try and keep the temperature above zero in hard winters. There was no water supply, no taps. Water had to be carried from the public pump 200 metres away. My mother anyhow was not very good on her feet and could just about carry one bucket. I, of course, carried two at a time and I did this ten or twelve times in succession that first summer to water the garden. There was also no drainage but we already had electricity; I remember that this was already laid in 1944 in spite of all the difficulties. But there was only one meter for about sixty connected cottages.

'When I returned, my mother was living alone in this house. My father had died less than a year before, but my brother, then thirty-six, married and with three children, of ten, seven and four, was living very near, about 100 metres away, in a similar, mostly self-constructed cottage. There were other relatives and friends in this garden settlement, who had made it their home after they had lost their own homes during the war. Many of them are still living there, but now in nice comfortable houses.

'I had about 15,000 Reichsmark on my own account, but it was impossible to buy anything over and above the very small official food rations – or only at exorbitant prices on the black market or by bartering against other goods. A joke at that time which might perhaps have had some kernel of truth said that farmers (who had food) were carpeting their cowsheds with valuable oriental rugs – obtained from people who had not lost them during the bombing. The others could not get anything: no extra food; no tools, nails, screws, wood; no fuel, clothing or soap.

'Electricity was supplied officially and therefore the price was fixed at a comparatively low rate. Of course, it did not always work, and then there was no light. However, in general this bottleneck in electricity had already been overcome by the time I got back to Hamburg. We had one meter for sixty households and the total bill was shared equally, whether somebody was only using one hot plate for a single person or whether he was catering for a large family, preparing the potatoes and vegetables from the garden for six or even ten people. Before the currency reform, the price of electricity was no problem.

'This currency reform, I think, took place on 20 June. Everyone got DM 40 as a basic allotment and, of course, their next salary or pension in this new money. Our bank accounts were practically worthless, devalued to 6 per cent of their previous value, and after a time one could collect these. People who had amassed large fortunes in Reichsmark bills on the black market, could not, of course, convert them. I was left with about DM 1000 in my account. My discharge money of 80 Reichsmark was then worth DM 4·80!

'I could have lived on this for a couple of months; my mother had a small pension. As I had no job before the reform, I can only illustrate the situation from what my wife recalls! In 1948, before the reform, she had a salary of 380 Reichsmark. After the reform, she got DM 160 a month as a secretary. My mother only had a small pension, but the rent of the cottage was quite moderate and we could manage. However, the first electricity bill was a shock, as in Deutschmark it was now too high. I tried every means of obtaining a meter of our own. I succeeded with the help of the coffee and cigarettes I had brought from Europe. We were then free to use the electricity we wanted and did not have to pay as much – as we used much less than people who had saved more apparatus than we had.

'My brother, handicapped as he was with only one leg, had a comparatively good job as a machine typesetter on a newspaper – though it only appeared twice a week and consisted of only one sheet! you could not just go out and buy this paper, as only a limited number of copies were printed, because of the shortage of paper, but we, of course, got a copy through my brother. Compare this with my personal situation as a POW in England, when I had the opportunity to subscribe to several dailies and as many weeklies as I wanted and had funds to pay for them!

'After the reform, many commodities reappeared and were offered for the Deutschmark. Today you can hear people say, "Immediately after the currency reform you could get everything if you only had the money." This, of course, is not true. The fact is that, compared with the present, it was still an extremely poor time and that was not only because nobody had money to pay for things. The situation did gradually get better, but officially it still took a couple of years before rationing was abolished and industrial commodities were more easily obtainable, of better quality than those we got during the war, and competition made things cheaper than they were directly after the reform.

'In summer, life generally is always easier. We neighbours and friends had some potatoes, vegetables and a few chickens, and some had rabbits, though it was not easy to get feed for the animals. Our chickens, I remember, did not lay eggs – probably their diet was too poor. There was no meat, no fish, no fat whatsoever; a small ration of bread. Everybody tried to get a bit extra. Queueing was normal but not always successful. People stood all night to get *Wurstbrühe* – water in which some sausages had been boiled. Of course, you only got sausages on your ration card and the ration worked out at less in one month than a good eater would like as a steak for supper now.

'I endeavoured to get my own pump in the garden, so that we should not have to carry water from the well. I had already tried to get the material in England, but it proved impossible to get everything, including tubes to a depth of about 30 metres, and then I would have needed experts to drill the hole. A year later I was glad that I had not succeeded, as we were able to be connected directly to the city water supply. The expense was high and not everybody could afford it. We had to dig the ditches and holes ourselves. I was among the first to get it.

'I lived there with my mother from April 1948 to January 1953.

'My certificate of discharge shows a stamp: "Leave for a fortnight until 3.5.1948." Leave from what? I had no job, but ten years before, I had finished my apprenticeship as an export merchant. The firm still existed or, rather, had managed to survive in spite of the fact that there was no export business at that time. They did not need me and nor did other firms. Friends could join their former employers – for instance, banks and government authorities – but their pay was also not very good. I remember when I was still in England, in January 1948, I celebrated my thirtieth birthday. It was not a nice feeling, not knowing at the time what the future would bring. But I have never been a pessimist, and now, thirty years later, I am in general quite satisfied and grateful for what has happened to me. Other friends at that time did not even have a profession. They had gone into the army straight from school. Some had no home, however modest, to go to when they were repatriated. There were quite a number whose families lived in East Germany, and who, as they did not want to live there, had somehow to manage to stay in the West. For them it was even difficult to get permission from the authorities to stay in Hamburg, for example.

'Soon after my return, a friend who lived 200 kilometres north of Hamburg invited me to stay with him for as long as I wanted. He was about twenty-two and had inherited a cinema, a hotel and a coal and fuel business in a small town near the Danish border. There had never been any bombing there, and therefore the standard of living was far and away better than the average in a big city where over 50 per cent had lost their homes. He had been a POW, but only for six months in Schleswig Holstein. I shall never forget my friendly reception by his family. Though they were not farmers, they kept their own cow in the garden for milk, and for his business my friend had a lorry and he could even use it for trips when he managed to spare some petrol for this purpose – and he did. This shows how different it could be for some people when they were repatriated.

'Apart from that one, I had several friends who were far better off than I was at that time. One had to take over his father's bakery, though formerly he had wanted to study medicine. Ten years later, he committed suicide. Another could not follow his original wish to become an engineer: circumstances forced him to take over his father's farm. He had enough food in the time of general shortage, or, rather, famine. Later he gave up the farm and could only get a job far below his intelligence, as an ordinary worker.

'It was not easy for me to find a job, in spite of many attempts. At last, a Mr Pannier employed me as an assistant. There was nobody else in his firm trying to sell tools, especially those for machines, such as heavy drills, and reamers, which no one could use at that period, as the shipyards had been dismantled by the army of occupation. The tools Mr Pannier had in stock had been in his possession since wartime and were officially quite valuable but it was impossible to sell them then. My salary was DM 150 per month. My task was to try and sell the tools abroad and to correspond and negotiate with British and American firms in the future. At that time, immediately after the reform, it was still too early. My net income per month was about DM120, out of which I had to pay DM10 for transport. Anyway, my mother and I could just manage. I worked from nine till four and it was difficult enough to fill this time with work. I should have liked to do more and use my initiative, but, with too little experience in those days and limited by practically no funds, there was not much that could be done to boost the business. Several times my boss had to apologise for not being able to pay my modest salary. I remember he had to pay a bill of DM 300 and he could have saved a cash discount of 2 per cent or DM 6 if it were paid immediately. He could not. I paid instead and thereby increased my income by 6 DM.

'I remained with him until the end of June 1949. He could not afford to pay my salary any longer. I joined my present firm in May 1950. Then thirty-two, I had finally caught up and could start a normal life.'

Normal life had indeed resumed. But in various ways it had been enriched through the sojourn in Britain. Not only were there the intangible lessons learned about democracy and constitutionalism, but, in addition, real contacts had been established and friendships of enduring value made with British people. Strong links still survive till this day.

Griselda Fyfe writes, 'After Fritz returned home, he wrote giving us his address. I still have the tail-end of this letter, and a letter he wrote in 1949 saying he had all his family with him again. My parents sent him a *Scotsman* calendar for 1948–9; I think at that time one couldn't send more. Christmas 1950, I received a large marzipan pig, decorated with green ribbons and red and white toadstools, with a mark-piece in its mouth. It was quite a pig! I still have the toadstools and the gift tag. He also sent a Christmas tree one year: it never arrived.

'My father took ill in autumn in 1950 and from then on I always sent a Christmas card to Fritz, whether or not he sent one in return. My father died early in 1952, but the Christmas card was still sent. Then, early in 1957, I received a letter and an invitation to go to Germany and see Fritz and his family. This has led to friendship with his family, his brother's family and his sister's family, even to friendship with a nephew and family in Kenya.

'I have visited him and his family six times since 1957 and will go again this summer. He came here in 1972 and was really pleased to be back . . . .'

C. V. W. Tarr tells of similar such relationships.

'From the end of 1947 onwards, the German boys were gradually repatriated, and, after all our friends had gone back, we continued in touch with them by correspondence, exchanging greetings at Christmas time and, in fact, getting to know all about their families, engagements, weddings, christenings, and so forth. Then in 1952 came the great day of reunion. My wife and I and the Parkins were invited to meet the boys and their friends and families in the main square in Düsseldorf. It was our first visit to Germany, and, indeed, our first visit abroad, except for my wartime service in the First

World War. The married German boys brought their wives, the unmarried brought their girlfriends, and we had a marvellous time sight-seeing and feasting.

'Ever since those unforgettable days, we have kept in touch with our German friends and have visited them in their homes. And I know that many people in this county of Devon have had similar experiences to ours, especially farmers' families . . . .

'The lovely daughter of one of the Germans comes to stay with us often. We love her as if she were our own daughter. These firm roots of friendship are spreading underneath the surface and constitute a real and lasting growth binding our two countries.'

Bibliography

Place of publication London in all cases.

Balfour, Michael, *West Germany* (1968).
Burt, Kendal, and Leaser, James, *The One that Got Away* (1956).
Faulk, Henry, *Group Captives: The Re-education of German Prisoners of War* (1977).
Longmate, Norman, *How We Lived Then: A History of Everyday Life during the Second World War* (1973).
Scotland, Lt Col. A. P., *The London Cage* (1957).
Sulzbach, Herbert, 'Inside Featherstone Park', in *Total War to Total Trust. Personal Accounts of 30 Years of Anglo-German Relations – the Vital Role of Non-governmental Organisations* (1976).
Taylor, A. J. P., *The Second World War: An Illustrated History* (1975).

Index